# Dragon Unravelled

*A new perspective on China*

# DRAGON UNRAVELLED

*A new perspective on China*

*Mathew John*

PENTAGON PRESS

*Dragon Unravelled: A new perspective on China* / Mathew John

ISBN 978-81-8274-499-8

First Edition 2011



*Typeset and Layout*
Geetanjali Pandey, Delhi.

*Published by*
**PENTAGON PRESS**
206, Peacock Lane, Shahpur Jat
New Delhi-110 049
Tel.: 011-64706243, 26491568
Telefax: 011-26490600
email: rajan@pentagon-press.in
website: www.pentagonpress.in

*Printed by*
Syndicate Binders, A-20, Hosiery Complex
Phase-II, Noida-201305

# Foreword

China is a fascinating puzzle.

For those of us who remember the ancient words of wisdom recorded in the **Arthasastra** of Kautalya, immediate neighbors are natural enemies, and therefore China cannot be merely an abject of idle curiosity.

Throughout history India has suffered from a strange psychological block—indifference towards the developments of the world outside. When Alexander's cavalry from Macedonia crossed the Himalayan passes and arrived in the north west corner of our country after destroying the great Persian empire, the leaders of the little principalities in the border area were taken by surprise. Even when Purushottama (Porus of the Greeks) was humbled, the inland kingdoms failed to recognize the threat and combine their forces to fight the new menace. Luckily the invader himself turned away.

History repeated itself after many centuries. The rise of a new power center in Arabia following the birth of Islam and the aggressive designs of the new rulers escaped the attention of Indians until the conquest of Sind in the 8th century. Even after this the complacency of Indian rulers continued until Ghazni Mahmud bombarded the cities and temples and destroyed Somnath temple in the 10th century. Then the Rajput rulers relapsed into their mutual conflicts until Mohammad Ghori pounced upon Delhi and Kanauj after two centuries.

Much later, the rebirth the Europe accompanied by the discovery of sea routes which planted imperialist aspirations in the minds of petty kings of Western Europe did not prompt Indians to prepare for meeting the new threat from the sea. The advent of the Portuguese in the 15th century shocked the rulers of Malabar, but other parts of India continued in their blissful ignorance about Europe. Even the Mughal emperors did not wake up to the possibilities of sea power in the new age. All Indian rulers failed to assess the potential danger from small mercantile groups which sent their feelers to India and infiltrated into the countryside.

More recently, Indian leaders' complacency left us ignorant about the real character and designs of Chinese communist rulers resulting in humiliating military reverses on the north eastern frontier. Thank God! This time the adversities have given rise to a group of China watchers among bureaucrats, journalists and academicians in recent years. The need to understand the political and economic changes in that huge country teeming with population and bursting with new energy is now recognized in India. China has always remained a closed society which introduced wonderful things like the silk industry, mariner's compass, gun powder and printing technology. The Modern European imperialists attempted to put them down through the opium way, but failed eventually. The Chinese differ from the rest of the world in race, religion, script and language. They are in all continents today; they have taken giant leaps in science and technology, and their sudden shifts in politics from hardcore Communism to high-tech Capitalism has left the whole world wondering about the implications of their new steps for the future of Asia. The present book is a product of this new intellectual climate.

Mr. Mathew John is an experienced IPS officer, widely travelled, who did not look upon retirement as a passport to the realm of idle pleasures. On the other hand, his energetic spirit found a new field of activity. He started explorations in the newly opened territory of China both in the real world and the virtual world. He devoured books on Chinese history, politics and culture. The enormous volume of data that he collected had to be digested and organized into usable convenient units for the consumption of people who are interested in coming to grips with the massive reality of modern China. He does not claim originality; he does not propound any new theory or interpretation of China, but he carefully and systematically places all the relevant facts to the best of his knowledge before the reader. It is up to the reader to formulate his own attitude.

This reference book will, I am sure, be a boon companion for tourists, traders, businessmen, teachers, and to some extent even to diplomats who have to deal with different aspects of China. It is also an indispensable tool for researchers as a ready reference.

This writer does not brand China in some way, call it good or bad and paint it in black and white. He does not accuse of defend, advocate or judge. He cites different views and also presents them in the form of diagrams and tables to satisfy the modern taste for information in capsules. His language is matter of fact as it should be in such a work, avoiding flourishes and flamboyance. As you follow him, you can experience the thrill of exploration and also access the information collected by others in the course of several journeys before. Mr. John tells me that he has kept a more detailed analysis of the material for another volume.

Here is a new kind of travelogue in which the traveler's direct narrative is minimal, though he has taken two trips to China. Much more is conveyed through extracts from other books. In short here is a new age travel book on the new age China.

**M.G.S. Narayanan**

# Preface

China has always been an enigma because of the 'bamboo curtain' and insularity which existed for a long time. In India there is a lack of authoritative information available on China because of the 1962 India-China war and the consequent unhappy India-China relations. China has emerged on the international scene with a 'big bang', with about 10% growth in GDP p.a. since 1981. As India has also of late shown remarkable economic resurgence on a similar track, there is a growing feeling that the 21st century may see China and India emerging as major global players, as was the case with the US in the 19th and 20th centuries. Hence, it was tempting to see the realities. So, recently my wife and I spent a few days in Beijing, Xian, Guilin and Shanghai, important places from the cultural and economic development point of view, to satisfy the curiosity and interest generated about China. My interest in China got multiplied after the visit. Hence, I started reading more on various aspects of China-past, present and projections about its future. Some friends suggested that they would also like to read a book, simple and general, but realistic and holistic, on China. It motivated me to make such an attempt. The following account based on the places visited, facts seen, impressions gained, study of relevant literature available from the internet, publications, etc. is the result. It is meant to give an educated Indian a general picture of China which has already emerged as a major economic power and also in Susan L Shirk's words a 'Fragile Super power'.

The term 'Dragon' in the title has different meanings and interpretations. It generally means a legendary mythical creature with reptilian traits. While the European dragon is seen as evil, the Chinese one, with five claws on each of its four legs, is seen as a symbol of the Chinese race, a symbol of imperial power, prosperity, good fortune, greatness, goodness, success, excellence, boldness, etc. It is also seen by some as a symbol of divine vigilance or protection, or an angel or symbol of auspicious power. Some see it as a national emblem of China though rarely used so in China. Many in China also use the term as a sign of Chinese ethnic identity. In the representation of Chinese culture, it is used for decorative purposes. It is even regarded as a supreme being among all creatures. Disrespect to the dragon is disliked even by the Communist Government. It, however, likes to avoid the impression of aggressive or war-like connotations given to it in European cultures. Dragon is also closely linked to 'Brand Hong Kong'. It is used in the title in a very generic and holistic way to mean all the impressions the word 'China' invokes-its long history and culture, philosophies and China centric world-view, picto-phonetic language, huge Diaspora, virtually unparalleled low-cost manufacturing capacity, political leaders who believe that fast economic growth will keep people happy even with out individual freedom or democracy, and a whole lot of other mixed feelings, mostly positive. 'Unravelled' is used in the sense of made simple for the common man, especially an Indian who may have heard of China only in a very limited sense-first in terms of its communism, later of 1962 India-China war and of late about its rapid economic advancement.

The book has essentially seven sections besides the 'Introduction'. In the 'Introduction', some details of its geography, administrative structure and other pieces of information of general interest are given. In the 'Historical Perspective', though some account of China before it became an Empire under the First Emperor Shi Huangdi has been given, the focus is on its recent history, especially the developments after 1911. The section on 'Socio-Cultural Scene' covers philosophical, cultural, educational, religious and linguistic fronts. Relatively more attention has been given to culture, education and religion with only marginal coverage of the linguistic aspects. In the Political Perspective, the current power structure and also issues relating to Human Rights have been covered at some length. Some Human Rights related issues have also been touched upon under Religious and Economic Scene as these relate to these fields. The issues on which China has been at the receiving end of attacks and criticism, mainly from the Human Rights Groups of democratic countries have been Suppression of Religious freedom, Arbitrary Detentions, Torture and Ill-treatment of Prisoners, Absence of Freedom of the Press, Absence of Individual Trade Union Rights, Lack of Judicial Independence and Due Process, Inadequate Efforts to stop ill-treatment, abduction and trafficking of women, Forced Evictions, Environmental Damage, Increasing Inequalities in Income and Development, Lowering of Water Table, and Arms Sales and Support to some Controversial Regimes. While some of these are systemic and relate generally to all communist systems, others are more specific for China.

The economic, tourist and military related topics follow. Fairly detailed coverage of the Economic scene commencing from the imperial days to the current scenario has been attempted. The highlights of the main tourist attractions with some photos have been given. The details of the attractive sights we saw in Beijing, Xian, Guilin and Shanghai and adjoining areas and other worth seeing sights in these cities and other parts of the huge country have been briefly provided. In the 'Emerging Scenario', the effort is to make some projections about the likely scenario in the coming years with the primary focus on the economic front.

This is a humble effort to familiarize an average Indian reader with China as interest in China is fast growing. Serious researchers, journalists who cover the area with some depth or diplomats who specialize on the country are advised to read further on specific areas of interest. Despite the limitations mentioned above, it is hoped that a reader will get a general idea of what China is today and what India can learn from its successes on many fronts. Successes have their own costs too. The Chinese system has its own weaknesses and limitations. It is hoped that this effort would generate more interest in people to read further on China more discerningly and also prepare them to better appreciate other articles and publications. The aim of the efforts put in will be achieved if the book serves any of the above causes.

I dedicate this book to the memory of my late father K.M. John, a teacher of rare dedication whom Providence took away at the blooming age of 46. I also dedicate royalty of the book to the educational upliftment of the capable Below Poverty Line children of the school where he taught till his demise in Dec 1965 and where I too studied.

March, 2011

**Mathew John**
Calicut

# Contents

# Acknowledgements

It would not have been possible for me to write this book but for the timely motivation, guidance and help given by a large number of people. It, however, is not be possible to mention all here due to limitations of space. However, it will be a great injustice if I do not acknowledge with pleasure the valuable help given by the following persons. I very sincerely thank them and document my gratitude to them for the pains taken for me.

a. Dr. Shashi Tharoor, M.P. (Formerly Union Minister of State for External Affairs, India and Under Secretary General, U.N.) and distinguished Author for agreeing to spare his valuable time to release the book.

b. Shri. K George Kizhakekkuttu (Kurumpanadom, Changanacherry, Kottayam Dist., Kerala, my uncle, who himself has written a number of books on science and health-care related topics), for inspiring, motivating and encouraging me to pursue the work.

c. My daughters Teena (Dr. Teena Mathew, M.D.), Neena (Neena Acharya, M.S.) and my son-in-law Dr. Anil Ramachandran (Consultant Urologist), for various types of assistance and help in improving the language, style and presentation. Similarly, my nephew Ranjit Rajan, a computer engineer and MBA helped me a lot in the design of the computer graphics and formats for the pictures. I thank my wife (Mrs. Mary Mathew) for putting up with all the troubles caused by my involvement in the difficult task of concentrated work for over two years.

d. I am thankful to my close relative in New York Shri Sebastian Antony (M.Arch., M.S.,) a Senior Functionary of Bank of America, for all the tips about modern writing in US, esp. about communicating more through pictures and graphics rather than through words as people have no time to read, computerized index for each part, references at the end of each chapter, etc.

e. My friend Dr. P.S. Zacharias (formerly Vice-Chancellor, Goa University) for all the time spent with me in revising many chapters and making valuable suggestions about improvements needed. The chapter on 'Emerging Scenario' was included based on his suggestion.

f. Dr. P.K. Michael Tharakan (Vice-chancellor, kannur University, Kerala) for his kind suggestions about improvement of my draft.

g. Dr. P. Joseph, Senior Prof. of Physics, Louisville University, Kentucky, USA, for his comments about the contents of some chapters and improvements in language.

h. Shri C.N.S. Nair, IAS (Retd.) for his valuable suggestions about new points to be covered in the comparisons between China and India, especially in the economics scene. His views helped me to adopt a more balanced approach by better coverage of the points of criticism of China by Human Rights groups and environmentalists. He educated me on many economics related topics.

i. Justice Cyriac Joseph for his suggestions about inclusion of some topics for making the coverage more comprehensive and balanced.

j. Dr. M.G.S. Narayanan, eminent historian and writer (formerly Chairman, Indian Council for Historical Research) for his valuable guidance and comments on certain aspects of writing and revision of the draft, especially the ones on history, culture and philosophy. I am also thankful to him for writing the Foreword for the book.

k. Shri A. Abraham Kurien IPS, DGP (Retd.) and my friend for about 50 years and also now Director/Academic, St. Thomas Academy for Research and Training, Calicut, for sparing his time to improve the contents of the Chapters on Linguistic and philosophical Perspectives, Cultural Scenario, Preface, etc. His daughter Rakhee took great pains to go through each word and suggested many improvements.

l. Dr. Sukumaran (Prof of English) for correcting the draft and improving the quality of the book.

m. Mr. Saji Isaac and Mrs. Elizabeth Varkkey, Advocates, Errankulam High Court, for their advice on copyright related issues.

n. Mr. V.A. George, President and CEO, Thejo Engineering Ltd, Chennai, for his advice on coverage of certain areas of concern and criticism of China.

I have liberally made use of the materials from Wikipedia. I have mentioned them at the appropriate places in the References. I have also drawn on materials and pictures of the CIA World Fact Book, World Bank data bases, Nationmaster.com, etc. Sources of other materials used are Tourist literature of Government of China, Encyclopaedia Britannica, articles in 'Time', 'Newsweek', 'Business week', 'Business world', different news papers, magazines and other publications, some books like' Coming Collapse of China' (Gordon Gong), 'China, the Fragile Super Power' (Susan L. Shirk), 'India: the Rising Giant' (Aravind Panagariya) and a large number of internet sites listed at the end of each chapter. A number of studies on specific topics taken from the internet have also been used. The details of sources, linkages etc.have been provided to the best of my ability both on the relevant pages and under each chapter. I gratefully acknowledge their help and usefulness in compiling this book meant for the common man. Wikipedia's rules about copyright in respect of materials taken from Wikipedia will apply.

In some cases, it has not been possible to get the latest data. Getting data, especially reliable ones about China is a known problem. Hence, the coverage is not full and upto date as I would like it to be. As the collection of materials was undertaken over a long period, some references may have not been noted down in time and hence there could be some unintentional omissions. I genuinely regret this failure and apologise for this lapse. If and when these are brought to my notice, it would be corrected at the earliest. I thank all copy right holders who have permitted me to use their product.

This is basically a compiled product with some analyses and comments added to give better clarity for those who do not have much idea about China. The primary aim has been to give an overall picture with out bothering much about total accuracy or specific details. Hence, absolute accuracy and reliability is not claimed, especially as different standards would have been applied by different sources. The problem about Wikipedia sources is known and this limitation too has to be kept in mind.

I am also thankful to all those who have in some way contributed to the book by their suggestions. I am solely responsible for the failures and drawbacks of various types.

**Mathew John**

# Abbreviations Used

ACFTU - All China Federation of Trade Unions
BBC - British Broadcasting Corporation
CC - Central Committee
CDSA - Central Department of Social Affairs
CIA - Central Intelligence Agency
CID - Central Investigation Department
CMC - Central Military Commission
CNN - Cable News Network
$CO_2$ - Carbon Dioxide
CPC/CCP - Communist Party of China/Chinese Communist Party
CTBT - Comprehensive Test Ban Treaty
CWC - Chemical Weapons Convention
DGP - Director General of Police
FBI - Federal Bureau of Investigation
FDI - Foreign Direct Investment
G-7 - Group of 7 nations viz. USA, Canada, UK, Germany, France, Italy and Japan
GDP - Gross Domestic Product
GNP - Gross National Product
HDI - Human Development Index
IAEA - International Atomic Energy Agency
IAS - Indian Administrative Service

| | | |
|---|---|---|
| ICBM | - | Inter Continental Ballistic Missile |
| IPS | - | Indian Police Service |
| Km | - | Kilometer(s) |
| MBA | - | Master of Business Administration |
| MD | - | Doctor of Medicine |
| MTCR | - | Missile Technology Control Regime |
| MNC | - | Multi National Corporation |
| MPS | - | Ministry of Public Security |
| MSS | - | Ministry of State Security |
| NPC | - | National Peoples' Congress |
| NPT | - | Non-Proliferation Treaty |
| PB/PBM | - | Polit Bureau/Polit Bureau Member |
| PLA | - | People's Liberation Army |
| PRC | - | Peoples' Republic of China |
| MS | - | Master of Surgery |
| RAB | - | Religious Affairs Bureau |
| RMB | - | Renminbi |
| SALW | - | Small Arms and Light Weapons |
| SEZ | - | Special Economic Zone |
| SOE | - | State Owned Enterprise |
| TFP | - | Total Factor Productivity |
| UAV | - | Unmanned Aerial Vehicle |
| UNDP | - | United Nations' Development Programme |
| UNESCO | - | United Nations' Educational, Scientific and Cultural Organization |
| USSR | - | Union of Soviet Socialist Republics |
| UFWD | - | United Front Work Department |
| WB | - | World Bank |
| WTO | - | World Trade Organization |

# Introduction

China is perhaps the oldest on going civilization. It is also the most populated country with over 1.33 billion people. It is three times bigger than India and slightly smaller than the US. With unprecedented economic growth nearing 10% for the last three decades, it has emerged as an economic giant among the developing nations. As a result of huge Foreign Direct Investments (FDI) for nearly two decades and cheap, disciplined and educated labour, it has virtually become the manufacturing capital of the world. With the second largest economy and huge foreign exchange surpluses, it is now an economic superpower. It has become virtually the fund provider to the US economy, the richest, by its investments of nearly a trillion dollars in US Treasury Bonds.

The opening and closing ceremonies of the 2008 Beijing Olympic Games, watched by at least 200 million people each, showcased its amazing cultural power. China's superb performance in the games marked its emergence as a sports power too. China has demonstrated its clear dominance over the sports field in Asia by bagging the maximum number of medals in the Asian Games, 2010 recently held at Guangzhou with no other country coming anywhere near it. It is also remarkable how market economy and changing communism co-exist in a fast growing country.

## 1. TERRITORIAL DIVISIONS

Administratively, China is divided into three tiers:

- The first tier comprises of 22 Provinces, 5 Autonomous Regions, 4 Municipalities directly under the Central Government and the Specially Administered Regions of Hong Kong and Macao.
- The second tier consists of 17 Prefectures, 30 Autonomous Prefectures, 283 prefecture cities and 3 Leagues.
- At the third tier, there are 1464 counties, 117 autonomous counties, 374 county level cities, 852 districts, 49 banners, 3 autonomous banners, 1 Functioning area and 2 special districts. Below these are townships (14677), ethnic townships (1092), townships (19522), sub-districts (6152), district public offices (11), Sumu (181) and Ethnic Sumu (1).

The area, capital, population and its density, GDP in US $ in 2008, nominal GDP per capita in 2008 in US $, major urban centres etc. of different Provines/ Muncipalities/Autonomous Regions/Specially Administered Regions are given in the Appendix-1[1], 2 and 4. The GDP per capita could be used to see the stage of development, inequalities in income and development, etc.

A closer look at the data will show the following salient features:

1. Beijing (11361), Shanghai (10537 $), Tianjin (9136) cities and Provinces like Zhejiang (6082 $), Jianxi (5695 $) and Liaoning (4506 $) have the highest per capita GDP. These are in the eastern part of the country. The lowest per capita GDP is in interior Provinces like Guizhou (1293 $), Gansu (1745 $), Henan (1823 $), Yunan (1840 $) and Tibet (1997$). Among the Provincial level cities, Chongqing (2597$) has the lowest per capita GDP.
2. Most populated Provinces are Guangdong (113 m), Henan (99 m), Shangdong (92 m), Sichuan (87 m) and Hebei (68 m). The least populated are Tibet (2.74 m),

Ningxia Hui ((5.88 m), and Qinghai (5.39 m). The density of population per sq.m. is highest in the Areas/Provinces of Macao (17310), Hong Kong (6352), Shanghai (2622), Jilin (1450) and least in Tibet (2), Qinghai (7), Xingiang (12) and Inner Mongolia (20).

3. The Provinces smallest in area are Shaanxi (20560 sq.m), Hainan (34000 sq. m) and Ninxia Hi (66400 sq. m) and the biggest are Xinjiang Yogurt (1660400 sq. m) Tibet (1228400 sq. m) and Inner Mongolia (1183000 sq. m). The map given below[2] shows the Territorial divisions of the country.

China-Provinces (22), Municipalities (4), Autonomous Regions (5) and Specially Administered Regions (2) and their capitals.

The Pie diagram[3] on the next page shows the distribution of population at the first tier level. The map further down[4] shows the density of population in different provincial level units with the darker colour showing

## China-Distribution of Population

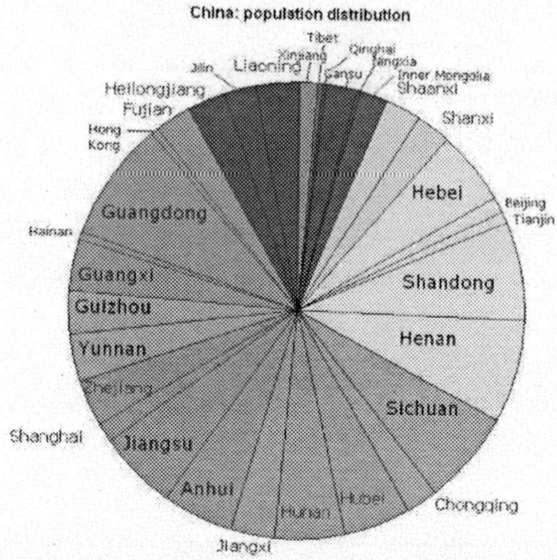


A population distribution map of the People's Republic of China. Population density map of China[4]

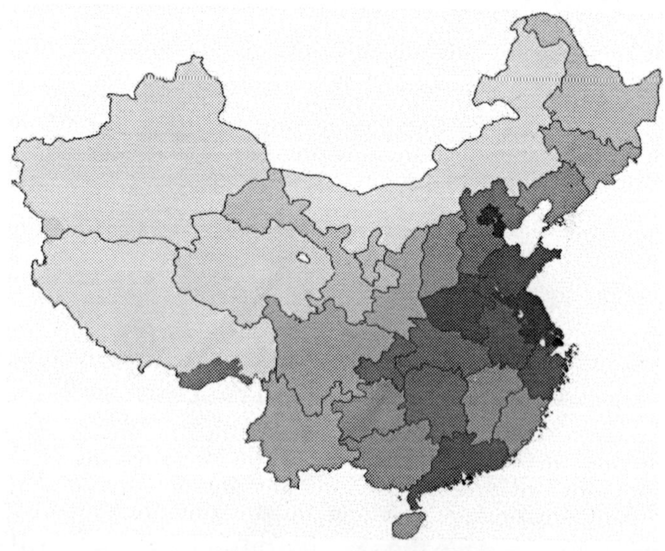

N.B. The map above wrongly shows Arunachal Pradesh in India as part of China.

higher densities and lighter colour lesser ones. The eastern, coastal provinces are much more densely populated than the western interior areas.

Superimposition (as given below) of the satellite maps (Google) of China over that of U.S. will show that US is only marginally bigger. But, Canada and Russia are much bigger than China.

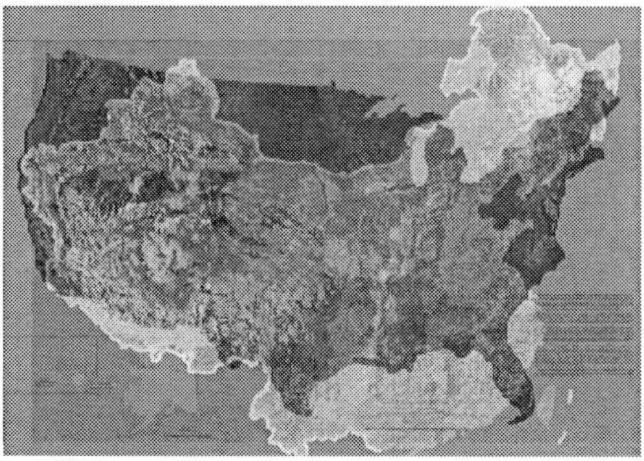

The Heihe-Tengchong Line,[5] also called the Aihui-Tengchong Line, is an imaginary line from Heihe to Tengchong County diagonally across China dividing it into two roughly equal area parts. Chinese population geographer Hu Huanyong who "invented" the line in 1935 called it a "geo-demographic demarcation line".

In 1935, the western part had 57% of the area, but only 4% of the population and the eastern part with 43% of the area, but 96% of the population. After 75 years, the statistics remain more or less the same but for some shift of population from east to west. According to the 2000 census, 9.2% lived west of the Line and this increase of 5.2% is attributed to Han Chinese migration to urban areas in autonomous regions of Tibet and Xinjiang. Still, the western part remains relatively rural and poor.

2. **People.** China now has a population[6] of over 1.33 bn with age groups 0–14, 15–64 and 65 and above constituting

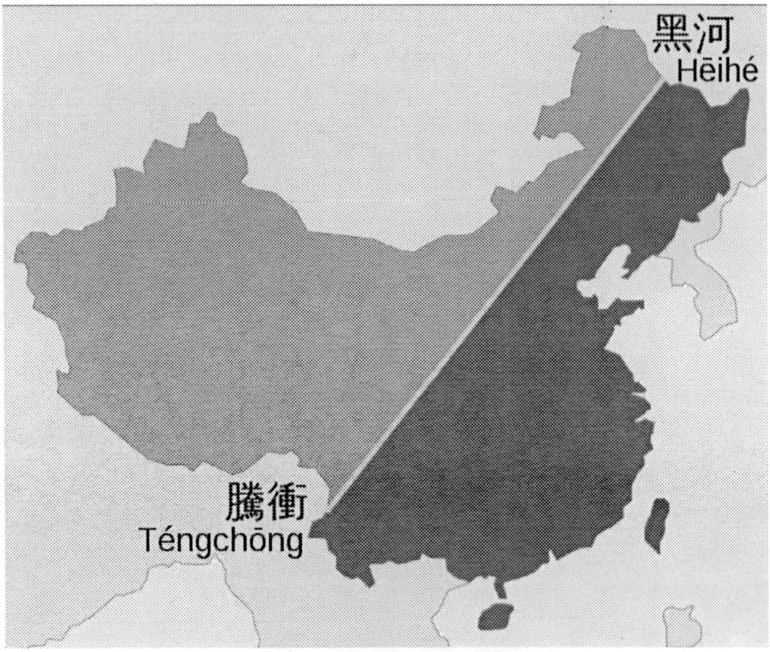


The Heihe-Tengchong Line

19.8%, 72.1%and 8.1% respectively. The median age for the whole population is 35.2 (male-34.5 and female 35.8). The population has a growth rate of .494% with a birth rate of 12.17 births/1,000 population (2010 est.) and 6.89 deaths/ 1,000 population (2010 est.). The urban population is about 43% which has been consistently going up in the recent past. The sex ratio at birth is 1.14 males/female and for the total population 1.06 males/female. The Infant mortality for the whole population is about 16.51 deaths/1,000 live births and life expectancy is 74.51 years (male-72.54 years and female-76.77 years-2010 est.). The average fertility rate is 1.54 children born/woman (2010 est.). The prevalence of Aids is 0.1% (2007 est.), people living with Aids about 700000 and 39000 deaths p.a. due to it (2007). The basic ethnic group is Han (91.5%) and the minority groups Zhuang, Manchu, Hui, Miao, Uighur, Tujia, Yi, Mongol, Tibetan, Buyi, Dong,

Yao, Korean, etc.constitute 8.5% (2000 census). Though officially atheist, Daoism (Taoism) and Buddhism have more believers followed by Christianity (3–4%) and Islam (1–2%). The main language is Standard Chinese or Mandarin (Putonghua, based on the Beijing dialect-official). Other dialects are Yue (Cantonese), Wu (Shanghainese), Minbei (Fuzhou), Minnan (Hokkien-Taiwanese), Xiang, Gan, Hakka and a few other minority languages. The literacy (definition: ability of age 15 and above to read and write) of the people has gone up remarkably in the recent decades as the educational expenditure reached 1.9% GDP (1999). It has further gone up in terms of percentage of the GDP and also in quantitative terms because of the rapidly increasing GDP. It has raised the total literacy to 91.6 % (male: 95.7%, female: 87.6%) (2007). The school life expectancy (primary to tertiary) is now about 11 years (Male: 11 years, Female: 12 years) (2008). *(pl. see Appendix-5 also).*

3. **Physiography.** China lies in the Pale-arctic and the Oriental zoogeographic regions[7]. All areas north of the Huang He, the Qing Zang Plateau, Xinjiang and Nei Monggol autonomous regions and northeastern China are in the Pale-arctic region. Central, southern, and southwest China lie in the Oriental region. Two-third of China is covered by Mountains*, hills, and highlands. In the southwest, the Himalayas and the Kunlun Mountains enclose Tibet, which has an average altitude of 4000 m above sea level. The Himalayas on the southwest and the Altai Mountains on the northwest form a natural boundary. On the eastern side are the densely populated low-lying areas of China with intense cultivation. All the principal rivers of China originate from the mountains some of which like the Kunlun have several branches rising eastward from the Pamir Mountains. The Qin Ling* mountain range, a continuation of the Kunlun Mountains, divides the North China Plain from the Yangtze River

Delta. It is the major physiographic and cultural boundary between the northern and southern parts. The topographical map of China below, with the greener color showing low lying areas, will help to better understand the physiographic features.

South of the Qin Ling divide in the middle are the densely populated and highly developed areas of the lower and middle plains of the Yangtze River. The Sichuan Basin is on its upper reaches. A high barrier of mountain ranges encircles it. Southeast of these mountains lies a coastal, hilly region of small deltas and narrow valley plains. This drainage area of the Pearl River and its associated network of rivers occupy a large part of the south. A southern branch of the Kunlun Mountains* divides the watersheds of Huang He. Towards the south is the largest loess plateau in the world, covering 600,000 square kilometers in Shaanxi Province, parts of Gansu and Shanxi provinces, and some of Ningxia-Hui Autonomous Region. As the river level drops precipitously toward the North China Plain, the river becomes sluggish and a heavy load of sand and mud from the upper the reaches gets deposited on the flat plain. The river hence flows on a raised ridge fifty meters or more above the plain requiring continuous efforts to protect the embankments. Water logging, floods, and course changes have recurred over the centuries.

4. **Rivers.** The *Yangtze River,* also called 'Yangtze Kiang', 'Yangtze Jiang'and 'Chang Jiang' is the country's longest and most important waterway. The name 'Yangtze Jiang', considered a poetic name in Chinese, is from Sui dynasty days. It comes from an ancient name for a ferry crossing in its lower reaches. The modern name 'Chang Jiang' means Long River. At its origin, in Tibet, it is called 'Dangqu' meaning marshy river. It is navigable over much of its length and has a vast hydroelectric potential. Rising in the Qing Zang Plateau in Qinghai province in Tibetan Plateau, it flows through the Provinces of Qinghai, Sichuan, Yunnan, Hunan, Jianxi, Anhui and Giansu and

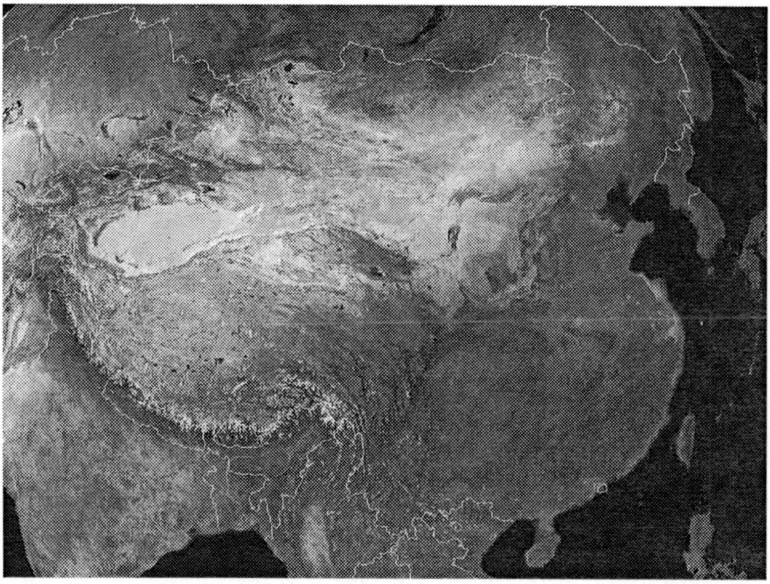

Topography of China[8]

finally Shanghai city before joining the East China Sea. It drains an area of 1.8 million square kilometers. While traversing 6,300 kilometers through the heart of the country, water from thousands of lakes, including four fresh water lakes and several tributaries joins it. Some regions are heavily polluted. Roughly 350 million people live along its middle and lower reaches cultivating rice and wheat. The Sichuan Basin produces a rich variety of crops. It is also a leading silk-producing area and an important industrial region with substantial mineral resources. It is hence called a 'golden water course'.

Yangtze is considered a dividing line between north and south China. The Three Gorges (collectively called Sanxia gorge and separately as Qutang, Wuxia and Xiling -. pict. page 231) hydel, irrigation and flood saving project is a gigantic one meant to generate huge quantities of hydel power, improve water transport and control floods. With its 600 ft high and 1.5 miles long dam, it is the largest power project generating 1/9th of China's hydel power. It is alleged that the gains would be at the cost of flooding many existing towns, cultural relics, and large-scale changes in ecology. Yangtze valley has many mountains, rivers, lakes and also the Grand Canal. It is one of the busiest waterways and is flanked by many industrial belts, which also pollute it in a big way. It provides internal link to international shipping to many provinces and is an internal artery for transportation for coal, manufactured goods, passengers, etc. Now luxury liners are available with international help. Tours in three gorges area are quite popular. From Han dynasty days, the river region was very important for China's economy. The difficulty of crossing the river had made it a boundary between North and South China.

*Yellow River (Huang Hai,* the 2$^{nd}$ largest in China (5464 km) after Yangtze and 6$^{th}$ largest in the world, is considered the cradle of Chinese civilization and hence is called the 'Mother River'. The name 'Yellow River' comes from the perennial ochre-yellow colour of the loess or yellowish soil blown in from the Nei Monggol deserts, suspended in water, which choke the Huang He with silt. Originating from two lakes in the Bayan Har Mountains of Qinghai province, traversing through the North China Plain, the historic center of Chinese expansion and influence and passing through 7 Provinces, 2 autonomous regions and major cities like Lan Zhou, Wuhai, Kaifeng, Baotou and Jinan, it empties into Bohai Sea. It has a drainage basin of 752,443 sq.km and maintains 120 million people in an east-west extent of 1900 km and north-south extent of 1100 km. It was often subject to devastating floods because of its elevated bed and is hence called China's 'pride and sorrow'. 1593 floods are said to have taken place during the last 3000–4000 years with the river changing course at least 8 times. The fluctuations of the North China plain contribute to deadliness of the floods. As fine-grained silt is continuously getting deposited down stream, the river flows above the surrounding farmland. A proposed

'South to North water transfer project' involves several schemes to divert Yangtze water where the two rivers are close to one another and another for the upper reaches of Hai River and a third using the Grand Canal.

*Other important Chinese rivers* are: *The Hai He,* located between Yangtze and Yellow Rivers, flows from west to east over 1000 km in length and has a basin of 185,700 sq.km. It is also vulnerable to flooding and its upper course consists of five rivers that converge near Tianjin, and then flow seventy kilometers before emptying into the Bo Hai Gulf. *Pearl River (earlier called Canton River),* also called Yue Jiang/Guangdong River, is the 3rd longest in China with 2nd largest volume. It is formed by the convergence of Xi Jiang (West River) and Bei jiang (North river) and, flowing through the provinces of Guangdong, Guanxi, Yunan and Guizhou and parts of Hunan and Jianxi, empties into the South China Sea between Hong Kong and Macao. It has a basin of 409480 sq. km and is very Polluted. *Songhua River,* also, also called Surgari River, is in northeast China. It is the largest tributary of Heilong River. Originating from Changbai Mountains, it flows through Heilongjiang and Jilin provinces and is navigable up to Harbin and for smaller vessels up to Jilin. *Tarim River* (tarim means 'bank of a river that flows into a lake' or 'that is not differentiated from sands of desert') is the longest inland waterway and also the principal river of the Xinjiang Uygur Autonomous region. It is formed by the union of Aksu and Yarkand Reservoirs and is located north of the Tibetan Plateau. Muzat River is one of its tributaries. It is 1,321 kilometers long and runs west to east along the northern edge of the Taklimakan Desert (China's largest) before flowing into Taitema Lake. Its basin is about 55700 sq. km, mostly the desert region of Eurasia with very low rainfall. In its valley 10 million people, mostly Uygurs and Mongolians, live. The River is shallow, silted and, hence is unsuitable for navigation. *Lijiang River* in Guanxi province originates in Mao'er Mountains and flows through

Guilin, Yangshuo and Pingle into Xijiang River. Its 437 km length is flanked by green hills. Cormorant fishing is associated with it. Karst topography of the region provides very beautiful scenery. Reed flute limestone caves, seven star park, mountain of splendid lives, mountain of many layers of variously coloured rocks, Elephant Trunk Hill (a hill that looks like a giant elephant drinking water), lingqu canal (a 214 B.C. canal), etc. are its main attractions. *Nanxi River,* a pure water river in Zhejiang Province, provides a good scenic zone with natural landscapes. The river first flows into Qujiang River and then empties into East China Sea.*Jin Sha Jiang River* flows southward and then turns eastward and eventually becomes a tributary and flows into Yangtze River. *Nu Jiang River* is about 1,500 miles (2,450 km) long. It flows south to become partly the border between Myanmar and Thailand. After leaving China, it is called Salween River. *LanCang Jiang River (Mekong River*) flows southward from China to Laos, Myanmar and Thailand. After leaving China, it is called Mekong River.

There are about 20000 lakes and of these 2300 have over one sq. km. size.Lakes cover a total area of 70988 sq. kms i.e. 8% of the area of China. The quantity of water in these is estimated to be 707.7 bn. cubic meters of which fresh water alone is 225 b. cubic meters. The presence of lakes is greater in Qinghai—Tibet plateau (51.4%), eastern Plains (30.2%), Mongolia-Xinjiang plateau (13.1%) and North-eastern plateau and mountains (3.3%). Other famous lakes are West, Poyang (Jiang), Dongting (Hunan), and Qinghai lakes. The others are Abe (Xingjian), Dagze Co (Tibet), Chao (Anhui), Deanship (Shanghai), Dian and Ethan (Yunan), Luoma, Hongse, Yangcheng (Jiangsu), Dong Quien and Qiandao west (Zhejiang).

5. **Climate.** China's climate* varies from subtropical in the south to sub-artic in the north. The monsoon climate dominates. The advance and retreat of the monsoons generally account for the timing and the amount of

rainfall. Tremendous differences in latitude, longitude, and altitude result in sharp variations in precipitation and temperature. Most of the country is in the temperate belt, but its climatic patterns are complex. The northernmost parts are in the cold-temperate zone while the southernmost parts near the Hainan Island have a tropical climate. Temperatures in the north can vary from -40 degrees Celsius in winter (December-March) to 38 degrees in summer (May-August). Rainfall varies more. Regions south of the Qin Ling have abundant rainfall, mostly in summer monsoons. In the north and west, rainfall is uncertain and the farther north and west one moves, it becomes scantier and uncertain. The northwest has the lowest rainfall and no rains in desert areas.

6. **Vegetation.** All the major types in the world except those of the equatorial rainforest and polar tundra are present. The natural vegetation can be divided into 29 types, 52 subtypes, and well over 600 principal colonies. It has all the woody temperate species. In a general way ,it can be divided into Coniferous forests, Mixed needle leaf and broadleaf forests, Broadleaf forests, Bushes, Grasslands, Savannas, Deserts, Alpine tundras, Alpine cushion plants, Meadows and Swamps. Of China's seed plants, 46 families are cosmopolitan, 168 families tropicopolitan, 77 families temperate, 7 families paleo-Mediterranean, and 3 families peculiar to China. There are numerous ancient or primitive families and many remnant plants of the Tertiary Period like some gymnospermous plants, common China fir, water pine, some some of fir family, some of the pine family, Chinese tulip tree, lily magnolia, cottonrose hibiscus, and banana shrub of the magnolia family, and several other plants of the Chinese witch hazel family. It has the 3$^{rd}$ largest variety in vegetation after Malaysia and Brazil.

7. **Wildlife.** China has most species of wild animals, with the number of terrestrial vertebrates alone exceeding 2,000, nearly 10 percent of the world total. Birds make up the largest, followed by beasts. Bird species so far discov-

The giant panda[9]

ered total 1,189; beasts, 500; amphibians, 210; and reptiles, 320. Many of the terrestrial vertebrate species in China are peculiar to, or are mainly found in the country. There are 19 species of the pheasant family, such as bamboo partridge, tragopan, blue pheasant and white-crowned king pheasant. There is also Pere David's deer, which is of special value to zoological studies and whose wild species has been extinct. Other rare species include takin, tufted deer and sika deer. China also has abundant species of resource animals, with more than 70 fur-bearing species, accounting for 17 percent of total beast species nationwide. It has rare animals like the giant panda, South China tiger, golden lion tamarin, Tibetan wolves, yak, Chinese alligator, snub nosed golden monkey, brown-eared pheasant, red-crowned crane, red ibis and white-flag dolphin. The giant panda, extremely rare with just over 1,000 left and symbol of the world's protected wild animals, weighs about 135 kg and lives on tender bamboo leaves and bamboo shoots.

8. **Natural resources.** Among the land resources, there are more mountains than plains, with cultivated land (10%)

and forests (14%) constituting only small proportions. Permanent pastures constitute 43 percent and other types constitute 33 percent. Irrigated land is about 498,720 sq km. The land resources are unevenly distributed also. The cultivated land is mainly in plains and basins in the monsoon regions of east China, while forests are mostly found in the remote mountainous areas in the northeast and the southwest. Grasslands are chiefly distributed on inland plateaus and in mountains. China has over 2.17 million hectares of coastal tidal-flat areas, an important kind of land and space resources, as they contain various mineral, biological and marine resources. China now has more than 50 salt fields along its coast, with a combined acreage of 337,000 hectares. Sea salt constitutes over 70 percent of China's total production of crude salt, with its annual output exceeding 20 million tons, ranking first world wide. A total of 20,278 species of marine organisms have been verified as living in China's offshore waters. Aquatic farms along the country's coast now cover 164,000 hectares, mainly breeding such shellfish as scallop, oyster and clam, and laminaria. China's tidal energy reserves amount to 110 million kw, 21 million kw of it being exploitable, which can be used to generate 58 billion kwh of power annually. Zhejiang and Fujian provinces account for 80 percent. The Qiantangjiang estuary in Zhejiang has a tidal range of 8.9 meters and is an ideal place for a tidal power plant. Coal, iron ore, petroleum, natural gas, mercury, tin, tungsten, antimony, manganese, molybdenum, vanadium, magnetite, aluminum, lead, zinc, uranium, phosphate, sylvite and hydropower potential (world's largest) are the other major natural resources.

9. **Constitution.** Under the present Constitution promulgated on 4 December 1982, the National People's Congress (NPC), a unicameral body with 2,979 members who are elected by municipal, regional, and provincial people's congresses to serve five-year terms is the

highest legislative body. The NPC elects the President and Vice-President of the country for five-year terms. The Prime Minister is nominated by the president and confirmed by the NPC. He is in charge of the State Council, the Cabinet, and is responsible to the NPC. The Chinese Communist Party or CCP with, Hu Jintao, as General Secretary of the Central Committee, is the only Party active in the country though there are eight registered small parties controlled by CCP also functioning. There are no substantial political opposition groups although the government has identified the Falun Gong sect and the China Democracy Party as potential rivals and banned them. Direct elections are held only at the lowest level of County based on universal suffrage for all above 18 years. There are restrictions on the number of candidates who can contest the elections with a maximum of 50% more at the lowest level where only direct elections are held. Above County level, elected representatives elect members of the higher legislative body (Peoples' Congress) with the number of excess candidates getting progressively reduced to 10% at the level of Province.

10. **Legal System.** Chinese legal code is a complex amalgam of statutes largely focused on criminal law. A rudimentary code is in operation since Jan 1987. Efforts are on to improve civil, criminal, administrative and commercial laws based on the guiding principles of Marxism-Leninism and Mao's thoughts. After the Cultural Revolution, efforts were made to develop a legal system to restrain abuses of official authority and revolutionary excesses. In 1982, the NPC adopted a new constitution that emphasized the concept of rule of law by which the party and state organizations are subject to law. A 1999 constitutional amendment also stressed the rule of law. These in no way weaken the CPC which is in a good position to change the law to suit its needs.

    Laws are essentially made to change the economy. Besides the NPC, Provincial and local Congresses can also make laws, but there is no guarantee that they will be implemented. Even court decisions are seen as something to be negotiated by Provincial governments, SOEs, etc. Since 1979, more than 301 laws and regulations have been promulgated. After the entry into WTO, many laws and regulations have been amended. Use of mediation committees of informed citizens who solve about 90% of all disputes and some minor criminal ones is an innovative measure. Legal reforms are considered a priority now. A Legislation to modernize and professionalize the nation's lawyers, judges and prisons was enacted. A 1994 law allows citizens to sue officials for abuse of authority or malfeasance. The criminal law amendment abolished the crime of counter-revolutionary activity. Procedures are being made more transparent and more adversarial trial process is being implemented. Laws on fundamental human rights, due process, etc. are also covered in the constitution though with limitations. Although the human rights situation has improved sine 1960s, the Government allegedly remains authoritarian and determined to crush any opposition to its rule like those from Tibetan and Xingjian separatists. The public sentiment in China is overwhelmingly in favour of continuance of death penalty as crime is seen as a serious problem.

Finality of trial is reached after two trials, if not appealed against with in the permitted appeal period or the Supreme Court hears a case directly. At each level there are Judicial Committees of courts appointed by the local congress or it's Standing Committee on the recommendation of the President of the Court to supervise courts. The President heads the Judicial Committee with the Divisional Chiefs and a few experienced Judges selected by the Standing Committee of the People's Congress as members. The committee can decide important cases or issue directions to judges or panels of judges. Each court has a President as presiding officer and several Vice-Presidents and different divisions for civil, criminal, administrative, enforcement and economic cases. Each division has a Chief and several associate Chiefs. It is the court and not a judge, which is vested with powers. Normally, a panel of judges will consist of 3 to 7 members. In simple matters, only one judge may constitute a court. At the second trial, a panel may be of 3 to 5 members. The President or Divisional Chief decides the presiding judges. The Standing Committee of the people's congress may prepare panels of assessors and give to courts. Such assessors have power to decide on facts and also on law unlike in a jury system. Again, unlike in adversarial system, judges are not silent listeners, but are dominant parties who ask questions to bring out facts. President and divisional Chiefs have powers to suggest changes in decisions taken by courts, which are often seen as interference in the western world. The Judicial Committee itself may decide on a case on completion of trial, again seen in the West as undue interference.

11. **The Criminal Justice System** consists of the People's courts under the relevant People's Congress and Higher Courts, Procuratorates (in charge of Prosecution, supervision of certain police roles, Prison systems, etc.), Police, Prison and correctional services. At the highest level is the People's Supreme Court headed by a President selected by the National People's Congress for a term of 5 years. He is assisted by Vice-Presidents, Heads and Assistant Heads of Divisions, Judges, etc. selected by the Standing Committee of the NPC. The Supreme Court has separate divisions for criminal, civil, economic, etc., cases assigned by law, other very important cases, appeals and Protests from Higher Courts and Special Courts, etc. It can give guidance to lower courts on important points or doubts raised ("Judicial legislation").

**Courts.** According[10] to the Chinese Constitution and the Organic Law of the People's Courts, the Chinese courts are divided into a four-level court system:

- At the highest level is the Supreme People's Court in Beijing as the premier appellate that supervises the administration of justice by all subordinate "local" and "special" people's courts.
- Local people's courts—the courts of the first instance—handle criminal and civil cases. These people's courts make up the remaining three levels of the court system and consist of "high people's courts" at the level of the provinces, autonomous regions, and special municipalities; "intermediate people's courts" at the level of prefectures, autonomous prefectures, and municipalities; and "basic people's courts" at the level of autonomous counties, towns, and municipal districts.
- Courts of Special Jurisdiction (special courts) comprise the Military Court of China (military), Railway Transport Court of China (railroad transportation) and Maritime Court of China (water transportation), and Forestry.

The court system is paralleled by a hierarchy of prosecuting offices called people's procuratorates, the highest being the Supreme People's Procuratorate. Hong Kong and Macau have separate court systems.

12. **Prosecution.** Procuratorate is the state organization for legal supervision of offences against the state, criminal cases, approval of arrests, prosecution/exemption from it, supervision over public security agencies, judicial activities in courts, prisons and detention centers, transformation through labour, supervision of prosecution in lower courts, etc. Its head, the Procurator General of the Supreme Court, is selected by the NPC. The Standing Committee of the NPC, based on the recommendation of the Procurator General selects Dy. Pro General, Members of the Procurator Committee and Procurators. The departments are decided based on needs. The decisions of the Procurator Committee are binding on all its lower levels. At each level of the court

system, there is a Chief Procurator, assisted by a number of Deputies and Procurators appointed by the relevant People's Congress or its Standing Committee.

13. **Crimes** are categorized generally into eight groups based on their objectives like against Communist revolution, Public security (arson, use of explosives, involving arms/ammunition, traffic accidents etc), socialist order (smuggling, speculation, trade marks related, etc), democratic rights of citizens (homicide, rape, abduction, forcing people into prostitution, unlawful detention, insults, humiliation etc), property, social order, marriage/family, duty/work, etc. Crime is not registered against those below 16 and in cases involving 16-18 years, lighter punishments are given. Death penalty is not given below 18 years.

14. **Police.** Police is involved in every aspect of life. Besides the pre-trial investigation, traffic control, detention centers, etc. supervised by local governments and procuratorates, reporting on all persons living in its jurisdiction, births, deaths, divorces, etc, regulation of hotels, arms, ammunition and explosives, poison, issue of Id. cards to all above 16, counseling and acting as role models, etc. are among the police jobs. The Police can normally arrest people only with a warrant approved by the Procuratorate.But in special/emergent circumstances, it can do so even with out it. Families are to be notified of arrest in 24 hours. Maximum detention under arrest is for 2 months. The conviction rate was nearly 83% in 1991 and 91% in 2000. The trials are normally fast and conviction quick. There are allegations of not notifying arrest in time, not giving enough time with defense lawyers, collusion between ruling party, police, and procuratorate and courts for quick disposal of cases and pre-decided convictions on extraneous considerations. Police in China has 13 levels-2 in constable, 3 in Sergeants, 3 in Inspectors, 3 in Dy. commissioner and 2 at the level of Commissioner. Police vehicles have black colour for the bottom half and white for the upper part.

15. **The National Security system** consists of the Ministries of State Security and Public Security, the People's Liberation Army (PLA), and the state judicial, procuratorial, and penal systems. The Ministry of State Security deals with activities of enemy agents, spies, subversion, revealing of state secrets, political dissenters, social advocacy, domestic and foreign Intelligence, etc. The Ministry of Public Security deals with police functions (including People's Armed Police, and PLA), Criminal Justice System (including Procuratorates, and penal systems), Security of Government offices, vital installations, VIPs, and Embassies, border Security, etc. The 1.5 million strong People's Armed Police deals with most of the pure security roles including border defense and assists the civil police when needed. At the Provincial level, Public Security Departments are under the dual supervision of Ministry of Public security and also the Provincial Administration. Below this, Public Security Bureaus in Prefectures/Cities are again under the dual control of the Local Administration and the Provincial Public Security Departments. There are Sub-Bureaus at the county level and Public Security Stations at the town level again under the dual control of the next higher levels and also the local Administration. The Public Security organization leads and directs the police and state security in matters of investigation, arrests, preliminary hearings, etc. Committees appoints its Heads at different levels.

16. **Local Government.** The local govt. is now structured in a hierarchy of four levels[11] (*Pl see Appendix-3*). The four levels are the township, county, prefecture or municipality and the Province. **Province level.** In 1996, China had 31 provincial-level administrative units, including 22 provinces, 5 autonomous regions and 4 cities of Beijing, Shanghai, Tianjin and Chongqing. **City level.** This category includes cities under the jurisdiction of the province, prefectures, autonomous prefectures as

well as leagues and districts under the jurisdiction of the apex municipalities. **County level.** This level includes county, autonomous county, county-level city, banner, autonomous banner, special zone, forest districts, industrial and agricultural districts, districts of the city under the jurisdiction of province, sub-districts of the apex municipalities, etc. **Village (town) level.** These include county, autonomous village, town, sub-district (excluding those of the municipality) and are the lowest levels of local government. Each level has its own People's congress, which elects its Government for 3 to 5 years and also has the power to pass local legislations. Bureaucracy at lower levels has to obey the higher levels. Each level is responsible for organizing the work of lower levels. At each level, there are two important officials- a figure reporting to the CPC termed party chief acting as the policy maker appointed by the supervisors. The second is the head of the people's government appointed in theory by the people and is usually called a Governor, Mayor or Magistrate. The second figure carries out the policies and most ceremonial functions. The party Secretary is always in precedence over the leader of the people's government. A central ministry and Province are at the same level. PM's orders have to be obeyed by them.

The **power** has now become more institutionalized after Deng Xiao Ping who was never the President or Secy. of the CPC, but was the 'leader' for a decade. The Regional power lies with party secretaries from Beijing, Shanghai, and major provinces like Guangdong, who are also in the P.B. Bigger and wealthier regions have growing power. Guangdong and Zhejing Provinces enjoy more autonomy on economic issues. Autonomous Regions and Prefectures are meant to give greater autonomy to ethnic groups. Now the Central Government has to build consensus for new policies among local, regional and influential non-party members and the population at large. As transition from public ownership to private ownership is increasing through privatization of the economy, freedom to make choices about education and employment is also increasing. It has weakened the CPC whose cell in the work unit was the control centre. Over economic issues, more and more control is being lost.

Sometimes, conflicts come up between municipalities and central leaders, esp. in Beijing and Shanghai. The removal of the Shanghai Municipality party secy. in Sept. 2006 and President Zemin's conflict with the Mayor of Beijing are some examples. Generally, Beijing appoints loyal party leaders, usually Hans Chinese, to over see the local work as party secretary while the chairman of the region's government, the nominal head, will be from the local ethnic group concerned. The management of the Provinces and townships is done through about 7000 party and government leaders who are appointed by the Organizational Dept. of the CPC to ensure implementation of the party line. Senior party cadres are transferred across the country. Hence, a high-ranking leader's career would include roles as party secy. or governor of different Provinces.

Conflicts between the way of the comrade wanting continuance of controls and the way of the citizen aspiring for more freedom resulting from the market reforms are being manifest. It is perhaps felt by the party thinkers that gradual political reforms and repression of those pressing for rapid change over the next 30 years will be essential if turbulent transition to a middle class dominated polity is to be avoided. The Cultural Revolution and its adverse impact, the Russian experience and the bitter experience of the Tiananmen Square revolt of June 1989 perhaps explain the robust system of monitoring and control in place to control the growing pressure for political changes.

17. **Relations with Neighbors** China has borders with Afghanistan (76 km), Bhutan (470 km), Burma (2,185 km), India (3,380 km), Kazakhstan (1,533 km), North Korea (1,416 km), Kyrgyzstan (858 km), Laos (423 km), Mongolia (4,677 km), Nepal (1,236 km), Pakistan

(523 km), Russia (northeast 3,605 km, northwest 40 km), Tajikistan (414 km), Vietnam (1,281 km) and regional borders with Hong Kong (30 km) and Macau (0.34 km).

The country had border problems mainly with Russia and India. The 6,542-kilometer frontier with the **Soviet Union** was, at one time, a source of friction. In 1954 China published maps showing substantial portions of Soviet Siberian territory as its own. In the northeast, border friction with the Soviet Union produced a tense situation in remote regions of Nei Monggol Autonomous Region (Inner Mongolia) and Heilongjiang Province. In September 1986, Soviet leader Mikhail S. Gorbachev offered the Chinese a more conciliatory position and the two sides resumed border talks that had been broken off after the 1979 Soviet invasion of Afghanistan. In 1991, the Sino-Russian Border Agreement was signed apportioning territory that became contested during the Sino-Soviet border conflict. The Russian government agreed to transfer Tarabarov Island and one half of Bolshoy Ussuriysky Island to China in 2004, ending the long-standing border dispute.

A major dispute between China and **India** remains unresolved. It concerns the northern edge of their shared border, where the Aksai Chin area of northeastern Jammu and Kashmir is under Chinese control but claimed by India. Eastward from Bhutan and north of the Brahmaputra River (Yarlung Zangbo Jiang) is a large area of Arunachal Pradesh in India, but claimed by the Chinese in the aftermath of the 1959 Tibetan revolt. The British McMahon Line, drawn along the Himalayas in 1914 as the Sino-Indian border, demarcated the area. India accepts and China rejects this boundary. In June 1980, China made its first move in twenty years to settle the border disputes with India, proposing that India cede the Aksai Chin area in Jammu and Kashmir to China in return for China's recognition of the McMahon Line. India did not accept the offer preferring a sector-by-sector approach to the problem. Several rounds of border talks have not produced any worthwhile results. Each side, but primarily India, continues to make allegations of incursions into its territory by the other. Despite this, trade relations has been improving with China becoming a major trade partner. Pakistan's closeness to China and China's suspicions about the US becoming closer to India as a counter weight against China are also relevant factors.

China and **Pakistan** have enjoyed a solid strategic relationship since the 1960s and China has provided Pakistan with a wide range of major conventional weapons. The two have various defence co-operation programmes to counter Soviet and Indian closeness on security issues. Pakistan has relied on China as an ally in dealing with India because of its military weakness. Beijing also values its close ties with Islamabad to extend its influence to South Asia and to balance against India. Bilateral trade between China and Pakistan today stands at around US$ 2.5 billion, with Chinese exports to Pakistan accounting for US$ 1.5 billion. In April 2005 a Free Trade Agreement, under which both sides have agreed to cut down excise duties and bring the tariffs to zero on a range of commonly used commodities, was signed by the two countries.

Though **Nepal** had always favoured its links with India, China is offering new prospects to Nepal as part of China's plan to develop its own western region. When high speed rails and express highways connect Tibet with mainland China, tourist flow to Nepal would increase from easier access to Nepal benefitting its economy. China has also already mentioned Nepal in its outbound tourist destination list for Chinese people. In May 2005, a bus owned by the Nepalese Government launched weekly coach trips between Kathmandu and Lhasa for nine months of the year. Enhanced trade possibilities and Joint venture programs (such as hydro-power generation) are also expected to flourish.

**Bangladesh** has long established diplomatic ties with China. Over time, China has set up in Bangladesh power plants, fertilizer factories, marine fisheries, and infrastructure developments including six "friendship" bridges and a Bangladesh-China Friendship Centre. But, Bangladesh had to dump Taiwan to facilitate this. Bangladesh still has a negative trade balance with China.

**Bhutan**'s foreign relations are Indo-centric and managed by India. Bhutan does not have any diplomatic ties with the People's Republic of China, despite sharing a contiguous northern boundary of 470 kilometers which is largely undemarcated. Relationship with China has been described as "indifferent". Traditional trade relations with Tibet remains suspended since 1960 when Tibetan refugees came to Bhutan. An agreement signed by Bhutan and China in 1998 to "Maintain Peace and Tranquility on the Bhutan-China Border" reiterated China's position "to fully respect the independence, sovereignty and territorial integrity of Bhutan".

**Mongolia** as a small nation situated between China and Russia was under the protective umbrella of Russia because of historical reasons. After the improvement of the China-Russian relations, both the countries recognized their shared strategic interests and improved relations. Though Russia continues to have political and economic influence in Mongolia, China is emerging as the main political and economic partner despite fears of Chinese expansion as Chinese regard Mongolia as a former part of its Middle Kingdom and view Mongolians as an ethnic minority.

**Myanmar.** China has since 1989 supplied weapons for the re-equipment and expansion of the Myanmar military. It is also deeply involved in economic and trade co-operation like upgrading of the port at Hyanggi and the communications facilities at Coco Island in the Bay of Bengal 45 kms from Indian Territory.

**Tajikistan, Kazakhstan and Kyrgyzstan.** In Xinjiang province of China, people are mostly Tajiks (Uyghurs) who speak an Iranian language and cultural-linguistic affiliations are considered important. **Uzbekistan** bordering Afghanistan also has a lot of Uyghurs too. The Uyghur ethnic group numbering about 9 million is the most dissimilar to the majority Han Chinese and speaks Turkish language almost like that spoken by the Uzbeks. As both are Muslim, they share a commonality. **Kazakhstan and Kyrgyzstan** lie adjacent to Tibet. The Uyghur people consider the Han Chinese presence in Xinjiang, or Eastern Turkistan as an occupation of their ancestral homeland. This places a bias on all affairs with China and consequently causes problems to the Chinese Government. In view of these, despite the absence of any major issue between China and countries like Tajikstan, Kazhakistan and Uzbekistan, sensitivites exist in the relations in view of the links of people of these countries.

**Vietnam** has differences with China about sovereignty over Hoang SA and Truong SA archipelagos. Though these archipelagos at present do not have favorable conditions for tourism as they are far from inland areas (Hoang SA 220 kilometers from Vietnam's inshore island of Ly Son and 260 kilometers from China's Hainan Island). Vietnamese suspect that China's plans to construct and develop International Tourism Island of Hainan incorporating these archipelagos under the management of the province of Hainan is meant to establish its claims for sovereignty on the basis of continuous occupation. China had in the past claimed these as part of its continental shelf.

**Afghanistan** and China in 1963 November signed a boundary treaty finally completing the determination of the boundaries of the two countries. Bilateral relations were very poor and hostile under the Taliban regime which had strongly backed the Uyghur rebels and and given sanctuary to the East Turkestan Islamic Movement and the East Turkestan Liberation Organization. China was also angered by the fact that the Taliban regime had also provided sanctuary for terrorist groups active in Central Asia and China. As a result, China had strongly supported the Northern Alliance which played a key role in the overthrow of the Taliban in 2001. After the fall of the Taliban regime and the United States' intervention in 2001, relations between China and Afghanistan have greatly improved. China has been continuously supporting the peace process, reconstruction, deepening cooperation in counter-terrorism, communication and coordination in international affairs and taking steps to raise bilateral ties to a new level.

There are some minor problems with **North Korea** created by the nuclear ambitions of N. Korean regime, growing presence of North-Korean refugees on Chinese soil and territorial disputes. China and North Korea share a 1,416-kilometre long border that corresponds broadly to the course of the Yalu and Tumen rivers. A dispute exists about Mount Paektu, a 2,744-metre high volcano lying at the source of the Yalu and Tumen rivers with a lake (Chongjin). Pyongyang claims 33 sq.km around the Mount Paektu because of a belief that the area is the birth place of founder of the first Korean state in 2333 B.C. North Korean authorities also consider Mount Paektu as the place of the most important guerrilla exploits in the 1930s under the command of Kim Il-Sung. Claims of Kim Jong-Il's birth on the Korean face of Mount Paektusan are also built-up to show symbolic closeness of his birthplace to the place dear to Korean people. Some problems about ownership of uninhabited islands in Yalu and Tumen, maritime boundary, etc exist stalling the economic development of the mouth of the Yalu and gulf Behai. China is avoiding increasing tensions with Pyongyang and inflaming nationalistic passions in South Korea.

**Thailand's** relationship with China is the closest balancing its good relations with US which is interested in its role in counter-terrorism, and peacekeeping contributions to both Afghanistan and Iraq. It gives Thailand access to advanced weaponry and annual Cobra Gold exercises, involving significant land, sea and air components of the United States armed forces. Both China and Thailand have a common interest in facing the separatist question in their troubled Muslim majority periphery areas—Patani in Thailand and Xinjiang in China. Convergence of interests exists over Cambodia and Vietnam too. Thailand had also supported China on the Taiwan issue, blocked entry to the Dalai Lama at one point and expelled members of the Falun Gong sect banned in China. Instances of bilateral tension over failure to aid Thailand in stemming the flow of drugs and people out of Burma, failure to restrain the Chinese-equipped Burmese army from the occasional border incursions, trade heavily weighted in China's favor which threatens a good deal of Thai businesses, etc.also are facts. Though unsure of the real implications and ultimate reach of China emerging as a superpower or China's ultimate intentions toward the region, Thailand hopes to accommodate China's rise.

Similarly, relations with **Cambodia** are very close. In the past five years, China has become Cambodia's most important source of foreign investment and invested $6 billion since 2006 in a $ 10 bn economy. China is seen as the region's strategic and economic hub. Both have agreed to cooperate on projects to develop Cambodia's agriculture, tourism and communications industries. The money China invests in Cambodia's infrastructure ends up going to state-owned Chinese companies that build the roads and hydropower dams. IMF has expressed concern over Beijing's insistence that Phnom Penh pledge to buy all of the power the hydropower dams generate for 30 years. Some criticize China's effect on Cambodia's environment, and the effort to improve governance and human rights. China's friendship provides Cambodia with a useful balance against countries such as Thailand, with which it has historical disputes.

China's relations with **Laos**, which had seen some deterioration after China's push into Vietnam close to Laos in 1978 has improved after 1989. China-Laos relations have been on trade and aid basically for road construction in the north. In 1992 an agreement delineating their common border was reached. China's commercial investments and trade with Laos have expanded since 1993. Some see China as the most powerful state to which Laos might turn for support against Thai or Vietnamese hegemony.

18. **Major Concerns.** China has the natural hazards of floods, tsunamis, earthquakes and droughts. Air pollution (greenhouse gases, sulfur dioxide acid rain),

water shortages, water pollution from untreated wastes, deforestation, soil erosion, desertification, etc. are major environmental issues. The democratic world, especially those who value human rights express concern over Suppression of Religious freedom, Arbitrary Detentions, Torture and Ill-treatment of Prisoners, Absence of Freedom of the Press and Individual Trade Union Rights, Lack of Judicial Independence and Due Process, Inadequate Efforts to stop ill-treatment, One Child policy, abduction and trafficking of women, Forced Evictions, increasing environmental damage, increasing inequalities in income and development, lowering of water table, arms sales and support to some controversial regimes. While some of these are systemic and relate generally to all communist systems, others are more specific for China.

## Endnotes

[1] Modified extracts from http://en.wikipedia.org/wiki/Administrative_divisions_of_China
[2] In Public domain.
[3] Ibid.
[4] Ibid.
[5] Released into the public domain by Author, Stefan Lew.
[6] CIA World Fact Book China, People.
[7] Modified extracts from CIA World Fact Book–China-Geography
[8] In Public domain–a NASA picture.
[9] In public domain.
[10] http://www.novexcn.com/organic_law.html
[11] From www.unescap.org/huset/lgstudy/country/china/china.htm

## References

a. en.wikipedia.org/wiki/Geography_of_China
b. http://en.wikipedia.org/wiki/Yangtze
c. * CIA FACT BOOK

d. 'Shangri-La', a booklet of China National Tourism Administration
e. http://en.wikipedia.org/wiki/Administrative_divisions_of_China
f. http://en.wikipedia.org/wiki/Heihe-Tengchong_Line
g. http://en.wikipedia.org/wiki/Court_system_of_the_People's_Republic_of_China
h. http://www.china.org.cn/english/Political/28842.htm
i. http://en.wikipedia.org/wiki/People's_Armed_Police
j. http://www.citymayors.com/government/china_locgov.html
k. http://www.unescap.org/huset/lgstudy/country/china/china.html
m. http://www.asianresearch.org/articles/2502.html
n. http://www.voanews.com/english/news/China-Cambodia-Ties-Grow-Tighter-88998402.html
o. http://en.wikipedia.org/wiki/File:PRC_Population_Density.svg

CHAPTER 1

# Historical Perspective

The History of China is briefly covered in three parts: Part I (Early or Pre-Imperialist Period up to 221 B.C.), Part II (the Imperialist Period from 221 B.C. to A.D. 1911) and Part III (the Post Imperialist/Republican/Modern Period from 1911).

## EARLY PERIOD

China is one of the oldest cradles of human civilization. The regions now comprising of China, even more than a million years ago, were perhaps inhabited by 'Homo Sapiens', or modern species of human beings. Stone tools found at Xiaochanliang (Hebei Province) are dated about 1.36 million years ago. The first evidence of use of fire in China, dated about 1.26 millions years ago, came from the archaeological site at Xihoudu (Shanxi Province). 'Peking Man' of the Old Stone Age discovered in 1923 is dated about 400,000 B.C. The other earliest sign of human life in China, perhaps dating back to about 600,000 B.C., was the discovery in 1963 of a fossilized skull (Shanxi Province). In the upper caves of the 'Peking Man' site, artifacts of a late Old Stone Age man (50,000–35,000 B.C.), an early form of modern man, who had made tools out of bones and stones, clothes out of animal hides, and had known the use of fire were discovered. There are claims that the 'Damaidi cliff carvings' in Ningxia Hui Autonomous Region showing characters like stars, sun, moon, gods, scenes of hunting, grazing, etc.could be as old as 20000 to 30000 years. These are similar to the earliest written Chinese characters.

Neolithic/New Stone Age in China perhaps started around 10000 B.C. The earliest evidence of Chinese civilization is associated with the 'Yangshao'culture along the Huang He (Yellow) River in Henan Province. It is dated 5000 to 3500 B.C. In Northern China, farming is believed to have commenced with millet culture. With agriculture increased population, storage and distribution of crops, specialized crafts men, etc. came up. Larger numbers of people began living together at settled places, cultivating millet and domesticating animals. These people made polished stone tools and built shelters in pit-dwellings and beehive-huts that were covered with reed roofs. They had developed the art of making pottery for storing food and drink. Red clay pots with black designs in the north-west near Yangshao village, and smooth black pottery in north-east China near Lungshan, Shandong Province showed further refinements in pottery. Such villages closely resembling those in the Nile valley in Egypt were found mostly in the area of the great bend of the Huang He (Yellow River) on the North-China Plains, good for agriculture. The culture, generally termed 'Yangshao' culture, shows that these Chinese who had settled in the Huang He (Yellow River) valley of northern China by 3000 B.C. had pottery, wheels, farms, and silk, but had not yet discovered writing or the uses of metals. The 'Long Shan culture' (Shandong Province) dated 3000 to 2000 B.C., perhaps a successor of the 'Yangshao culture', was more advanced with evidences of use of refined silk, fine fabrics, potter's wheel, and houses built with strong baked bricks. They also used irrigation and flood control systems.

According to one Chinese tradition, many tribes existed along the 'Yellow River' about 4000 years ago. Huangdi, s/o Shaodian, was head of one important tribe with bear as its totem. Huangdi, it is said, was a leader with high morals and great wisdom. Under his leader ship, Chinese way of life improved a lot and a new civilization emerged. Chinese believe themselves to be off-springs of Huangdi. As he had a great liking for yellow, he was also known as the 'Yellow Emperor'. His family, it is believed, lived in Henan Province. He is believed to have lived for 100–118 years (reigning from 2607 to 2598 B.C.) and then ridden a dragon to heaven to join the immortals. According to one belief, a dragon from heaven came to take Huangdi away. He emerged as the chief deity of Taoism during the Han dynasty. Generally, he is regarded as the legendary sovereign and cultural hero-ancestor of all Chinese. All the families of the nobles of the first three dynasties, Xia, Shang and Zhou, were said to be his descendants. He was buried in Mt.Qiao in Huangling county, Shaanxi province. During Qing Ming festival people pay homage to him at his Mausoleum (First Mausoleum).

**Xia dynasty (2100–1600 B.C.)** The history of ruling dynasties is traced back to 2100 B.C. commencing with the quasi-legendary 'Xia' dynasty (2100–1600 B.C.), the first to be described in the 'Records of Great Historians' written between 109 B.C. and 91 B.C. and unofficial bamboo annals. No written records are available; but, indications of commencement of dynastic rule are seen. There were 17 Xia kings ending with Jei who was notorious for corruption. He was overthrown by Tang, leader of the Shang people from the east.

**Shang Dynasty (1600–1100 B.C.)** The written history of China began with the Shang dynasty which was established in 1600 B.C. by Tang who overthrew Jei, the last Xia ruler. Tang was a compassionate ruler with his capital at Yin (the current Xiatun village in the Anyang city of Hinan province). It was also called 'Yinshang'. The dynasty gave great importance to agriculture, fishing, arts, sculpture, porcelain and metal works, etc. Bronze work reached high levels of excellence. Belief in God, worship of ancestors, sun, moon, rivers, etc.and fortune telling were prevalent. Records of solar and lunar eclipses and other celestial happenings, advancements in astronomy, calendar system, mathematics with odd and even numbers, etc. were other features of this period. A complex system of picture writing using forms called ideograms, pictograms, and phonograms was developed by 2000 B.C. Records of the Shang dynasty were written on animal bones and tortoise shells.Libraries connected with palaces and temples were also in existence. The last emperor led a luxurious life. There were many attempts to overthrow him and the royal power declined considerably. He was finally overthrown by Zhou, chief of the Zhou tribe.

The highlights of the periods and developments till the establishment of the first Empire by Qin Shi Huang Di in 221 B.C. are summarized in table 1.

## IMPERIALIST PERIOD (UP TO 1911)

**Qin dynasty (221–206 B.C.)** period was short lived, but is well-known for the unification of China under one ruler Qin Shi Huangdi, the First Emperor. This period started the centralized bureaucratic and imperial rule which carried on till the fall of the Qing dynasty in A.D. 1911 Qin Shi Huangdi,

First Emperor Qin Shi Huangdi[1]

**Table 1**

| *Dynasty* | *Period* | *Founder/Other prominent Persons* | *Highlights* |
|---|---|---|---|
| Western Zhou dynasty | (1100–771 B.C.) | Setup by King Wu with capital at Haojing, near Xian. Had 13 kings. | Feudal set up with slavery. Known for strong military. Constant wars with barbarians. Chariots, iron etc. in use. Nobles dominated agriculture and industries.Agriculture, canal systems, astronomy, bronze work, handicrafts, etc. developed. The concepts of Kings as 'Sons of Heaven' ruling with 'mandate of Heaven' emerged. Height of splendour of pre-historic times. |
| Eastern Zhou dynasty | (770–221 B.C.) under two periods of Spring and Autumn and warring States. | | Capital at Luoyang (Henan province). A 'Period of Hundred Schools' referring to different schools of historical Chinese intellectual thought (Confucianism, Taoism, Mohism and Legalism) contributing to the decline. Rise of a new social group of scholars (shi), as forerunners of the scholar-officials of the Chinese Empire. |
| Spring and Autumn period | (770–475 B.C.) | | Emergence of 140 states and loss of royal authority. Five war lords/over lords declared supremacy and later two became more powerful. One of them regrouped and defeated the other. There were 480 wars and 52 vassal states were vanquished. 36 kings were killed. |
| Warring States Period | (475-221 B.C.) | | 7 states of Qi, Chu, Yan, Han, Zhao, Wei and Qin emerged with their chiefs as overlords. Qin claimed hegemony in the west and annexed all the others. New routes to remote areas like the 'Silk' route to Europe emerged. Waves of expansions and assimilations merged together to form the modern Chinese culture. |

to strengthen himself, relied on legalism and centralization of authority through ruthless methods. Dissenting Confucian scholars were put to death. Weapons were confiscated and stored at the capital. Frequent expeditions were made to the north and south to quell rebellions and ensure peace.

To guard against barbarian invasions from the north, walls of the Warring States periods were connected to form a 'Great Wall' (The present 4858 km long Great Wall, however, emerged during the Ming period only). Canals, bridges, etc. were also set up. The Terracotta Warriors near Xian were made by him because of his belief in life after death.Qin's behaviour became erratic because of excessive drinking, obsession with after life, use of mercury to prolong life, etc. He did not develop a successor. Nomads were active in the north and were expanding in the west and east. His youngest son forged a will in his own favour causing his elder son to commit suicide. The youngest son killed all his brothers and in the end, he was also killed by the eunuchs. With in a few years of Qin's death, the dynasty came to an end. He had two enduring legacies: the name China (from his name Qin/Chin) and a structure for the empire which lasted for more than 2000 years.

The highlights of the periods and developments till the establishment of the Tang Empire are summarized in table 2.

**Tang Dynasty (A.D. 618–907)** is clearly associated with the Sui dynasty and is often seen as an extension of the dynasty. Administration was expanded and the first common criminal code was formalized linking the degree of crime to the relationship of the people involved. Rural families were given plots to raise food grains and taxes were paid based on the number of people. It helped to have a correct census too. Rice production increased and people began to shift to areas good for rice cultivation. Ploughs, chains with paddles and harrow were in use. Common granaries helped to transport grains from the north to the south during periods of famines/shortages. The Tang army

**Table 2**

| *Dynasty* | *Period* | *Founder/Other prominent Persons* | *Highlights* |
|---|---|---|---|
| Western Han dynasty | (206 B.C.–25 A.D.) | Set up by Lin Bang, a noble, who became emperor 'Gao Zu'Capital at Changán (Xian). | Most prosperous period was during the reign of Emperor Wu (141–87 B.C.). Held sway over Korea, Vietnam, Japan and parts of Central Asia. Diplomatic relations with Rome and India. History of the empire from Huangdi to Western Han emperor Wu was documented. One of the greatest periods of China with its culture reaching unparalleled heights. Even today, the ethnic majority claim themselves to be Han people. Western Han ended with Liu Ying when revolts erupted |
| Eastern Han Dynasty | (A.D. 25–220) | Continuation of Western Han dynasty. Set up by Liu Die who became 'Emperor Guangwu'. Capital at Luo Yang in the East. 12 rulers over 195 years. | Middle of the first century A.D. was the most prosperous with economic, cultural and scientific advancements surpassing that of the Western Hans. Paper making was known. Seismograph was in use. In medicine, operations using anesthetics existed. After a rebellion of farmers, a minor war lord Cao Cao seized power. |
| The Three Kingdoms Period | (A.D. 220–280) | | Disunity, power struggles and sophisticated military strategies. Three kingdoms of Wei, Shu and Wu thus came up. One of the bloodiest periods in Chinese history with a large part of the population wiped out in internal strifes. But, had advancements in technology like use of wheel barrow, water powered puppet theatre, square pallet chain pumps for irrigation of gardens, south pointing chariot and compass. |

*Table contd..*

*.contd.. Table*

| *Dynasty* | *Period* | *Founder/Other prominent Persons* | *Highlights* |
|---|---|---|---|
| Jin Dynasty | (A.D. 265–420) | Western Jin was founded by Emperor Wu (Sima Yuan) with capital at Luoyang. | Wn and En Jins. When Emperor Huai was captured by rebels in A.D. 311, remnants of Jin groups went to the south and established a court at Jeankang and an Eastern dynasty was set up (311–420). 16 kingdoms of the north annexed south too. |
| Northern and Southern dynasties | (A.D. 386–581) | | Followed the Sixteen Kingdoms. Despite wars and disunity, culture flourished. Poetry, calligraphy, painting, music, medicine, astronomy, mathematics Buddhism became more popular and Daoism spread. Sinicization was accelerated. Migration from the north to the south also continued. Navy was used effectively in the south, cavalry was the main source of strength in the north. |
| Sui Dynasty | (A.D. 581–618) | Founded by Emperor Wen with capital at the present Xian. | End to four centuries of divisions. Dynasty marked by ruthlessness and tyrannical methods. Reunification of China. Though business spread and coinage improved, construction of the Grand Canal, Expansion of the Great Wall, etc impoverished the country. Popular revolts and break up of the empire. |

had both aristocrats and peasants. While aristocrats on horse back were used to fight nomads, peasants were used to occupy forts, do public works and serve as infantry. During this period, the Chinese empire expanded into Iran, Manchuria, and Korea and became a great power in Asia.

The dynasty had the only female ruler (Wu Chao) in A.D. 690. She was a concubine who ruled China for 15 Years with the indirect support of Buddhist monks and her relatives who were kept in key positions. After her rule, there was a brief disruption of the Tang rule and then a golden age emerged (710–755). Poetry became very popular. New opera styles emerged. Tea drinking emerged. Reorganisation of the army and military leadership took place. Military leaders became very powerful and this ultimately led to the destruction of the Tang rule. Peasant rebellions, retreats from all occupied areas, etc. also took place and one of the rebel leaders (Huang Chao) declared himself emperor. This led to division of the empire into five dynasties.

The highlights of the periods and developments from the end of the Tang Dynasty to the establishment of the Yuan Dynasty are summarized in table 3.

**Yuan Dynasty (A.D. 1271–1368).** From the latter part of the 12th century, Mongols had been strengthening themselves in northern parts of China. In A.D. 1204, one of the leaders called Tiemuhan alias 'Genghis' khan (Leader of the world) acquired supremacy over all other tribes in the region. A Mongol empire was established which later captured the Jin dynasty. Kublei Khan, grandson of 'Genghis Khan', ascended the throne in 1271 and changed the name of the dynasty to' Yuan' and made Yuandadu (Beijing) his capital. His territory was not really all of Mongol as 3 parts had broken away. In 1276, he captured the Southern Song areas too and unified China. Siberia, Tibet, south sea areas, etc. were also under him. This was the first of the two times when China was ruled by a foreign power. Though Genghis' Khan had also captured most of China, Kublai Khan was the first Mongol emperor who ruled over the country and founded a dynasty. It was the superior military skills, esp. superior cavalry, which gave them supremacy.

**Table 3**

| *Dynasty* | *Period* | *Highlights* |
|---|---|---|
| Five dynasties and Ten Kingdoms | (907–960) | A period of political upheaval beginning in the Tang dynasty and ending in the Song dynasty. Five dynasties came up in the north one after another while the Ten Kingdoms existed concurrently in the south. Power shifted from the imperial govt. to the military governors. One of the bleakest periods of the Chinese history characterized by anarchy and disunity Warfare and official corruption were endemic. Barter replaced monetary system. A positive development was widespread use of printing of Confucian, Buddhist and Taoist literature. |
| Song dynasty | (A.D. 960–1279). | Northern Songs with capital at the present Kaifeng controlled most of inner China. Southern Song came up south of the Yangtze River with the capital located at Linán (present Huangzhou) after the Northern period lost power to the Jin dynasty. The first to issue bank notes/paper currency and build a permanent standing navy. Population doubled through improved rice cultivation. Social life was unbound. Science, mathematics, philosophy, and engineering flourished. Neo-confucianism emerged. Many foreign missions visited China and foreign trade, ship building, etc. prospered. But lost power to the Jin dynasty. After two decades of warfare, Kublai Khan who had conquered the northern region was able to defeat the Songs. China was again unified under the Yuan dynasty of the Mongols. |

During his rule, Mongols held all the important positions though education and culture-wise Chinese civil servants were superior. Education, science, mathematics, literature, theatre, operas, etc. improved and the country progressed commercially too. Agricultural techniques, astronomy, mathematics, medicine, etc. also progressed. Trade and diplomatic activities also improved. Foreign trade was allowed and private traders could trade abroad. Marco polo had arrived from Spain.

Chenghis Khan[2]

Kublai Khan[3]

Gradually, the Mongols grew weak and weary in getting adjusted to the Chinese requirements. Popular uprisings came up and internal contradictions, natural disasters, unreasonable grading systems, etc. angered people. Excessive spending and trade restrictions depleted the economy as also building of canals and palaces. Campaigns against Japan resulted in the loss of many ships. A large number of non-Chinese personnel also weakened the government The Chinese nobility despised Mongols as even foreigners were treated better. Impoverishment of China led to popular uprisings. The Mongols also did not show great enthusiasm in maintaining their hold. In 1367, a rebel captured the Yuan capital ending the dynasty.

**Ming dynasty (A.D. 1368–1644)** was founded by a peasant known as 'Hongwu' Emperor. He had led the revolt against the Mongols. His capital was at Nanjing (later shifted to Beijing by his grand-son, the third emperor). This was the last dynasty of the ethnic Hans. It had a vast navy and a one million strong

Emperor Hongwu[4]

army. Emperor Hongwu tried to create a society of self-sufficient rural peasant communities and reduced the taxes on peasants. This improved rural life. Granaries were kept stocked to guard against famines. The dykes on the Yellow and Yangtze rivers were kept well maintained. Hunger was eliminated. Many economic projects of reconstruction like that of the Grand Canal, the Great Wall and construction of the 'Forbidden City' were undertaken. The Great Wall was strengthened. The scholarly bureaucracy helped to stimulate maritime trade with Spain and Portugal. New global trade of plants, animals, goods and food crops, esp. with Europe and Japan was established. These brought a lot of silver which improved the coinage, but, when the flow of silver declined, the currency was adversely affected.

Novels developed during the period from the story writings of story tellers in common people's language. Wood art and block printing became popular. Blue and white porcelain also became popular. Dictionaries and Encyclopedia were written. The number of Chinese characters was reduced from 540 to 224. Sea routes to Japan and South Africa were developed and naval expeditions to African coasts were organized. Huge ships which could

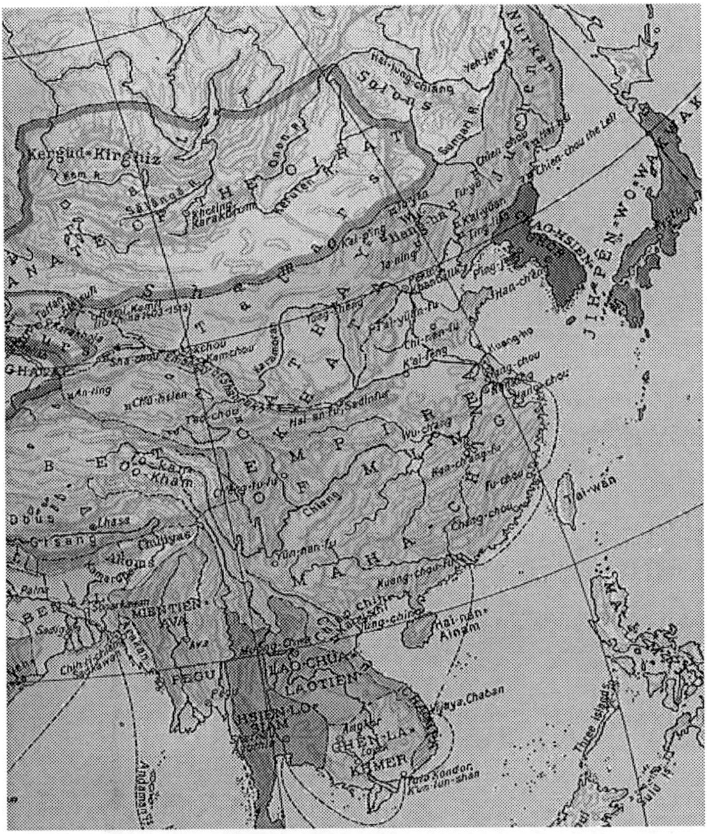


China[5] under the reign of the Yongle Emperor

carry 500 people were in use though in later periods only smaller ones were seen. This had made coasts subject to raids by pirates.

Internal power struggles led to the down fall of the dynasty. Nobles and eunuchs joined hands and kept weak rulers on the throne. Crop failures, famines, epidemics, etc. weakened the imperial authority. Rebel leaders began to challenge the Ming authority. When the flow of silver from abroad reduced, copper coins were issued which led to a lot of counterfeits using lead. Manchus from the north began to attack the much weakened capital eventually in 1644 gaining control over the whole of China.

**Qing Dynasty (A.D. 1636–1911)** was the last ruling dynasty founded by the Manchus who originally belonged to the north eastern China (Manchuria). In 1616, it was called the Later Jin dynasty. In 1636, it was changed to Qing.

The founders were from Jurchen tribe of North-Eastern China between Korea and The Great Wall. They were being used by the Mings to guard the northern frontier and to repel Japanese invasion of Korea. When the Mings declined, they gathered strength. Beijing was captured in 1644 and Emperor Shunzhi was enthroned as the first Emperor with authority over most of the China we know today. Complete pacification was, however, achieved only in 1683. Qings were completely integrated with the Chinese culture. Friendship with the Mongols on the west was maintained through inter-marriages. The Manchu language itself was based on Mongol script.

As Manchurians were only 2 m among 100 m Chinese, they made use of the existing administrative system and services of Chinese scholar civil servants. Originally, the southern China was under some generals who had shifted loyalties. By 1681, they were totally subjugated. In 1689, a treaty was signed with Russia limiting their boundaries. Throughout the 18th centaury, the Manchus continued to consolidate and Tibet was won from the Mongols in 1720. Later, Sinkiang was taken over and assaults were launched on Central Asia.

There were 3 important rulers between 1694 and 1796-Emperors Kangxi, Young and Qianlong. Emperor Kangxi made 6 tours to Southern China in 1670 and published 16 maxims based on Confucian teachings stressing respect for parents and elders, generosity, frugality, hard work, timely payment of taxes, etc. based on his knowledge of Chinese values. He also took up many irrigation projects and recruited 50 scholars to write a history of Mings. Dictionaries and Encyclopedia were also made. His son, the Young Emperor (1723–1735), strengthened the monarchy further by setting up an inner

Emperors Kangxi[6], Yongzheng[7] and Qianlong[8]

circle of Advisors. He also used a secret Memoranda system to bye-pass normal channels of Administration and imperial power was further strengthened. His son Qianlong combined his father's authoritarian and grand-father's cultured styles. Literacy was encouraged and scholars were rewarded. The period saw the zenith of Qing power which flourished in the 18th century.

European influence began increasing in the 18th century and gradually they began to ask for equal treatment vis-à-vis the locals who had preference in trade. In 1759, restrictions on trade by foreigners were imposed at Canton. Only Chinese were allowed to handle exports. The British wanted such unfair restrictions to be removed and over the issue a war ensued in 1842 and it was settled at a great cost to China. Five ports were opened to foreigners and an indemnity of 21 million pounds had to be paid by China. Hongkong also went to the British. Uneasy relation again resulted in the Opium war in 1856–60 with a humiliating defeat for the Qings. In 1860, the British and French troops occupied Beijing and forced the emperor to flee to the summer palace which was also looted. Loss of territory to foreigners continued and the Russians encroached on Sinkiang. In 1874, the Japanese raided Taiwan and in a humiliating defeat in the war that followed, Taiwan was lost. In addition, China had to open up several ports and pay a huge indemnity to the Japanese who were allowed to build several factories. In 1895, Korea ended the tributary relationship. In 1897, Germany took over some part of Shan deg peninsula. The French took Annan near Vietnam. Japan occupied Ayuku islands and began to encroach on Korea. Russians also annexed some areas. Emperor Qinlong's death in 1793 marked the end of Qing successes. Between 1796 and 1803, a large number of peasant uprisings took place. Costly military campaigns further drained the resources. In mid-19th centaury, there were many rebellions devastating many towns and cities. During the period 1861-1908, Dowager Empress Cixi was the de-facto ruler.

In 1911, Kuomintang led by Sun Yat–Sen overthrew the dynasty and founded the Republic of China.

Empress Cixi[9]

## REPUBLICAN/MODERN PERIOD (SINCE 1911)

**Sun Yat- Sen and the Republican Revolution.** Sun Yat-Sen was the key revolutionary leader in the over-throw of the Qing dynasty in A.D. 1911. Hence, he is referred to as the Father of modern China. He co-founded the 'Kuomintang', the revolutionary party which had spearheaded the campaign against imperialism and was selected in 1911 as the 'First Provisional President' of the newly founded Republic of China. He was a uniting figure in post imperial

Sun Yat-Sen[10]

China revered both by the Communists and Nationalists in Taiwan.

Sun Yat-Sen had troubles with the warlords who were controlling the army units, esp. the Beijing army, and hence could not see consolidation of the Republic. The provisional government, which had no army of its own, was weak. When the southern provinces declared independence, as a compro-mise, Yuan shikai, chief of the Beijing army, was made President of the new republic to force the emperor to abdicate. However, when Yuan declared himself Emperor six months later, Sun Yat-Sen unsuccessfully revolted against him and left for Japan to reorganize Kuomintang. There were a lot of war lords and no effective Central government. With his supporter Chiang Kai-shek as commandant, a military academy was set up by him near Guangzhou. He had to face challenges both from the local government and the Beijing Government. Comintern backed him and he co-operated with the communists to hasten the conquest of China. He died while making efforts for the Beijing expedition.

His chief legacy was in developing the political philosophy known as the 'Three principles of the people' viz. nationalism, democracy and people's livelihood/ welfare or socialism. He had drawn inspiration from the Gettysburg speech of Abraham Lincoln where Lincoln had spoken of "governmentof the people, by the people and for the people." Even the CPC accepts him as a revolutionary nationalist and the First Provisional President of China. The Governmentof Taiwan treats him as their foremost hero.

**Mao-Tse Tung and the Communist Revolution of 1949.** Mao Tse Tung is one of the most important leaders in modern history and a political and military leader of China who in the civil war led the communists to victory against Kuomintang. He is respected in China as a revolutionary strategist and a national leader who transformed China into a great power. He is, however, criticized for mistakes in the 'Great Leap Forward' and Cultural Revolution (1966–76), for the loss of millions of lives, damage to culture, society and economy. He has now been partly overshadowed by the political and economic performance of Deng Xiao Ping and others in the recent decades. He is respected as a poet and Calligrapher too.

He was born in 1893 in a peasant family of Hunan province and was a soldier in a local regiment in the fight against the Qing dynasty. Later, he worked as an Assistant Librarian in the Peking University where he learnt Marxism. He joined Kuomintang inspired by its nationalist and revolutionary ideas. Similarly, inspired by the Russian revolution, he co-founded the Communist Party of China (CPC) in 1921. He believed in eliminating feudalism and imperialism in China through a violent revolution.

Mao-Tse Tung[11] Mao's house at his native village.[12]

He joined various labour struggles of his area and was termed a radical activist. He found that unlike in USSR, where revolution was brought about by the organized labour, in China, which had only a small percentage of such labour, peasantry and rural areas had to be the focus. Hence, he organized peasants on Marxist lines and led peasant uprisings in Hunan area. Defeated in his attempts there, he left for Jianxi and organized soldiers who were scattered there. Each company was given a party cell to give ideological/political instructions which ensured absolute control of CPC over the military. After leading some uprisings in Jianxi area, he marched to Guanxi Mountains to join hands with insurgents, peasants and workers and to form a 'Red Army'. He used terrorist tactics to eliminate his rivals in the party in Jianxi area and gained absolute control. He also tried rural reforms, guerilla and mobile warfare tactics. In 1930, he clashed with Chiang Kai-shek who tried to encircle his areas of control. Chou-En Lai who was till then with the Bolshevik camp also joined Mao who started his 'Long March' from Jiaanxi to Shaanxi (9600 km) when surrounded by Chiang's forces. He however led the resistance movements against Japanese in the 1937–45 second Sino-Japanese war. While continuing the fight against the Japanese, conflicts came up with Chiang Kai-shek who was being supported by the US. USSR was giving weapons to Mao because of its conflict with US. In the conflicts that followed, Chiang led Kuomintang suffered increasing losses. On Dec 10, 1949, Mao laid siege to Chengdu, the last Kuomintang occupied city and Chiang, with US backing, evacuated that day from Mainland with his supporters to Taiwan. Mao declared China to be a Communist Socialist Republic.

His I Five Year Plan (1953–58) with focus on ending dependence on agriculture and rapid industrialization was fairly successful. The II plan, 'The Great Leap Forward', aimed at rapid collectivization, increases in literacy, land to the landless, etc.became ultimately a failure despite initial tall claims of success. Tall and false claims and exorbitant

Chiang Kai-shek[13]

demands from farmers led to famines wherein millions perished during 1959–62. Mao lost esteem and was forced to abandon the schemes. He lost some political power to Liu Shao Qui and Deng Xiao Ping.Liu became President with Mao as Chairman. The deaths due to faulty 'Great Leap Forward' are variously estimated between 20 and 72 millions.

There was a general agreement about its failure. A brief period of liberalization followed with Deng Xiao Ping reviving the economy, disbanding people's communes, introducing private holdings of farmers and improving production of food grains.

**Cultural Revolution (1966–76).** In the back ground of Mao's failure seen in the 'Great Leap Forward', Liu and Deng Xiao Ping's prominence was becoming a challenge to Mao's position. There were demands that he should be removed from actual power maintaining a ceremonial and symbolic role only. This prompted Mao to launch a cultural revolution against bourgeoisie elements, class enemies, etc. threatening the socialist frame work. It was in fact meant to strengthen Mao and allow him to reassert his supremacy giving power to 'Red Guards'—mostly students and youth—for whom Mao was a cult figure. Chaos reigned and millions were humiliated. It led to destruction of cultural heritage, and imprisonment of a large number of people besides economic and cultural chaos. Millions suffered and perished as the Cultural Revolution had entered every aspect of life. Mao chose Lin Biao as his successor.

Lin Biao[14]

Madam Jiang[15]
Qing Mao's wife, Who led the 'Gang of Four'

But, later Mao felt he was planning a coup or even his assassination and tried to curb his influence. Finally, Lin was killed in an air crash over Outer Mongolia when he was allegedly trying to fly to USSR. It was declared he had been trying to replace Mao. He was posthumously expelled from CPC in 1969. Mao also declared the Cultural Revolution to be over.

**Deng Xiao Ping and the new Economic Revolution.** Deng Xiao Ping was a prominent Chinese politician, reformer and de-facto leader of China between 1978 and early 1992 though he never held the position as head of state or head of Government. He was the main architect of Chinese economic reforms and the concept of "socialism with Chinese characteristics". Deng, at the core of the 'second generation Communist Party leadership', is credited with vastly raising the standard of living in China and developing China into one of the fastest growing economies.

Born on August 22, 1904 in Guangán County in Sichuan province, he discovered Marxism-Leninism in France where he was educated. After spending some time in USSR, he returned to China in 1926 and led the Baise uprising in Guanxi Province against the Kuomintang Government. He was a veteran of the Long March and, as a supporter of Mao, held several important posts in the new government, including that of Secretary General of the Communist Party, soon after the formation of the People's Republic of China. After supporting Mao in his anti-rightist campaigns of 1957, he became General Secretary of the CPC.

During the Cultural Revolution, Deng Xiaoping and his family were targeted by Red Guards who imprisoned, tortured and forced Deng's son out of the window of a four-story building, resulting in his becoming a paraplegic. But, when Premier Zhou En-Lai fell ill from cancer, Chou

Deng Xiao Ping[16]

En-Lai was able to convince Mao to bring Deng Xiaoping back into politics in 1974 as Executive Vice-Premier to run the daily affairs. But, the 'Gang of Four' led by Mao's estranged wife Jiang Qing, competing for power within the Communist Party saw Deng as their greatest challenge to power. When Chou En-Lai died in January 1976, Deng lost firm support within the party and was purged again at the instigation of the 'Gang of Four' for his "political mistakes".

But, Deng gradually emerged as the de-facto leader of China in the few years following Mao's death in 1976 by carefully mobilizing his supporters within the CCP. Deng was able to outmaneuver Mao's anointed successor Hua Guofeng and then oust him from top leadership positions by 1980. But, Deng allowed Hua to retain membership in the Central Committee and helped to set a precedent that losing a high-level leadership struggle would not result in physical harm. Deng then repudiated the Cultural Revolution and, in 1977, launched the "Beijing Spring" which allowed open criticism of the excesses and suffering that had occurred during the period.

Meanwhile, Deng gradually outmaneuvered his political opponents encouraging public criticism of the Cultural Revolution. Deng gradually consolidated control over the CCP and Hua was replaced by Zhao Ziyang as premier in 1980, and by Hu Yaobang as party chief in 1981. Deng remained the most influential leader, although after 1987 his only official post was that of Chairmen of the State and Communist Party Central Military Commissions.

The Tiananmen Square protests of June 4, 1989 were, however, a black mark on Deng period. These were triggered by a visit of Gorbachev and death of Hu Yaobang, a liberal and former party General Secretary who had been forced to resign from his position by Deng Xiaoping and other influential leaders. Use of military force to resolve the crisis ordered after ousting Zhao Ziyang

Chou En Lai[17] Zhao Ziyang[18] Hua Guofeng[19]

from political leadership resulted in large scale killings of students, youth and democracy advocates as armed forces were confronted by Chinese students in the streets of Beijing. The violent suppression of the Tiananmen Square protest attributed basically to Deng Xiaoping and other hardliners, especially Li Peng caused widespread international condemnation of the PRC government. Critics accused Deng of dictatorial powers and suppressing any signs of political freedom that would undermine the direction of his economic reforms. Deng justified the crackdown as a measure to enforce social stability for effective economic progress. Deng retired from top positions when he stepped down as Chairman of the Central Military Commission in 1989, and retired from the political scene in 1992. Deng Xiaoping died on February 19, 1997, at the age of 92, but his influence continued.

Though a pivotal figure in modern Chinese history, Deng Xiaoping's legacy is very complex and opinion remains divided. Deng changed China from a country obsessed with mass political movements to a country focused on economic construction. But, he was unrelenting on the political clout of the Communist Party of China, as evidenced by the 1989 Tiananmen Square Protests. China's significant economic growth in the 1980s and 1990s was largely credited to Deng's policies. Deng's socialist market economy was a largely novel concept. However, a large number of issues like unprofitable state-owned enterprises, regional imbalance, disparities in urban-rural wealth, official corruption, and the resurfacing of evils within a more liberal society, exacerbated during Jiang Zemin's term (1993–2003), remained unresolved. The re-emergence of significant inequalities was contrary to the founding ideals of communism. Social unrest was increasing. Some Chinese nationalists criticize Deng for embracing too many foreign ideas and making domestic industries insignificant. On the diplomatic front, despite many successes, he is being criticized for appeasement and forgetting war crimes by Japan.

## Endnotes

1 In public domain.
2 Ibid.
3 Ibid
4 Ibid.
5 Ibid.
6 A faithful photographic reproduction of an original two-dimensional work of art in the public domain.
7 In public domain.
8 Ibid.
9 Ibid.
10 Ibid.
11 Ibid.
12 Re: Request for permission to use Picture of Chairman Mao's House in his native village. Permission given by 'go_fox@163.com on Wednesday, Feb. 3, 2010 at 2:50:21 PM. With the reply 'Yes, as you like'.
13 In public domain.
14 Author-Government of the People's Republic of China.source-http://photocdn.sohu.com/20071211/Img253971020.jpg-*Author=unknown | Date=1955*
15 In public domain.
16 Ibid.
17 Ibid.
18 Ibid.
19 Ibid.

## References

*I. Early Period*

a. http://en.wikipedia.org/wiki/History_of_China (Dec. 10, 2009)
b. http://simple.wikipedia.org/wiki/Ancient_China (Dec. 10, 2009)
c. http://en.wikipedia.org/wiki/Four_Great_Inventions_of_ancient_China (Dec. 10, 2009)
d. http://en.wikipedia.org/wiki/Xia_Dynasty (Dec. 10, 2009)
e. http://en.wikipedia.org/wiki/Western_Xia (Dec. 10, 2009)
f. http://en.wikipedia.org/wiki/Shang_Dynasty (Dec. 10, 2009)
g. http://en.wikipedia.org/wiki/Western_Zhou_Dynasty (Dec. 10, 2009)
h. http://en.wikipedia.org/wiki/Zhou_Dynasty#Western_and_Eastern_Zhou (Dec. 10, 2009)
i. http://en.wikipedia.org/wiki/Warring_States_Period (Dec. 10, 2009)
j. http://en.wikipedia.org/wiki/Spring_and_Autumn_ Period (Dec. 10, 2009)

*II. The Imperialist Period*

k. http://en.wikipedia.org/wiki/Qin_dynasty (Dec. 10, 2009)
l. http://en.wikipedia.org/wiki/Western_han_dynasty (Dec. 10, 2009)
m. http://en.wikipedia.org/wiki/Eastern_han_dynasty (Dec. 10, 2009)
n. http://en.wikipedia.org/wiki/Three_kingdoms_period (Dec. 10, 2009)
o. http://en.wikipedia.org/wiki/Jin_Dynasty (Dec. 10, 2009)
p. http://en.wikipedia.org/wiki/Northern_and_southern_dynastes (Dec. 10, 2009)
q. http://en.wikipedia.org/wiki/Sui_Dynasty (Dec. 10, 2009)
r. http://en.wikipedia.org/wiki/Tang_dynasty (Dec. 10, 2009)

s. http://en.wikipedia.org/wiki/Five_Dynasies_and_ten_kingdoms (Dec. 10, 2009)
t. http://en.wikipedia.org/wiki/Song_dynasty (Dec. 10, 2009)
u. http://en.wikipedia.org/wiki/Yuan_Dynasty (Dec. 10, 2009)
v. http://en.wikipedia.org/wiki/Ming_dynasty (Dec. 10, 2009)
w. http://en.wikipedia.org/wiki/Qing_Dynasty (Dec. 10, 2009)
x. http://chinaculture.org (Dec. 12, 2009)

*III. The Republican/Modern Period*

y. http://en.wikipedia.org/wiki/Xinhai_Revolution (Dec. 10, 2009)
z. http://en.wikipedia.org/wiki/Mao_Zedong (Dec. 10, 2009)
aa. http://en.wikipedia.org/wiki/Cultural_Revolution (Dec. 10, 2009)
bb. http://en.wikipedia.org/wiki/Zhou_Enlai (Dec. 10, 2009)
cc. http://en.wikipedia.org/wiki/Lin_Piao (Dec. 10, 2009)
dd. http://en.wikipedia.org/wiki/Deng_Xiao_Ping (Dec. 10, 2009)
ee. http://chineseculture.about.com/gi/o.htm?zi=1/XJ/Ya&zTi=1&sdn=chineseculture&cdn=newsissues&tm=17&f=00&tt=14&bt=1&bts=0&zu=http%3A//wwwchaos.umd.edu/history/toc.html (Dec. 10, 2009)
ff. encarta.msn.com/encyclopedia_761595562/Republican Revolution (China).html (Dec. 24, 2009)

CHAPTER 2

# Socio-cultural Scene

## PHILOSOPHICAL SYSTEMS

Sorcery had great influence in the initial days of evolution of Chinese thought. Gradually logic began to replace it. A salient feature of early Chinese thought was the belief that Heaven guided the entire world including activities of human beings, especially the Government and frequently intervened in governmental affairs. In early Shang dynasty (1600 B.C.), thought was based on cyclism of day and night, change of seasons, waxing and waning of the moon, etc. It was believed that the departed continued to live among people and needed to be consulted, prayed to and appeased. When the Shangs were over thrown by the Zhous (1046 B.C.), the "Mandate of heaven (tien Ming)"concept was introduced to mean that over throw of rulers unworthy of their positions would get the approval of Heavens. It was a shift away from faith in "Shangdi" (supreme God associated with Heavens) and ancestor worship increased.

Chinese philosophy is often traced back to "yi Jing" (the book of changes), an ancient compilation of divination attributed to King Wen about 1000 years B.C. The book of changes evolved over the next 8 centuries with the first recorded reference in 672 B.C. When the Zhous got weakened and Spring and Autumn periods came, the classical period of Chinese philosophy began with "Hundred Schools of Thought". Of these, Taoism, Confucianism, Mohism and Legalism were the dominant ones.

Kongxi/Confucius[1]

Lao Zi[2]

Wang Yang Ming[3]

Analects' of Kongxi/Confucius and 'Tao Te ching' of Leo Tzu/Lao Zi, a short text of 500 characters, came around 600 B.C., before Buddhism and Socratism. Confucianism based on 'Analects' is a system of moral, social, political, and religious thought which has tremendously influenced Chinese history, thought, and culture. Its basic ideas are rén (humanity or humaneness), zhèngmíng (rectification of names, e.g., a ruler who rules unjustly is no longer a ruler and may be dethroned), zhMng (loyalty), xiao (filial piety), lĐ (ritual) and the concepts 'Yin' and 'Yang' (two opposing forces that are permanently in conflict with each other, leading to perpetual contradiction and change). The Confucian idea "get rid of the two ends, take the middle" is a Chinese equivalent of Hegel's concepts of "thesis, antithesis, and synthesis", a way of reconciling opposites and arriving at some middle ground combining the best of both.

'Analects' was not written by Confucius, but compiled after his death. It is a collection of his teachings and is not an analysis of any new doctrine. It is believed that he compiled and edited existing texts into their classical form. A lot of his teachings centered on the themes of virtue of the individual and the stability of society. The Lunyu (one of the four books of Confucius/'Analects' in dialogue form) is primarily concerned with the first. Moral self-cultivation has great social implications. If there are more good people in a society, especially among the rulers, the more likely it is to be good society. However Confucius' understanding of virtue is based on the observance of prescribed norms of social behaviour and rituals. Moral self-cultivation is essential and has beneficial effects on others. Altruism, special concern for children, respect for elders and central position of family are key factors of Confucian thought. Thus, Confucianism can be called a school of active morality.

Wang Yangming/Mengzi (Mencius-391–308 B.C.) who followed Confucius defended his ideas. Mengzi focused on goodness of human nature. While Confucius was vague and non-committal on the subject, he stressed its importance. He believed that compassion, altruism, moral discrimination, etc. were basic characteristics of human beings. For him becoming virtuous meant developing what already lies within. Xunzi (3rd century B.C.), another important Confucian thinker, believed that desire was the most significant human characteristic. He disputed Mencius' view that man is innately good and taught that individual desires, if unchecked, would cause social conflicts. He wanted social rules to teach people which of their desires might or might not be satisfied. He was more pragmatic and favoured education and rituals to curtail man's inborn tendencies. Though both Mengzi and Xunzi are Confucians, for Mengzi people become moral because of innate tendencies, while for Xunzi, they become so despite their desires.

Legalism dominated under the Qin dynasty and Confucian and other philosophical schools suffered. The ancient period of classical Chinese philosophy ended with the fall of the Qin dynasty in 206 B.C., but, legalism continued to dominate till Hans adopted Taoism and later Confucianism as official doctrines. At the end of the Eastern Han days, Confucian concepts and values had waned as the society went through major turbulences. Buddhism came in the first century A.D. and it was accepted mainly due to its similarities with Taoism. From Tang to Song days (A.D.960–1279), traditional values declined and Hans people blended with other ethnic groups. Confucians tried to integrate Confucianism, Taoism and Buddhism and establish an

Mengzi[4]

Zhou Dunyi[6]

Zhu Xi[6]

integrated philosophical approach for the people. Thus, during the Song dynasty, Neo-Confucianism came up as a revised version of Buddhism, Taoism, Confucianism and Legalism and continued so during the Ming dynasty period (1368–1644).

Zhou Dunyi/Chou Tun-i (1017–73)] is famous for introducing what is known as 'The Diagram of the Great Ultimate' into Confucian thought. It is Cosmology based on the principles of Yin and the Yang, the Five Agents, etc. It has constituted the core of Neo-Confucianism. Metaphysics achieved a far higher role in Neo-Confucianism and Zhu Xi's influence was behind the establishment of the basis of the Chinese civil service examinations from 1313 to 1905. Lunyu, the Mengzi and two additional short works, the Zhongyong (Doctrine of the Mean) and the Daxue (Great Learning) were key texts for the examination.

Daxue is an important text summing up the Confucian philosophy. It gives priority to regulation of families. Those who wish to regulate their families should first cultivate their personal lives. Those who wish to cultivate their personal lives should first rectify their minds. Those who wish to rectify their minds should first make their wills sincere. Those who wish to make their wills sincere should first extend their knowledge. The extension of knowledge consists in the investigation of things. The first step for this is metaphysical reflection on the nature of the world and its contents. Zhu Xi objected to this and, citing the original version, gave priority to making the will sincere. He believed every person knew the difference between good and bad and hence people should first look inwards to uncover their own innate knowledge. This is to be done through the elimination of desires. Both Zhu Xi and Wang Yangming subscribe to the traditional Confucian ideal of moral self-cultivation. Both believed in its benefits to the individual and the society. However, they differed on how it is to be achieved, with one taking a more intellectual and the other a more mystical approach.

Taoism (Daoism) is a philosophy (which later also developed into a religion) based on the texts the 'Tao Te Ching' ('Dào Dé J+ng') and the 'Zhuangzi' (partly ascribed to Zhuangzi). Tao (Dao) literally means 'path' or 'way', a force that encompasses the entire universe but which cannot be described or felt. All major Chinese philosophical schools have investigated the correct 'way' to go about a moral life, but in Taoism it takes on abstract meanings. It advocates non-action (Wu Wei), the strength of softness, spontaneity, and relativism. Its motto is "if one must rule, rule young". It believes that human attempts to make the world better actually make the world worse. Therefore it is better to do nothing and Wu Wei is exactly this. Though it serves as a rival to Confucianism, a school of active morality, many go by the idiom "practice Confucianism on the outside, Taoism on the inside."

"Dao, the way, is perhaps the most important term in Chinese philosophy with each Chinese philosophy advocating its own 'way'. Those who came to be known as Taoists were only proponents of one particular way. Its understanding is more intuitive or experiential. The direction in which one must search for the way involves not doing certain things rather than doing them. Two human habits in particular are singled out for regular criticism. First, we should desist from attempts to impose our desires upon the world. Secondly, we should desist from making unnecessary distinctions. This is based on the idea that there is a natural order to the world, which we fail to appreciate and regularly violate. We should be more concerned with conforming ourselves to it. Making unnecessary distinctions means we see the world as a fragmented one. Since making of distinctions is basic to discursive knowledge, some criticize its anti-intellectual tendencies and primitivism. Some see it as a valuable resource for modern environmentalism. This worldliness and practicality are essential aspects of Chinese philosophical systems.

Gradually, a set of widely shared views about the basic nature of the universe evolved. The universe is run by a single principle' Tao' or Great Ultimate. The idea of Yin-Yang, two opposing principles found in the universe, is the major one. In their most primitive senses, Yin and Yang, perhaps meant something like 'dark' and 'light'. They oppose each other and produce change. Yin gradually came to be associated with cold, darkness, feminity, moon, completeness, material forms, submission and passivity while Yang with heat, light, masculinity, sun, creation, Heaven, dominance, and activity. Parallel to this, and in due course amalgamated with it, was the idea of the Five Agents/Elements, namely metal, wood, water, fire and earth. Five Elements too are seen as dynamic in nature.

Representation of [7]Yin and Yang.

Each is regarded as the dominating force at any particular time, and they cyclically succeed each other. Changes arising from their constant interactions are seen as essential nature and pattern of existence. It is thus a principle of duality with each phenomenon having seed of the opposite ("presence in absence") and cyclicity. That is why the most famous ancient compilation of Chinese texts is called the Yijing (I Ching), or Book of Changes. This notion of change is at the core of the Chinese world-view. Hence, Chinese philosophy is more concerned with the notion of 'becoming' unlike the western ones which are concerned more with the problems of 'being'.

Mohism (Moism), founded by Mozi (Mo Tzu, 480-390 B.C.), a radical thinker and social activist, promoted universal love for mutual benefit. His approach was more utilitarian than religious. He wanted everyone to love each other equally and impartially and avoid conflicts and war. He condemned aggression in relations among individuals, families, and countries. The moral guide must promote and encourage social behaviors to maximize general benefit. Belief in the power of argument and the impartiality of reason are other features. Human beings have free will and are persuadable. They could be expected to do that for which the strongest case could be made. Where Mengzi would take a positive attitude towards human nature and Xunzi a negative one, Mozi was more neutral in outlook. Emphasis on the importance of reason and argument has prompted some to see him as the first recognizable genuine philosopher in Chinese history. He rejected Kongzi's great concern for traditional ways and views on family and rituals. Centralized political power, universal love, anti-war and anti-extravagant sociological notions, respect for heaven and gods, indeterminism in religious thoughts, and rational and practical attitude in science are its essential features.

Legalism upholds the rule of law and is thus a theory of jurisprudence. A ruler should govern his subjects based on Fa (law or principle), Shu (method, tactic, art, or statecraft) and Shi (legitimacy, power, or charisma). The most important among legalists was Han Feizi (d. 233 B.C.) who was primarily a political thinker concerned with the question of how the state might best be preserved and serve the interests of its people. He believed that it was best achieved by the establishment of efficient institutions of government based on a sound understanding of human nature and society. The principal mechanisms to be employed were the law and punishment. It was a source of inspiration to the totalitarian-minded Qin Shi Huangdi (210 B.C.), the first emperor of a unified China.

Emergence of the Ch'an (or Zen) school of Buddhism, which drew much from Daoism is seen as a product of the medieval period of Chinese philosophy. It was a forward movement in the eleventh century and marked the beginning of 'modern' Neo-Confucianism which became the dominant philosophy for the next nine hundred years of imperial China. It was a new version of old Confucian principles with Buddhist, Taoist, and Legalist features and hence the name Neo-Confucianism. Despite Confucianism losing to Taoism and Buddhism, its concepts of li (principle), qi (vital or material force), taigas (the Great Ultimate), and xin (mind) remained relevant in Neo-Confucianism."

Though Buddhism, a religion, psychology and a practical philosophy based on the teachings of Buddha, originated in India, it has had a lasting effect on China. 'Buddha' is generally considered to be someone who discovers the true nature of reality. Because Chinese tradition focuses on ethics rather than metaphysics, it has developed several Buddhist schools like Salons, Tiantai, Huayan and Chan which are different from the Indian schools. They investigate consciousness, levels of truth, whether reality is ultimately empty, and how enlightenment is to be achieved. Buddhism has a spiritual aspect that compliments Neo-Confucianism with prominent Neo-Confucians advocating certain forms of meditation.

The logicians (School of Names) were concerned with logic, paradoxes, names, actuality, etc. Li-Si was its proponent. Logician Hui Shi was a friendly rival to Zhangzi of Taoism. It did not thrive because the Chinese then regarded subtle reasoning and logical argument as impractical.

Some of the terms commonly found in Chinese philosophy are: Tao (the Way, or one's doctrine), De (virtue, power), Li (principle), Qi (vital energy or material force) and Taiji (Great Heavenly Axis) from which the concepts of Yin and Yang originated. There are some commonalities and also controversies in Chinese philosophical systems. The commonalities are belief that the big questions can be answered even if the answers are not currently known (epistemological optimism), the tendency not to view man as separate from nature, the belief that the purpose of philosophy is primarily to serve as an ethical and practical guide, absence of focus on a personified and supernatural God unlike in western thought and generally a political focus. The controversies are about analysis of human nature, method of discovering truth and relation between matter and principle.

The foci of mainstream Western and Chinese philosophies are different. Western philosophies emphasize ambition, individualism, rationality, power, and liberty. The Chinese philosophies, on the other hand, emphasize benevolence, harmony, wisdom, family, and honoring one's ancestors. Chinese philosophies are primarily more internally focused unlike the western ones which are more externally focused. Thus, in many aspects, the Western and Chinese philosophies are the antithesis of each other. For example, while western Platonism stresses rule of law, Confucianism preaches a society ruled by ethics. While Enlightenment Thinking calls for liberty and democracy, Legalism demands unquestioned loyalty to imperial authority. While competition is essential in the ideology of Capitalism, cooperation is seen as the key for harmony in the philosophy of the East. Western philosophers primarily value reason and rationality, while the Far Eastern philosophers generally emphasize meditation and wisdom. There were philosophers like logicians in China who made scientific rationality their chief focus. There were philosophers in the West like Marcus Aurelius who saw meditation as the path to knowledge.

Therefore, the differences were only in the mainstream philosophical schools.

The Chinese philosophical thought was always closely related to societal changes. As social issues dominated during periods of great unrests, philosophical responses were also more. This was seen earlier in the evolution of the 'Hundred Schools of Thought'. At the junction of the Ming and Qing dynasties (14th to 17th cent), a generation of religious people who had secluded themselves in temples and mountains dominated. Later, when China was defeated by external powers, philosophers searched ancient, eastern and modern philosophies to inspire Chinese thought and brought in mixed approaches. This remained till the 20th century. In the communist system, initially, all except Legalism were despised and also purged during the Cultural Revolution. The Present government encourages market socialism, but the influences of old systems remain. The 1978 constitution allows freedom of religion with restrictions and no threat to the CPC is tolerated.

Chinese philosophy, which has profoundly influenced thought in East and South East Asia, has been a melting pot of ideas. Generally, it has been tolerant towards other views except during the Qin days when legalism dominated. Even when one philosophy was accepted as official, others were debated and new ideas were evolved. Neo-Confucianism, which has spread around the world, was such a product. Even during the modern times, this has continued with May Fourth Movement (around 1911) asking for total abolition of imperialist institutions. Sun Yat-Sen tried to integrate Democracy, Republicanism and Industrialism. Mao similarly tried to incorporate Marxism, Stalinism and Communist thoughts. Today's Chinese leaders talk of 'Socialism with Chinese characteristics' integrating socialist and communist principles and market economy of the capitalist system.

There were some minor foreign influences on Chinese

philosophy. The most important of these was that of Buddhism. In the seventh century, Nestorian Christianity and Islam impacted. From the thirteenth century onwards, Catholic missionaries began to arrive bringing with them philosophical and religious texts. In the latter part of the nineteenth century, some works of modern Western philosophies like John Stuart Mill were translated. Bertrand Russell had some following from 1920s. The influence of Marxism on Mao Zedong is well-known.

Though when the Communist Party of China took over power, previous schools of thought, except Legalism, were denounced as backward, and even purged during the Cultural Revolution, their influence on Chinese thought remains. Pure spiritual and philosophical institutions are not perceived as threats to the power of the CPC, though their activities are monitored. The 1978 Constitution of the People's Republic of China even guarantees "freedom of religion" with a number of restrictions. The current government, while encouraging market socialism with Chinese characteristics since the days of Deng Xiao Ping, is more tolerant towards traditional beliefs because of their deep roots in Chinese culture. It also helps its efforts to find a unifying force in growing Nationalism.

The greatest Philosophers of China are Confucius, Lao zi; Mozi, Shang Yang, and Lin-chi (a great Buddhist Ch'an thinker and teacher). Mencius, Zhu Xi and Wang Yangming were prominent Confucians with their own variations in ideas. Similarly, in Taoism, Zhuangzi, and Lei zi are also quite prominent. Among legalists, Han Fei and Lisi are important. Mao is probably the most recent Chinese philosopher who has changed China radically. Today the modifications or tactics of Deng Xiao Ping on the economic front rule the roost enabling the country to reach unprecedented rates of growth during the last three decades and thereby improving the lot of the people.

## Endnotes

[1] In public domain.
[2] Ibid.
[3] Ibid.
[4] Ibid.
[5] Ibid.
[6] Ibid.
[7] Ibid.

## References

a. http://en.wikipedia.org/wiki/Chinese_philosophy (Dec. 12, 2009)
b. http://urantiabook.org/archive/readers/601_taoism.htm (Dec. 12, 2009)
c. http://en.wikipedia.org/wiki/Confucius (Dec. 12, 2009)
d. http://en.wikipedia.org/wiki/Yin-Yang (Dec. 12, 2009)
e. http://en.wikipedia.org/wiki/Mohism (Dec. 12, 2009)
f. http://en.wikipedia.org/wiki/Category:Chinese_thought (Dec. 12, 2009)

## CULTURAL SCENE

By 'Culture' we mean the whole spectrum of human development and achievements resulting from it. It would include the sum total of beliefs, behaviors, manners and ways of living, excellence in crafts, arts and letters, scholarly pursuits, characteristics of a people transmitted from generation to generation, etc. Owing to its large size, in China customs and traditions vary considerably between regions, cities and towns. It has many ethnic groups with the Hans constituting about 92%. Many subgroups within Hans have maintained their separate linguistic and cultural identities with the family names often indicating them.

Chinese culture is an embodiment of a philosophical concept that upholds the unity of human beings with heaven and earth. This holistic philosophy influences language, literature, art, medicine, education and daily lives of people. Humanism, personal ethics, self-cultivation and pursuit of moral perfection are its essential aspects. Inheriting early humanism, Confucius (551–479 B.C.) emphasized benevolence (ren), individual self-criticism and propriety (li), social ethics and order, moral human relationships between the ruler and subjects, father and son, etc. Traits of moderation, courtesy, respect for elders, etc. generally seen in Chinese society even today flow from these. Taoism advocated by Lao Zi (770–476 B.C.) and Zhuangzi (369–286 B.C.) has 'Dao' (the way) as its basic concept. It believes that though all things are constantly transforming, they have a basic order with 'yang', the positive force (for.eg, the sun) and 'yin', the negative force (for eg, absence of sun) as the basic elements of the universe. Both Taoism and Confucianism stress the importance of good relationships-Taoism between man and nature and Confucianism among men.

Buddhism which came from India between 202 B.C. and A.D. 9 blended with the prevalent Chinese culture and gradually took the form of Zen Buddhism. While traditional Buddhism advocates strict asceticism, solitary meditation on scriptures, etc., Zen Buddhism believes that self-cultivation, isolated from the society, can never be successful. It can be done during the course of normal work and life and even illiterate farmers, if they work hard and fulfill their responsibilities to the best of their abilities, can achieve enlightenment. It has its own belief systems and encourages free thinking and debates as a means to knowledge. In its temples, Buddha is featured in Chinese styles. Chinese culture today is the result of integration of Zen Buddhism with Confucian and Daoist thoughts.

Chinese art consists basically of calligraphy, painting, sculpture, architecture, music and drama, and folk arts. Porcelain work is the oldest art. Traditional brush writing is still part of the curriculum in Chinese schools and a person who can produce beautiful calligraphy is considered highly cultured. Seal cutting is a unique traditional art. Making stamps or seals with exquisite miniature sculptures to enhance the artistic effect is common. Calligraphy involving use of Chinese characters on cylindrical or rectangular blocks of bronze, stone or jade is also very old. In China, seals are used more as evidence of personal identity than signatures.

Fine arts, folk arts and performing arts had acquired prominence from very early days. Folk arts like puppetry, folk painting, folk dances, sculptures, crafts, folk music, acrobatics, etc. existed for thousands of years. Shadow puppetry is 10000 years old. Story telling, ballad dance, doll making, embroidery, kite making, etc. were also popular. During the Han period, paper cutting became a new art and later, opera and a variety of others also came up. China is the home of eastern martial arts with 'Kung Fu' as its original name. It is home to the Shoaling monastery and Wudong Mountain famous for these. A variety of weapons were also in use in these martial arts. Extraordinary physical skills of common people were a form of palace entertainment.

Traditional Chinese painting uses minimum lines to portray the subjects. Classical Chinese artists believe that

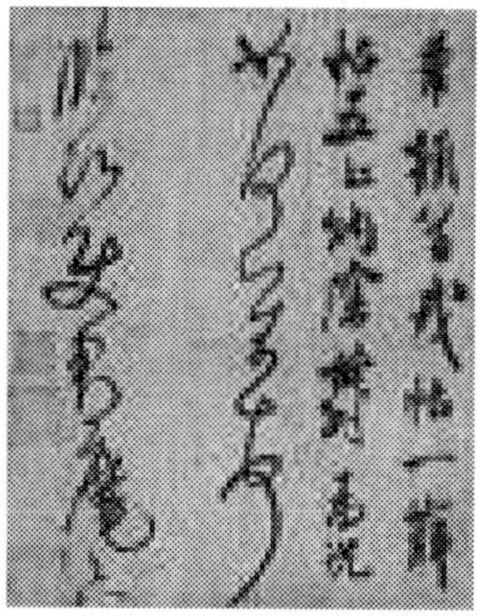

Chinese calligraphy[1]

painting should not be limited by the actual colour of their subject. Most landscape paintings use a shifting perspective to portray a continuous sweep of connected use. These paintings bounded on long horizontal/vertical scrolls, allow the viewer to appreciate panoramic views that cannot be seen from a single perspective. During the Tang-Song days (7–13th centuries), 'mountain and water' landscapes became primary features of Chinese painting which was influenced by philosophical thinking. In the recent past, artists have been combining the spirits of Chinese and western arts to create new styles. It was an accepted belief that to be cultured, knowledge of stringed musical instruments, Chinese chess, painting and calligraphy was essential.

1. Painting by Ren Xiong[2]

2. Three symbols of Chinese culture[3]

1. Painting by Ren Xiong, a pioneer of the Shanghai School of Chinese art.
2. The Chinese Dragon, Fu dog and incense comprise three symbols within traditional Chinese culture.

Music has played an important part in Chinese culture from the dawn of Chinese civilization, especially from the days of the Zhou dynasty. Perhaps, even from the Neolithic days, bone flute and pottery wind instruments were in use. Written music dates back to Confucianism. Early music was based on percussion instruments and later involved string and wind instruments. Others were various wind, string and percussion instruments like drum and gong. Tang period was marked by flowering of music. From 10th century onwards, traditional opera had become representative music. It changed later taking cues from western systems and instruments.Music was intertwined with dance for 4000 to 5000 years. Dance was used initially in religious rituals, palace ceremonies and banquets. It was used to recreate motions of planting and hunting. It was often performed by slaves and by priests to train children of the nobility.

Folk dances were common in festivals, marriages, celebrations of change of seasons, invocation of good weather, abundant harvest, etc. for a long time. In addition to revival of these during the Tang period, western techniques also came up. Opera developed from 3rd century B.C. to 14th century A.D. combining dance, vocal and instrument music, acrobatics and martial arts to create an integrated form of theatre art. In it, emotions were freely expressed. It gradually became an important form of entertainment. The Beijing Opera which emerged during the Qing dynasty period emphasizes symbolism and stylized representations of space and time.

Extensive books prepared since the Zhou dynasty (1100 B.C.) are the touch stones of Chinese cultural development. The classical tests covered poetry, astrology, astronomy, calendar, constellations, etc. Confucius believed that essay writing was most appropriate for connecting ethics and ideology and hence it was known from very early days. Poetry is the most representative class of Chinese literature used to express emotions and give voice to aspirations. Poetry and prose reached their heights during Tang-Song period (A.D. 618–1276). Modern Chinese poetry, however, uses straight forward and easily understandable language following western styles. Story telling evolved during the Song-Yuan period between 10th and 14th centuries. Drama developed during the Yuan dynasty (A.D. 1271–1368). During the Ming dynasty (14–17th centuries), romantic writing emerged and took newer forms in later periods. Chinese novels depicting the lives of common people evolved. From the 20th century, Chinese writers have been using styles of other modern languages.

From early days, Chinese were accomplished in Technology and the 'four great inventions' of gun powder, paper, compass and moveable type came from China. Gun power was made mixing charcoal, sulphur and potassium in A.D. 600. Seismograph is said to have existed in the 2nd century A.D. Paper making was known during the Western Han Dynasty period (202 B.C.–A.D. 24). Moveable type was in use in the 11th century. South pointing needle/compass was invented in the Warring States period (475–221 B.C.).

Traditional medicine used inspection, listening, enquiry and pulse taking as the method of examination. Theory of 'Yin' and' Yang' (receptive and reactive) permeates traditional Chinese medicine. Traditional methods of acupuncture and moxibustion use methods like stimulating particular points, puncturing with special needles and heat. During Tang period, a government sponsored compilation of pharmacopoeia was done. In the Ming period, 1982 medical substances and 10000 different prescriptions were compiled.

Crafts embody blending of art and life, aesthetics and practicality. Ceramics, porcelain and lacquer work epitomize Chinese crafts. Pottery made its first appearance in China about 7000 years ago. The 'Yangshao' culture which flourished approximately between 5000 B.C. and 3000 B.C. was characterized by high quality painted pottery in Xian. Chinese had made dragon their totemic animal. Porcelain, also called 'China ware' emerged during the Shang dynasty (1600–1046 B.C.). Glazed pottery using yellow, green, and white colours came during the Tang period. Blue and white glazed porcelain became famous in the 13th and 14th centuries A.D. during the Qing period. Lacquer ware was famous from ancient days as it resisted corrosion, retained heat and withstood acid. It was used on wooden furniture in daily life and on fancy objects and also to symbolize status of rulers. Chinese bronze sculpture flourished between 1600 B.C. and 256 B.C. Artifacts belonging to Shang and Zhou dynasties have been excavated in many places. These were basically ceremonial musical instruments used by nobility to make offerings to the deities, ancestors, etc.

The Terracotta Army of Qin Shi Huang Di, the first Chinese Emperor, massive Buddhist sculptures, etc. show China's extra-oriental sculptural traditions. Chinese carvings of Guanyin, Buddhist goddess of mercy and compassion, in expression of sanctity and serene beauty perhaps can rival Raphael's painting of Madonna. The 'monument to People's heroes' in Tiananmen Square is a representative work of modern Chinese sculpture. It has 10 engraved panels each representing a historical event and thus offers a comprehensive depiction of China's revolutionary history.

Architecture has existed in China for over 2000 years. A common feature of Chinese architecture is emphasis on width as seen in the halls of the Forbidden City. Western architecture emphasizes height. Pagoda architecture is an exception. Symmetry is another feature. Gardens are asymmetrical. Chinese gardens try to create an unending flow and let the viewers wonder. 'Fengshu' has also played an important part in architecture. Traditional Chinese architecture also emphasizes harmony between structure and its surrounding environment. Palaces, temples, parks, residences, etc. merge with adjoining landscapes to form an integrated scene. Chinese people believe that even inside the building, human beings and nature have to form a unified whole.

A lady in Baggy Qipao[4]

Chinese people are accustomed to living in extended families with several generations under one roof. The elders live in the more desirable south facing rooms usually located on either side of a central hall. The younger people live in the eastern and western wings reflecting the order of status within the family. Nowadays, though many western concepts are being used, most Chinese cities still follow a mixture of traditional and modern layouts of rooms, often on a central axis.

Traditional arts like 'Kungfu' enhanced ethics and morality and blows were controlled to avoid injury. It was used for entertainment too. Numerous physical exercises, five animals playing, shadow boxing, etc., were developed from ancient days. Even today, physical education forms an important part from elementary school to university levels. A number of calisthenics programmes for different categories of people are in use in China. Special timings are given to employees for such activities. 'Ping pong' is a national sport. Sword dancing, knife dancing, shadow boxing etc. were other items. By such methods, in the recent years, China has made tremendous progress in sports and games.

Ancient depiction of fighting monks[5] practicing the art of self-defense.

Ancient Chinese had shown great creativity and practical sense about food and eating. Food styles depended on available local resources. Plants and animals that were easily available dominated the food culture of a place. Knowledge of food was considered a basic requirement of a gentleman. In palaces, most employees were expected to have good knowledge of the food section. A lot of rituals also existed in respect of food habits.

The staple food in China is usually rice and wheat. The uniqueness of Chinese food is in its flavor. Type wise, food items could be divided into starch, vegetables, legumes, fruits, meat, and spices. Milk and diary products do not have much importance in Chinese cuisine. There are more than 600 types of vegetables that the Chinese eat. Processed products i.e., smoked, salted, singed, pickled, dried, soaked, items also have their place. Cooking is considered basically an arrangement of such resources with a local flavour. Essentially, two tracks—'fan' (for grains and starch) and 'tsai' (for vegetables and meat)—are involved in the preparation of Chinese food. For each meal, a component of both will be there. 'Fan' is considered indispensable. Separate utensils are used for cooking and serving these.Main food for monks and nuns, Taoists, etc. is vegetarian. In the northern and western Provinces, diets are hot and spicy because of the humid cold weather and high altitude.

Normally people share cooked food around round dining-tables with the most delicious food placed in the centre of dining-table closer to the main guest. By eating together and chatting, people promote friendship and solidarity. Guests commence eating normally after the host says something like 'Please enjoy yourself'. People also propose toast to each other to reflect mutual respect and comity. Earlier, the whole family used to eat together with all the family members sitting around a table. Each person will have one set of dining tools in front, including two bowls—one for rice and the other for soup, one pair of chopsticks and one plate for meat/vegetable. The aged,

An outdoor painting of a small Chinese banquet[6] hosted by the emperor for scholar-officials from the Song Dynasty (960–1279).

teachers and guests are shown great respect and consideration. Children are given special care. The best items are first given to seniors. The dishes in the central of table are shared with each person picking up only what he wants to eat. Rice is never picked up from the bowl, but the bowl is taken towards lips and rice put into the mouth using chopsticks. Soup is taken during or after dining. Returning home of a family member is celebrated with noodles while for departures dumplings are used, especially in the north-east. Birth of a child is announced by sending a red boiled egg with end painted black with even dots for a boy and odd for a girl.

Dress culture is the collective patterns or styles of behavior of people. Clothes had their roles in preserving Chinese identity. 'Xia', meaning grandeur of rites and social conduct, and 'Hua', meaning beauty and decoration, combine literally to from 'Huaxia often used to represent Chinese civilization. Dress styles were, over a period of time, influenced by central Asian patterns as a result of mixing of people. Three types of traditional items viz.'pien-fu' (a tunic like dress up to knees and a trouser extending up to angles), 'changpao' (one piece from shoulder to heels) and 'shen-i'(a cross between the two with a tunic from shoulder to knees and a skirt upto angles stitched together) are common. All have plain designs, wide sleeves, loose fits with little stitches, but often have embroidered borders, shoulder patterns, sashes, etc. Darker colours were used for higher classes and lighter ones for commoners. Clothing had also changed and evolved with the fashion of the days since its beginnings in the Shang dynasty.

Many of the earlier designs were more gender-neutral and simple in cuttings. Later garments incorporated multiple pieces with men commonly wearing pants and women commonly wearing skirts. Clothing for women usually accentuated body's natural curves through wrapping of upper garment lapels or binding with sashes at the waist. Many in the countryside still use distinctive peasant dress.

People wearing typical Chinese dress during Qing dynasty days.[7]

Han Chinese clothing is now worn only on festivals, coming of age/rite of passage ceremonies, as ceremonial clothing by religious priests, for cultural exercises, etc. The Han style has differences with the styles of other ethnic groups in China, especially the Manchurian ones like the 'qipao' now popularly assumed to be the solely recognizable style of "traditional" Chinese garb.

On top of the garments, hats (for men) or hairpieces (for women) may be worn. From the head ware, one can identify the profession or social rank. The typical male hat or cap is called a Jin for commoners and guan for the privileged. Officials and academics have separate sets of hats.

Taoists have a 'scarlet gown' which is made of a large cloak sewn at the hem to create very long deep sleeves. Buddhists have a cloak with gold lines on a scarlet background creating a brickwork pattern which is wrapped around over the left shoulder and secured at the right side of the body with cords. High priests may have further decorations. Those in academia or officialdom have distinctive gowns, typically round collared gowns closed at the front. The most distinct feature is the headwear which has 'wings' attached. Only those who passed the civil examinations were entitled to wear them, but a variation of it could be worn by ordinary scholars and laymen.

Nowadays western influences on a traditional foundation dominate. Even brides these days use western gowns. Jeans are in common usage among the youth. Shorts are rare. Even in everyday life most educated Hans now wear western-style clothing. Some wear modernized traditional clothes. Some men wear traditional gowns and women 'Chipao'. Motifs of lion, dragon, clouds, guardian gods etc, decorative works in belts, shoulders, openings, seams, are also seen. Some preferences for colours are also seen. Green colors for spring, red for summer, white for autumn and black for winter is the general pattern. Chinese prefer black, yellow and brown colours with women preferring black. Brighter colours like red are preferred for special events. Children's uniforms normally have white, blue and green colours. Even modern men use traditional gowns and women chipao. Some other interesting aspects of Chinese culture also deserve mention.

1. In traditional Chinese systems, different colours represented different feelings. Red is a colour of happiness and is forbidden at funerals. Yellow represents good luck. Emperor's clothes were usually in yellow. In Buddhism, however, yellow is a mourning colour. Green stands for health, prosperity and harmony. It is sometimes associated with infidelity. White is associated with purity, chastity, cleanliness and holiness. It is also a colour associated with funerals. Silver colour can take the place of white. Black, as in western systems, stands for mourning. It is perhaps an adaptation of their western practices. Blue is also associated with funerals the western practices.

2. China is a country of etiquettes and ceremonies. About 2000 years back, people used to cup one hand in the other before the chest to salute. Now a days, such patterns are seen in Spring festivals only. Bowing is used by subordinates, students, attendants, etc. to show respect. Shaking hands is the common style now. Modern youngsters only nod as a greeting. During discussions, nod means only active listening and not necessarily agreement with the view expressed. A junior is introduced to the senior and familiar to the unfamiliar. In conversations, talking of the weather, food, hobbies, etc. is done to break the ice. Men talk on sports,

current affairs, job, stock market, etc. while women may talk about their families, jobs etc.Women are not asked private questions.

3. Gifts play an important role in courtesies, esp. on occasions of weddings, birth-days, festivals, patient visits, etc. Wine, cigarettes, tea, candles, fruits, pastries, flowers, etc. are given on family parties. Gifts to old people are sent in pairs. Gifts are not given in public and gifts in black and white colours, in odd numbers, etc.are avoided as taboos.
4. Most social values are Confucian or Taoist. Most accepted ones form part of Neo-confucianism, Buddhism, etc. The principle of Quanxi ensures primacy of relations over rules. In business, a letter of introduction at first is the norm though, of late, emails, faxes, etc. also go.
5. Chinese Dragon, Fu dog and incense are 3 symbols of traditional Chinese culture. The dragon which was a symbol for the emperor or high level imperial families during the Ming period is often seen as a replica of the general Chinese culture and is respected as such by the common people despite its imperial background. A gold fish is signature scenery depicted in countless art work.
6. After the adoption of one child norm in late seventies, there has been a drop in the proportion of women. There are now only 100 women for 120 men. There is an obvious preference for boys in rural areas as they add to the working hands in agricultural work and over 60% of Chinese live in rural areas. Female children being abandoned in public places do take place. In cities, however both boys and girls are treated as equal and a very large percentage of employees in shops, offices, hotels, tourism related activities, super bazaars, factories producing silk, jade, pearls, clothes and other textile items are women only especially in cities like Beijing, Shanghai, and Xian. In middle level shopping complexes, a large number of girls working as lobbyists or liaison people to take prospective customers to shops is a regular

sight. In big cities like Shanghai after 10 p.m. prostitutes in groups soliciting customers is quite visible. Modern women, it is said insist on 3 Cs- of cash, car and condominium (house) -as a precondition for marriage. In some rural areas, the prospective bride groom has to work for 3 years without wages in the land of the bride's family and prove desirability and commitment before the parents agree for the marriage and allow them to live as husband and wife. The shortage of girls has added to this problem. The one child norm is modified for minorities (55) and they are allowed to have a second child after 4 years of the birth of the first child. Dis-incentives of various types continue to exist for parents violating the one child norm.

7. For serious discussions, formal meetings are preferred. Such meetings are normally followed by dinner to show hospitality. Women do not demand separate treatment though courtesy is appreciated. Punctuality is preferred and the Chinese normally come a few minutes earlier to show their eagerness.
8. On the eve of the Olympics games, the Government had given the following pieces of advice to its people to improve their manners. While dealing with visiting foreigners: there should be no more than three color groups in clothing; wearing pajamas and slippers to visit neighbors is not to be done; dark-colored socks are recommended, and white socks should never be worn with black leather shoes; no public displays of affection; feet should be slightly apart or in the shape of a V or Y when standing; handshake should not last more than three seconds and don't ask foreigners their age, marital status, income, past experience, address, personal life, religious belief or political belief. These tips were added to the ban on spitting (in Beijing at least) and Queuing/ *Patience In Line Day* (the 11th of each month). Campaigns involving nearly a million volunteers had been launched to give etiquette tips at schools, universities and government offices. In some districts, university students

were encouraged to go to villages to educate rural people. Such campaigns and educational activities are now gradually improving the lives of Beijingers. More smiling faces and more properly and elegantly dressed people are seen in streets. People are learning the habit of queuing for buses.

9. 99% people in cities live in small flats. Most of the modern flats are occupied by foreigners, other business executives and others who have acquired wealth during the last 10 years. There were only a few who own individual villas in cities and these are mostly film stars, prosperous businessmen, and foreigners who have invested considerable funds in the country. A large number of foreign cars made in China like Volkswagen, Honda, Mitsubishi and a number of similar ones of Chinese design dominate the streets showing how fast prosperity is spreading.
10. Chinese society today is stumbling towards a more liberal attitude about sexuality. Pornography is banned, but the blocks on adult-oriented websites have inspired some Chinese users to acquire specialized software to circumvent the government's system of web censorship. Shops filled with sex toys, often called "adult health stores," are common in every Chinese city. People who have enthusiastically documented their promiscuity in writing have found wide readerships on the Internet. It's common for prominent and wealthy men to indulge in affairs, so much so that every story of a fallen corrupt official is paired with tales of his pampered mistresses. At least 90% of high-level party cadres convicted of graft also kept mistresses, according to a report by Chinese prosecutors in 2007. Prostitution is illegal, but most cities have brothels poorly disguised as 'hair saloons'.

## Endnotes

[1] In Public Domain.
[2] Ibid.
[3] Ibid.
[4] Ibid.
[5] Ibid.
[6] Ibid.
[7] Ibid.

## References


a. http://en.wikipedia.org/wiki/Chinese_culture (July24, 2009)
b. http://en.wikipedia.org/wiki/Chinese_art (Dec. 28, 2009)
c. http://en.wikipedia.org/wiki/Culture_of_China (July 11, 2009)
d. http://en.wikipedia.org/wiki/Four_occupations (July 11, 2009)
e. http://www.chinaculture.org/gb/en_madeinchina/2005-09/27/content_73485.htm (Jan. 5, 2010)
f. http://chineseculture.about.com/library/weeklyaa031901b.htm (Dec. 26, 2009)
g. http://chineseculture.about.com (July24,2009)
h. http://answers.com/topic/culture-of-china#Arts (Dec. 23, 2009)
i. http://chineseculture.about.com/od/minoritiesinchina/a/Uyghurs.htm (July 24, 2009)
j. http://www.chinaunique.com/educate/culture.htm#dress
k. http://www.chinaunique.com/educate/culture.htm#family
l. http://library.thinkquest.org/20443/clothing.html
m. http://www.chinatownconnection.com/chinese-traditional-dress.htm
n. http://www.travelchinaguide.com/intro/cuisine.htm
o. http://en.wikipedia.org/wiki/Chinese_cuisine
p. http://en.wikipedia.org/wiki/File:Song_Dynasty_Elegant_Party. JPG

## EDUCATIONAL SCENE

During the imperial rule education was not easily available to peasants and workers. Despite Sun Yat-Sen's support for education to common people, even after the Republican Revolution in A.D. 1911, it was limited to the elite partly due to the high inflation. Blind respect to traditions compounded the problem. The communist system chose to provide education for all children except of those under suspicion like the landlords and bourgeoisie.

To get an overall idea of the Chinese educational system, we can divide it into categories like Basic (pre-school, primary, junior and senior middle school), Vocational/Technical, Higher and Adult Education. The following items are covered in these categories.

**Basic Education.** In this, Pre-school, Primary (6 years), junior and senior middle school (3 + 3), special education for disabled and education for the illiterate are included. Pre–school education is from 3 to 6 (3 years). The academic year consists of 2 semesters with 19 weeks with one extra week as reserve. Secondary education may be regular one with 3 years each of junior and senior middle schooling with 39 and 40 weeks classes respectively.

**Occupational/Technical Education.** In this, Professional schools, Polytechnics, occupational middle schools and short-term occupational technical training programmes are covered. Vocational and Technical training programmes are after 9 years of schooling and vary from 2 to 4 years. Higher vocational schools, Medical technical schools, vocational high schools, employment training centers, adult technical training centers, social training centers, etc. come under this. Farmers, management and technical personnel, middle level skilled workers, etc. are the targets. Schools for skilled personnel are for 3 years.

**Higher Education.** Junior colleges (2 years), bachelor (4 years) colleges, masters (two/three years) and doctoral/Ph.D. programmes in universities come under this classification.

**Adult Education.** Schools for adults, Anti-illiteracy programmes, Radio and T.V. universities, workers and peasants institutions, colleges for management personnel, educational training institutions, correspondence colleges, advance Technical training, T.V educational programmes via satellite, etc. are covered. In respect of each category, it may cover basic, vocational/technical and higher education. Secondary schools and short and long courses for cadres are also encouraged. The grading system used may be A to E or A to D. There are 'Pass' or 'Fail' grading too. Private Institutions too make considerable contributions now to the development of education. In 2003, there were 60000 private schools with 11.16 million students and 1202 places of higher learning.

**Administration.** The State Education Commission oversees formulation of educational policies and co-ordination for higher education. 36 national colleges and universities are directly under it. Twenty-five Key Institutions like Beijing, Tsinghua and Fudan universities are also directly under it. Some institutions training personnel for sponsoring Ministries are also Key Institutions.Muti-disciplined Universities, colleges, teachers training colleges, special colleges, etc. are under local control. Schools are with local authorities. Short cycle colleges for volunteer training are under the administration of the cities.

There are Key schools for all levels-national, provincial and municipal. They get priority for funding and allotment of best students based on entrance examinations. But, there are also criticisms against the system on grounds of elitism with some Provinces opting against it. They are costly and technical graduates from non-key institutions get more pay than their products.

**Pre-school education** begins at $3^1/_2$ years. The schools are in buildings made available by public enterprises, production teams, municipal authorities, local groups and families. The government has decided that individual organizations should sponsor pre-school education as part of the welfare services of various institutes, government organizations, state and collectively operated enterprises, etc.

**Special education** is meant for gifted children and slow learners. Gifted children are allowed to skip grades. Slow learners are encouraged to reach minimum standards. Generally, those with learning problems, handicaps and psychological needs are the responsibility of parents/families. Extra provisions are made for the blind and seriously learning impaired children.

**Primary Education.** From 20% enrollment in 1949, reached 96% in 1985 and nearly 99% in 2007. The bar diagram given below will facilitate better understanding of the progress achieved between 1949 and 2007.

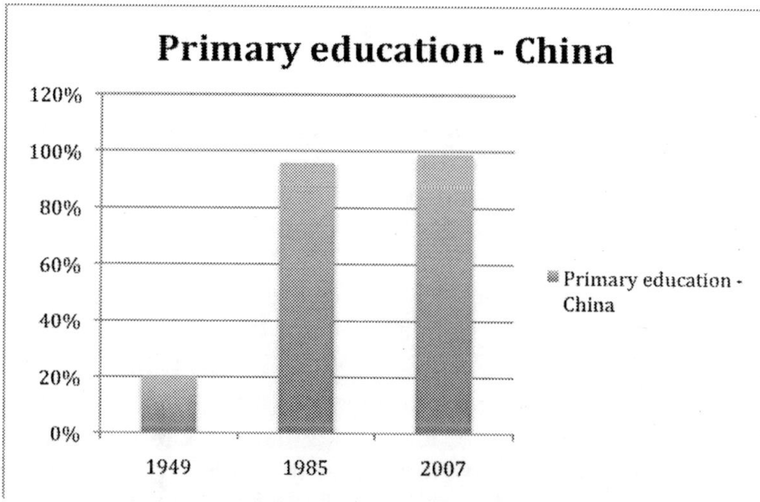


Primary education is free and is given in neighborhoods and villages. State enterprises and institutions are encouraged to set up primary schools. Parents pay a small fee for books and other expenses like transportation, food and heating. Children from poor families receive stipends.

The curriculum consists of Chinese, mathematics, physical education, music, drawing, history, geography and practical work experience in the school. A general knowledge of politics, moral training with stress on love of mother land, love of party and of people and a foreign language (often English), are taught from class 3. Chinese and Mathematics account for 60% of the class time and natural science and social science for 8%. "Pinyin" Romanization is taught in lower grades and kindergarten schools and "Putonghua" (common spoken Chinese) in regular schools. All schools impart education on morality and ethics from grade 4.Usually students have to perform productive labour 2 weeks every semester in workshops or on farms to relate classes with production experience. Most schools have after hour education one day/week in recreation and community service.

**Secondary Education.** In 1960s, the policy of 'walking on two legs' with regular academic schools and separate technical schools was followed. During the Cultural Revolution, many technical schools were closed and academic ones were expanded as it was felt that the system provided unfair education to children of workers and peasants. As a result, quality of education declined. By 1976, renewed emphasis on technical training established more technical schools and their enrollments increased. By 1986, junior middle education became mandatory. Emphasis was on increase in quality rather than enrollment.

In senior middle schools, 50% of the time is spent on natural sciences and mathematics and 30% on Chinese and a foreign language. Encouragement is given to senior school education if it would result in university education, which would provide an escape from village life. A senior school graduate is considered an educated person in China.

The bar diagrams below show the changes in the number of children admitted in Kindergarten in 1985 and 2003 and primary and secondary schools in 1985, 2003 and 2010. There was a decline in the total number of children admitted in Kindergarten schools between 1985 and 2003, may be due to the decline in the total births because of the 'One Child' policy. The increase in the Primary and Secondary school level admissions, particularly at the

**China : Progress of education since 1985**

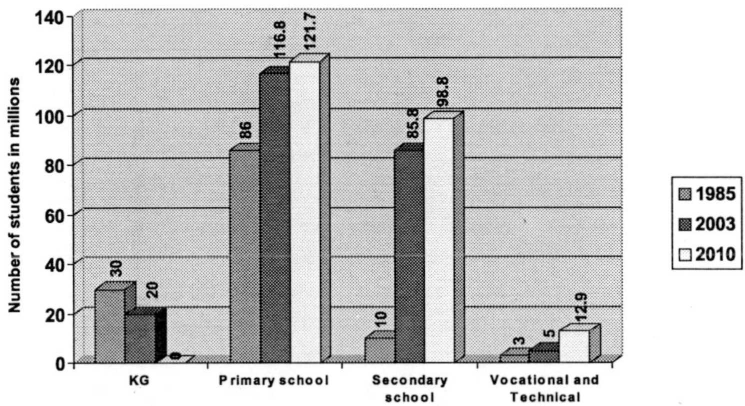


*Source of data:* CIA fact book, China, nationmaster.com, etc.

secondary level is substantial. This is a clear indication of the increase in literacy during the period.

The bar diagrams below show the progress in the Senior secondary school level between 1987 and 2007. The increase from 7.7 m to 25.2 m was quite remarkable.

**Sr. school education: 1987–2007**

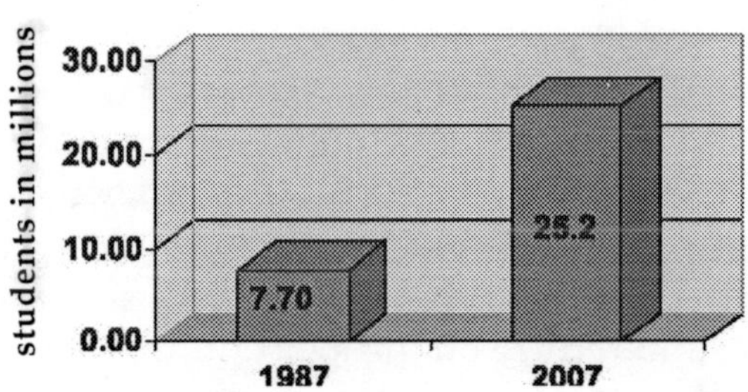


**Vocational and Technical Education.** This category includes higher vocational schools, secondary skill schools, vestibule schools, vocational high schools, job finding centers, other adult skill and social training institutions. Recently, these have been oriented towards employment focusing on the two demands for high quality workers in manufacturing and service industries and training rural labour moving into urban areas. Impoverished western regions received more attention. A number of technical and skilled worker training schools were opened after the Cultural Revolution for meeting the needs of industries, business, services and agriculture. Reformers were pressing for conversion of 50% of the seats for upper secondary education to vocational education. Students passing out from these were to work in rural areas. Regular senior middle schools were to be converted into vocational middle schools and vocational training classes were to be established in some senior middle schools. Diversion of students from academic to technical education was intended to alleviate skill shortages and reduce competition for university enrollment. To encourage this, vocational and tech school graduates were given preference in job assignments.

In 1987, there were 4 kinds of secondary vocational and technical schools:

1. Technical schools that offered a 4 year post junior middle school course and 2 to 3 year post senior middle school training in commerce, law, fine arts and forestry.
2. Worker training schools that accepted students with senior middle school education and provided 2 years training in carpentry and welding,
3. Vocational training schools that accepted either junior or senior middle school students for one to three years course in photography, trades and other services
4. Agricultural middle schools that offered basic subjects and agricultural services. They were to give in-depth training and reduce on the job training needs and long-term costs.

The progress in Vocational and Technical education betwenn 1985 and 2010 is shown in the last bar diagram above. The number of students increased from 3 m in 1985, to 5 m in 2003 and 12.9 m 2010 which is also quite substantial.

**Higher Education** figured in some of the crucial political struggles in China. The 'Great Leap Forward' and Cultural

Revolution saw focus on political re-education. During the Cultural Revolution, a large number of students joined the Red Guards effectively closing down higher educational institutions. Admission was restricted to those recommended by work units, possessed good political credentials and those who distinguished themselves in manual labour. By 1976, steps to improve quality were initiated. It also meant reduction of political contentions in university campuses. 88 institutions and universities were given special funding and other support and freedom to recruit on merit without regard to political activism and family background. "Four modernizations" scheme required improved quality of scientists and engineers and increased focus on higher education was considered essential. Universities and colleges were given freedom to change teaching plans, curricula and acceptance of projects from abroad. They were also allowed to receive funds from work units. Emphasis on television, radio and correspondence courses was also done.

**Merit based selection system for higher education.** National examination to select candidates for higher education was part of the change in culture, and selection was considered prestigious. Cadres with 2 years of experience were also recommended in a small number of universities on an experimental basis. Preferential treatment to minorities, students from disadvantaged areas and those who agree to work in less developed areas also existed. As shown in the bar diagram below, in 1977 when the national examination was reconstituted, 5.7 million candidates took the exam for 278000 seats. In 2003, 16 million were tested for 430000 places in 900 colleges and universities.

A minimum cut-off score for the national examination was set up for admission to specific departments in prestigious colleges and universities. Minimum cut-off score for others were decided by the provinces. Key universities had separate clauses for minorities. If candidates had the minimum scores, schools had the option to decide on selection. Physical examinations and political screenings were also done. By 1980, institutions of higher learning crossed 1000.

Adult students above 40 were also given some seats based on separate tests (cut-off scores were decided by the Provinces/Admin region/municipality). Approval of work units and senior middle school graduation were also insisted upon for adult students above 40. In 1985, 6% of the enrollment was from such groups. Payment of fees for tuitions, accommodation and miscellaneous expenses were required for teachers colleges. Those with financial difficulties, remote areas, etc. were given exemptions.

Employers were to pay a part of fees and adult students were to work for the units for some time. Those who paid their own fees and other expenses were also admitted. In 1986, colleges and universities were allowed to decide on their departments, majors and teachers needed. Institutions of higher learning were allowed to publish their curricula 2 to 4 years at a time. In 1985, posts of Teaching Assistant, Lecturer, and Asst. Prof. and Prof. were instituted on national basis after testing in Beijing and Shanghai universities. Presidents of the universities headed the selection committees based on the academic levels. A maximum retirement age was also introduced. From 1986, private schools were allowed when attainment of 9 years of compulsory education by 2000 was targeted. By 2003, 1552 institutions of higher learning (with Beijing, Tsinghua and 100 key universities as the most sought after), had 725000 teachers and professors for 11 million students.

The diagrams below show the number of seats that were available for higher education in 1977 and 2003, the

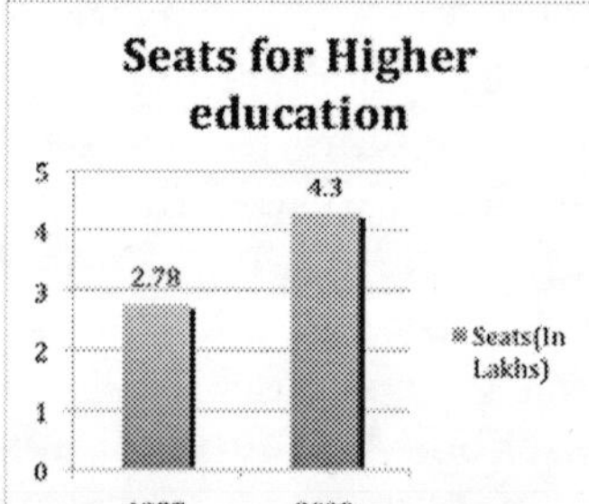

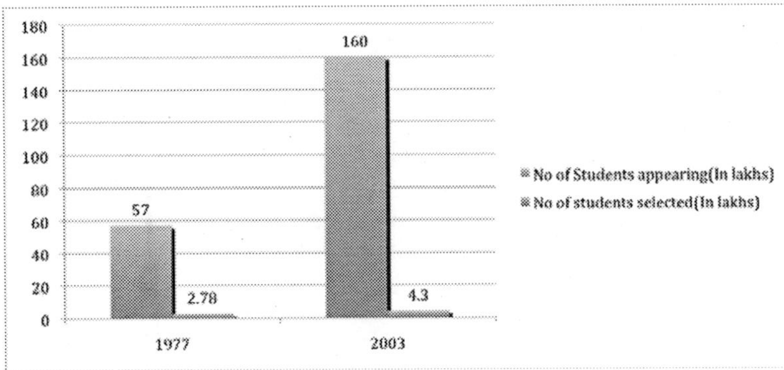


increase (about 55%) during the period,the numbers who had competed for entrance to univeresities and the high level of competition involved in the selection process. In 2003, out of the 16 million who competed only 4.3 lakhs could get admission.

Education especially at postgraduate level has been growing very fast. Projects for creating 100-world class universities began in 1993 and 708 schools of higher learning were upgraded (302 of them into universities). It produced far-reaching reforms in higher education management, with better standards and quality and increased availability of funds. Between 1999 and 2003, enrollment in higher education increased from 1.6 million to 3.82 million. In 2003, UNESCO reported that China had the highest number of students in higher schools of learning and the total had doubled over a few years. In 2004, 4473 schools of higher learning and research institutions enrolled 326000 P.G. students, 37000 more than the previous year There were 24.1% more recruitments and 25.9% more researchers. There were over 20 million students. 43 national universities scientific technical parks were started or approved as centers of commercializing research This produced good recruits giving rise to many new and high technical enterprises and innovations.

The bar diagrams below show the increase in tertiary level enrollments from 1999 and also the increase in total students in the recent past (in millions).

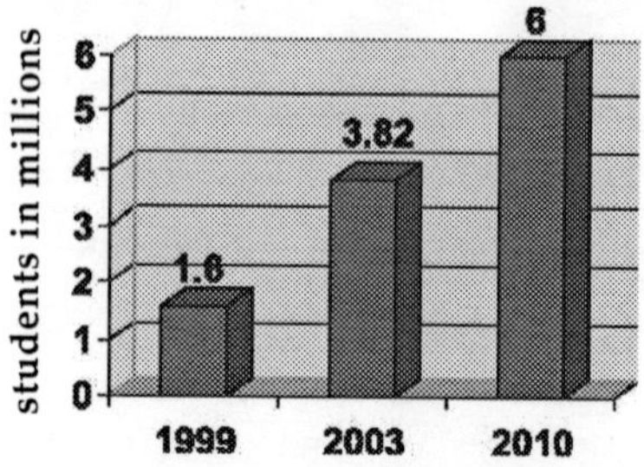


Enrollments/Tertiary-1999–2010(millions)

**source*: nationmaster.com

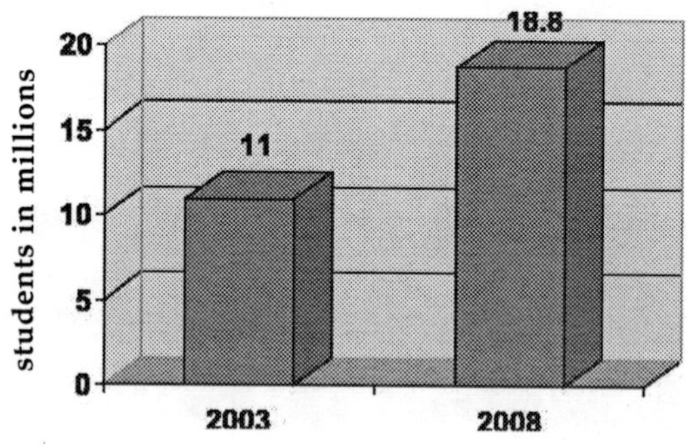


Total Students/Tertiary level-2003–08 (millions)

Today, 259 million Chinese get three levels of education doubling the rate of increase in other parts of the world during the same period. Net elementary school enrollment has reached 98.9% and gross enrollment rate in junior schools has reached 94.1%. Ten years ago, MBA graduates were virtually unknown, but by 2004, 47000 were trained in 64 management schools. Many also have international qualifications. About 100000 are enrolled in schools of higher learning like Beijing and Tsinghua universities. The educational field has skyrocketed with training and testing for professional qualifications and foreign languages. By 2020, 13500 in every one lakh would have junior college education and 31000 senior high school. Illiteracy would fall below 3% and average schooling duration would increase to 11 years from the current 8 years.

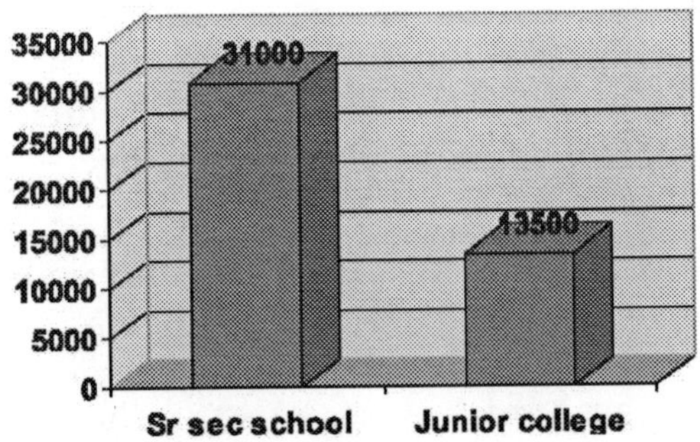


Educational Targets for 2020

**Changes in policies.** Marxist ideology overestimated the superior wisdom of workers and peasants whose hand skills were assumed to be the base for super structure of science and learning in general. These resulted in various experiments where workers were made teachers overnight. Education was made easier by simplifying many characters and focusing on skills common people could use. The system was, however, indifferent to the intellectuals during the 'Great Leap Forward' and' and 'Hundred Flowers' campaigns.

During the Cultural Revolution, higher education in general suffered tremendous losses and the system was virtually shut down. A generation of college students and teachers, academicians, technicians and professionals were lost. An irrationally structured education was unequal to the need of economics and technology too. Deng later realised that for modernization of China, development of science and technology and international resources were essential. Hence, his new reforms focused on new technology, advanced management expertise, etc. China also needed an educated labour force to feed its billion people.

Educational reforms being implemented now aim at more delegation from Government to Institutions, Institution to department/Faculty, etc., more specialized courses for agriculture, foreign languages, and media, diversification of financial channels with business, agreements with 160 countries and 14 International organizations to organize joint programmes in areas like Business administration, Economics, Marketing, Accounting, Financial Management, Human Resources, International trade, English, French and German, Computer Science, Technology and Electrical Engineering.etc.

**Literacy and Human Resource Development.** Literacy[1] (capability to read and write for those above 15 years) is 91.6% with males leading with 95.7% and females lagging further behind with 87.6%[2]. The following bar diagrams will show the rapid advancements in education in China after 1980 and the slower progress in India.

If we consider progress in adult literacy (15 years and above) after 1990, vis-à-vis the Indian scenario, China showed much better progress.

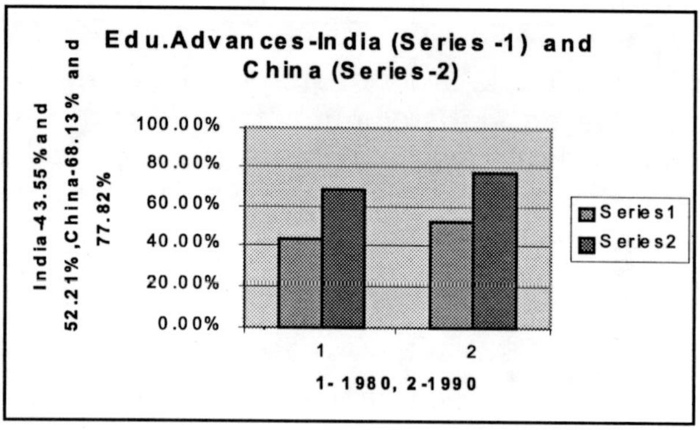


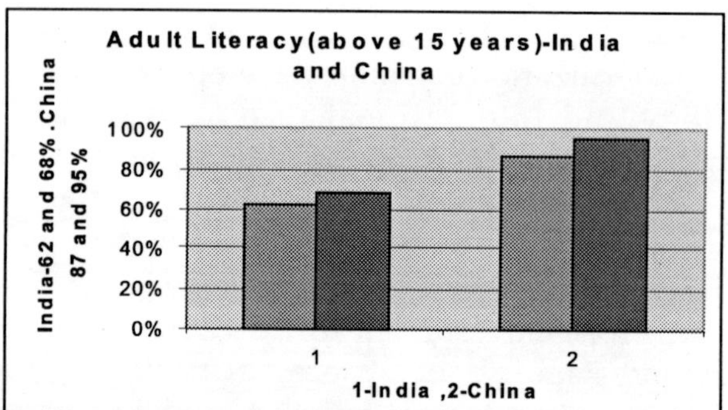


Adult literacy (15 years and above).

One analysis summed up the progress in Adult literacy, enrolment in primary, secondary and tertiary levels in the beginning of the 21st century in China and India as given below:

| *Country* | *Adult literacy ratio* | *Combined primary, secondary and tertiary enrolment* |
|---|---|---|
| India | 61.30% | 53.00% |
| China | 90.90% | 68.00% |

The higher educational levels in China enabled it to achieve higher levels of development of its people as a whole. The relative positions of different countries have been worked out by a comparative study On Human Resource Development based on certain selected parameters like Educational advancement and Per capita GDP as given below. India's position is now at 119 and China's at 88. The indices for the other factors are given in the Table below.

| *Country* | *Rank* | *Ed. Index* | *GDP* | *HDI* |
|---|---|---|---|---|
| India | 119 | 0.59 | 0.55 | 0.602 |
| China | 88 | 0.83 | 0.64 | 0.745 |

While India has been at rank 127 for a fairly long time, by 2003, China moved up from 104 to 94. Perhaps, because of China's socialist background, it gave more importance to education and health care attaining a better level of economic productivity. India in 2002 was in the same position as China in 1985 giving China a lead of 17 years in respect of Human Resources Development Index. The figures in respect of use of personal computers, telephones, mobile phones and internet per 1000 people show a much higher deviation vis-a-vis the educational gap showing how higher levels of educational achievements accelerate use of latest technologies/modern systems which are essential for faster growth today.

China-India: Use of Modern Facilities

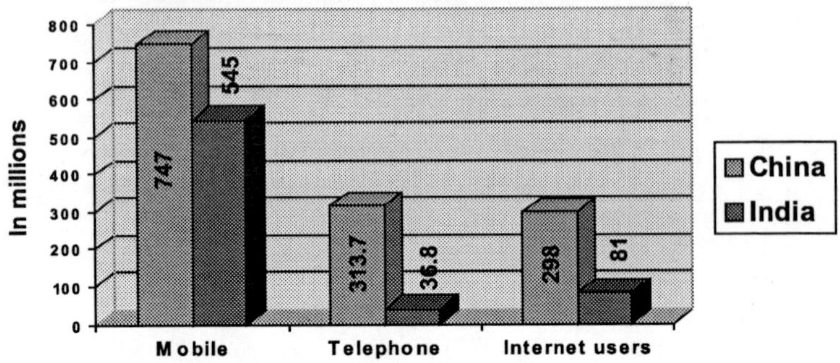


Comments: data 2010.

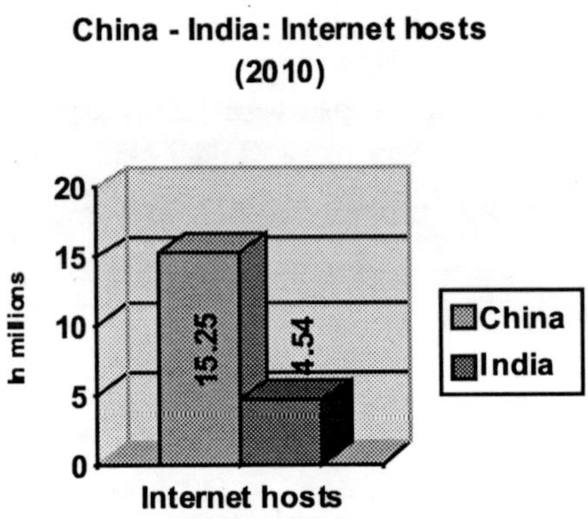


**Comparison with developed countries.** The first set of bar diagrams (i) below gives a comparative analysis of the literacy levels, literacy for men, tertiary (university level) enrolment and extent of public spending on education in China, India and developed countries like UK, and USA in 2003.

The second set of bar diagrams (ii) compare China and India with UK and USA in respect of Average years of schooling for adults, Years of compulsory education, Pupil teacher ration and number of universities (out of top 100). The Pie diagram below (iii) shows the distribution of top 500 universities of the world.

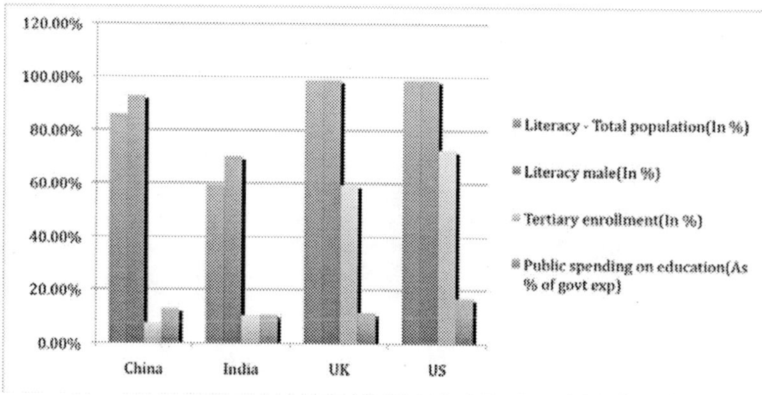


**(i)**

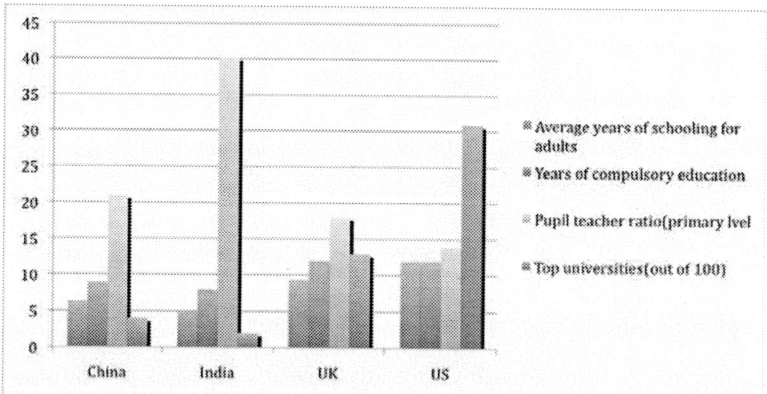


**(ii)**

According to Prof. Xiaohong Li, President and Professor of Chongqing University[1], the national gross rate of enrollment for Higher Education increased from 9.8% in 1998 to 15% in 2003. The diagrams below, in his view, will give a comparative view of China, India, US and Russia in respect of total college graduates, total doctoral degrees, ratio of doctoral degrees to undergraduate degrees and percentage of Science and Engineering doctoral degrees in 2003.

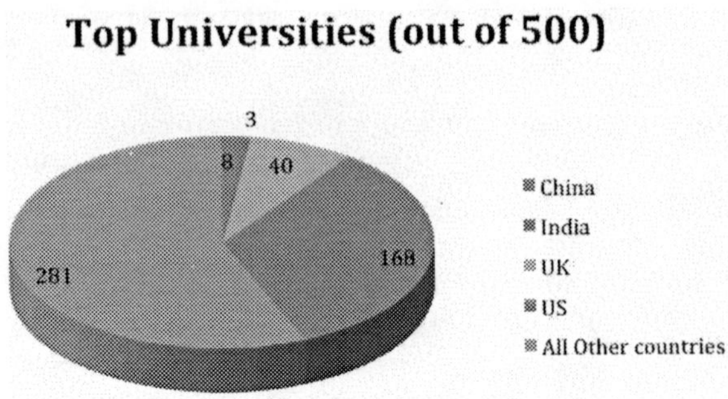
Top Universities (out of 500)
3
8
40
168
281
China
India
UK
US
All Other countries

(iii)

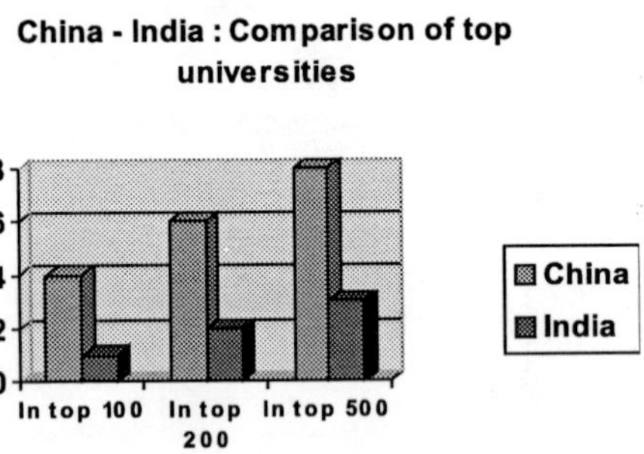
China - India : Comparison of top universities
8
6
4
2
0
In top 100
In top 200
In top 500
China
India

(iv)

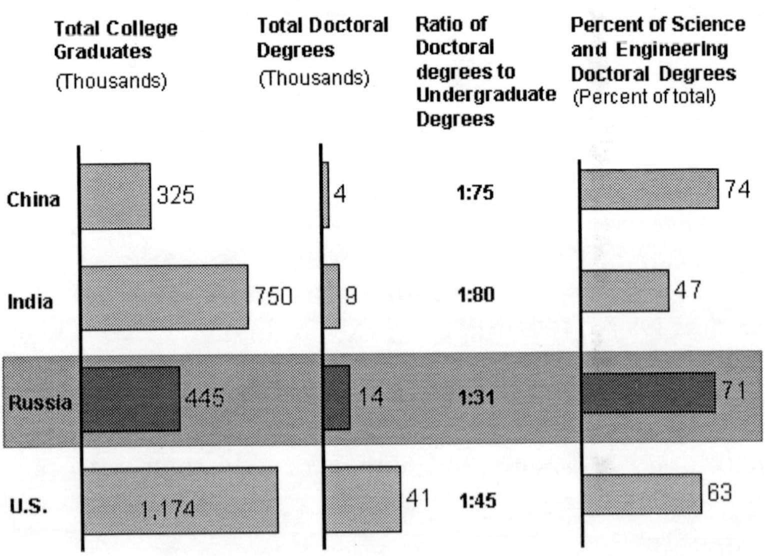
Total College Graduates (Thousands)
Total Doctoral Degrees (Thousands)
Ratio of Doctoral degrees to Undergraduate Degrees
Percent of Science and Engineering Doctoral Degrees (Percent of total)
China
325
4
1:75
74
India
750
9
1:80
47
Russia
445
14
1:31
71
U.S.
1,174
41
1:45
63

(v)

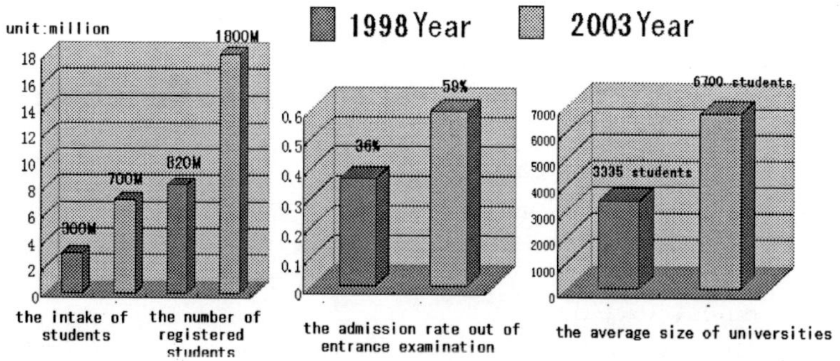


**(vi)**

According to Prof. Xiaohong Li, the bar diagrams above show the increases in intake of students, number of registered students, admission rate out of entrance examinations and average size of universities between 1998 and 2003.

Literacy (ability to read and write for those above 15 years) in China now, according to CIA world fact book, is 91.6% (men-95.7% and women-87.6%) against 61% in India (men-73.4% and women-47.8%). The targets set for 2020 shown earlier looks achievable. It would raise China's literacy level to nearly that of advanced countries, which would be a major landmark in the efforts to develop the huge human resources of the country, the main strength of China and India.

## Endnote

[1] http://universitiesaustralia.edu.au/documents/policies_programs/International/collaboration/Prof-Li-Xiaohong. ppt

## References

a. http://en.wikipedia.org/wiki/Education_in_the_People's_Republic_of_China (Dec. 15, 2009)
b. http://Nationmaster.com/country/ch-china/edu-education
c. http://universitiesaustralia.edu.au/documents/policies_

programs/International/collaboration/Prof-Li-Xiaohong.ppt

d. http://www-personal.ksu.edu/~dbski/publication/overview
e. http://math.ksu.edu/~dbski/publication/history.html
f. http://news.xinhuanet.com/english/2003-02/26/content_746294.htm
g. http://china.org.cn/living_in_china/studying/2008-12/08/content_16916351.htm
h. http://www.teachingtips.com/blog/2009/08/30/25-surprising-facts-about-chinas-education-system
i. http://www.unescobkk.org/fileadmin/user_upload/apeid/Conference/11thConference/ppt/5B_li.pdf
k. a number of other articles and websites on the subject.
l. Different issues of 'People's Daily'
m. Reports from Xinhua news

## RELIGIOUS SCENE

1. In China, in pre-historic periods, filial piety and ancestor worship were the basics of religion in China. People believed that their ancestors became god-like when they died and wished to be worshipped. Ancient Chinese looked upto their ancestors to get answers to questions about origin and nature of the universe. These extended to legendary or historical figures such as the patriarch or founder of one's surname, virtuous individuals such as Confucius or Guan Yu, or mythological figures like the 'Yellow Emperor'. Even today, major Chinese festivals like the Qing and the Double Ninth Festival involve Veneration of ancestors. It is conducted in many other ceremonies, including weddings, funerals, and initiations. Generally prayers are offered with food, incense, candles, and other offerings at the sites of ancestral temples, graves, tombs, household shrines, etc.
2. Later, during the Bronze Age (2205–256 B.C.), many gods and spirits used to be worshipped. During the Shang dynasty period (about 2000 B.C.), different gods like weather gods and sky gods were worshipped. By the time of the Zhou dynasty (about 1100 B.C.), a natural force called 't'ien', 'Shand–Ti'or 'Diety above' which translates into 'Heaven' began to be worshipped. It was believed 'Heaven' ruled over other gods and also decided who would be the Emperor or Empress. The Emperor, considered 'Son of Heaven', could only rule as long as he had the 'Mandate of Heaven'. When the Emperor lost the 'Mandate', he would be overthrown by somebody who would then succeed. The 'Temple of Heaven' in Beijing is such a place where the Emperor worshipped Heaven on whose behalf (as son of Heaven) he ruled. It was believed that Heaven punished people who offended him and rewarded those who pleased him. Spirits represented many things found in nature like

mountains, streams and stars. Belief in after life prompted even sacrifice of servants of kings following their deaths so that they could get their services in heaven too. Often worship was seen not as an individual exercise, but one for the society as a whole. Each family worshipped its ancestors as intermediaries. Later, priests came up as intermediaries to specific gods, for specific prayers, etc. Another feature was the augur system which asked the gods specific questions. Divination using bones was used to find answers.

3. After the advent of Taoism and Buddhism, public faith in Heaven monotheism faded. However, some of its concepts like the 'Mandate of Heaven', the Emperor's role as 'Son of Heaven', and the legitimate overthrow of a dynasty when its 'Mandate' ended remained relevant. These concepts, influenced heavily by Confucian theory, actually consolidated the authority of the Emperor. Some elements were also incorporated in Chinese folk religion. Execution by lightning, for example, became one of the roles of the thunder gods. The concept of the almighty Heaven remained in popular expressions. It is said that where an English man would say "Oh my God" or "Thank God", a Chinese might say "Oh Heaven" or "Thank the heavens and the earth".
4. Around 600 B.C. (Eastern Zhou) and for the next nearly two hundred years, different new religious ideas came up. A philosopher named Lao Tzu created a semi -religious philosophy called Taoism. It became very popular. 'Tao', path or way, is a wide force in nature which is the source of all things. Taoism asked people to follow Tao as it was essential for a happy life. It taught that people should do things with natural forces acting in their favour. Some less educated teachers later introduced magic and alchemy too. Taoism was well established in the late Eastern Han Dynasty (25–220) when it was made the official religion also. With the support of rulers, it reached its zenith during the Northern and Southern Dynasties (386–589). Taoist temples were

scattered all over the country. Taoism gradually became an integral part of Chinese culture.

Another thinker 'Confucius' created a different philosophical system popularly known as **Confucianism,** which disagreed with Taoism, but also became very popular. It stood for politeness, morality and social norms and order as the way to peace. It held that people should do their duty and faithfully follow their leaders and gods. If everyone just does what he or she is told, and what he or she is supposed to do, there would not be any quarrels. It asked people to do their duty to the ruler as good citizens. The Han Dynasty eventually made Confucianism the official state culture. Later, it became a basis for education too. Some changes were introduced centuries later by Confucius' followers under Neo-Confucianism. Though Confucianism is not a religion, there are temples where Confucius is worshipped. Under the Ming Dynasty, Confucianism was the main philosophy of the emperors, while Buddhism and Taoism remained popular among ordinary people. But, the old ideas of the Mandate of Heaven, traditional Chinese gods, and ancestor worship continued.

**Buddhism** came from India during the Han dynasty (1st cent.–9th cent.). It was quite popular during the ancient dynasties of Southern, Northern, Sui, Tang, Song, etc. Originally, it was seen as a kind of 'foreign Taoism' and its scriptures were translated into Chinese using the Taoist vocabulary. 'Chan Buddhism'is Buddhism modified by Taoism, integrating distrust of scriptures, text and even language and integrating Taoist stress on 'this life', dedicated practices, etc. In the Tang period, Taoism incorporated such Buddhist aspects like monastic life, vegetarianism, prohibition of alcohol, the doctrine of emptiness,etc. But, it was not universally welcomed, particularly among the gentry. The Buddha's Dharma seemed alien and amoral to conservative and Confucian sensibilities. Chinese officials questioned how a monk's monasticism and personal attainment of 'nirvana' benefited the empire. In China, Buddhism altered over time and concepts like return of some who attained 'nirvana' to help and guide humans were evolved. Chinese often believed in more than one religion with Taoism, Confucianism and Buddhism influencing one another. The Tang Dynasty Empress Wu, for example, was a Buddhist when Taoism was still very strong in China.

Under the Song Dynasty (about A.D. 1000), Confucianism combined with Buddhism became popular. Scholars re-read the old Confucian writings in Buddhist terms, and tried to get Buddhist meanings out of them. With the Mongol conquests around A.D. 1200, a new multiculturalism came to China. Kublai Khan, a Mongol emperor, a Buddhist, was very interested in all faiths and encouraged Christians, Muslims, Jews, Hindus and Tibetan lamas to come to his court and debate each other. But, most people in China remained either Buddhists or Taoists. The Chinese religious tradition of three religions (Confucianism, Buddhism and Taoism) combining into one was generally developed during Sui and Tang Dynasties.

Qing Dynasty (1644–1911) honoured Tibetan Buddhism and showed no interest in Taoism which eventually lost the support from rulers and upper classes. It became a secret religious organization practiced by mostly Hans and a few other ethnic groups. At present, many people in Honking, Macao and Taiwan believe in Taoism. It is undergoing a major revival now. In April 2007, at an international conference of celebrities and government officials, support to Taoism as one of the foundations of Chinese culture was expressed.

While estimates of the number of Buddhists in China vary widely, Chinese government statistics estimates the number of Buddhists at 100 million. Some recent surveys put the total number between 660 million (50%) and over 1 billion (80%), thus making China the country with the most Buddhist adherents. It is difficult to estimate accurately the number of Buddhists as they do not have congregational memberships and often do not participate in public ceremonies. Vast majority of Chinese Buddhists are of the

Mahayana sect. Some restrictions on Tibetan Buddhism are due to controversies about its hierarchy, especially the leadership of Dalai Lama who is in India. Chinese government has prohibited the 'reincarnation' of Tibetan living Buddhas without its permission. Buddhism is, however, deeply embedded in China's culture, philosophy, and way of life.

Apart from these, common people had their own belief systems and practices which may be called folk religion. It comprises of religious practices prevalent for thousands of years including ancestor worship and concepts within mythology. It is sometimes seen as a part of Chinese traditional religion and often, the two are taken as synonymous. It is a combination of religious practices, including Confucianist ceremonies, ancestor worship, Buddhism and Taoism. It has also traces of Neolithic belief systems like veneration of (and communication with) the sun, moon, earth, the heaven, and various stars and even animals. Worship of deities, cultural heroes, demigods and supernatural beings (particularly the Chinese dragon) that vary depending on geographical and local conditions, etc. are all its parts. Worship of secondary gods does not conflict with a person's chosen religion, but is accepted as a complementary adjunct to Buddhism, Confucianism or Taoism. Some mythical figures in folk culture have even been integrated into Buddhism as in the case of 'Miao Shan' who is generally thought of as having evolved into the Buddhist bodhisattva Kuan Yin. Other folk deities may belong to pre-Buddhist eras. It is not organized in institutions, has no clergy or formal rituals, but has its own temples. It is Popular in Hong Kong, Macau and Taiwan and perhaps has about 800 million adherents across the globe.

**In folk religion**, there are a large number of gods and goddess, saints, immortals and demigods who were traditionally venerated. Historical figures noted for their bravery or virtue are also venerated and honored with their own festivals. The following list represents some commonly worshipped deities:

1. Guan Yu is a symbol of trust, integrity and loyalty. He is worshipped mainly in the Fujian and Taiwan areas as a divine physician whose powers include even raising the dead. 2. 'Cai Shen'/'Gongming Zhao', with the shape of a giant blue whiskered cat, is worshipped as god of wealth. 3. The 'Eight Immortals' are important literary and artistic figures who became objects of worship after their death. 'Hu Ye' (Lord Tiger), is a guardian spirit while Jiu 'Wang Ye' (Nine Emperor God) refers to spirits of nine emperors, worshiped as 'Mazu' patron goddess of sailors. A festival is held in the first nine days of the ninth lunar month to celebrate the return from heaven of the Nine Emperor spirits. 4. 'Shangdi' (Supreme Emperor) was originally the supreme god, synonymous with the concept of 'Tian'. Later this title was used for the supreme deity of various religions, including Yu Huang Dadi and the Christian God. 5. 'Cheng Huang', is a class of protective deities. Each city has a Cheng Huang who looks after the fortunes of the city and judges the dead. Usually, these are famous or noble persons from the city. 'Sun Wukong' or The Monkey King is a stone monkey born from heaven and earth who wreaked havoc in heaven. 6. 'Tu Di Gong', is the "God of the earth" whose statue is found in roadside shrines and is considered the protector of a place. He is also known as the god of wealth by virtue of his connection with the earth. 7. 'Wenchangdi' (Emperor Promoting Culture), is a god of students, scholars, and examination. 8. 'Wangmu', the Queen Mother of the West, reigns over a paradisial mountain with powers to make others immortal. In some myths, she is the mother of the Jade Emperor. 9. 'Yuexia Laoren' (Old Man under the Moon) is a matchmaker. He pairs lovers together, and is worshipped by those seeking to find partners. 10. 'Zao Shen', the Kitchen God reports to heaven on the behavior of a family once a year on the occasion of

Chinese New Year. He is given sticky rice in order to render his speech less comprehensible.' 11. 'Zhusheng Niangniang' (Birth-Registry Goddess) is worshipped by the childless and those who want male heirs.

**Other religions.** During the Tang Dynasty, trade with the Persians and the Islamic Empire in West Asia resulted in Christianity, Judaism, Islam and Zoroastrianism, gaining followers in China. In 636 A.D., for instance, some Christians from Syria built a church in China. Jews settled at Kaifeng, at the end of the Silk Road, built a synagogue in A.D. 1163. Islam came through import and export trade which was dominated by Muslims for long. Some Zoroastrians also settled in China for a while. But, of these only Christianity and Islam took deep roots and others virtually disappeared with the march of time.

**Christianity,** consisting of basically of Catholics, some Orthodox churches and Protestants, has been a growing minority religion for the last 200 years. The first group to come to the country was the Assyrian Church of the East (A.D. 635). The next group was the Franciscan missionaries of Catholics in A.D. 1294 during the Yuan Dynasty. Not much progress was achieved till the Jesuits arrived in Beijing at the end of the Ming dynasty. They followed a policy of accommodation to the traditional Chinese practice of ancestor worship which was eventually condemned by the Pope. Roman Catholic missions then struggled for decades without much progress. Chiristianity began to take root in a significant way during the Qing Dynasty when waves of missionaries came to China as a result of contact with foreign powers. Russian Orthodox Church came in 1715 and Protestants in 1807. In the 19th and 20th centuries, missionary activities increased after the First Opium War in 1842 and Christian schools, under the protection of the Western powers, went on to play a major role in the westernization of China. Boxer Rebellion was in part a reaction against such activities.

Christians established modern clinics and hospitals and provided modern training for nurses and founded numerous educational institutions from primary to university levels. Some of the prominent universities began as religious institutions. Missionaries also worked for abolition of foot binding and unjust treatment of maidservants. Charitable work including distribution of food to the poor, campaigns against opium trade and treatment to opium addicts were other activities which won them support. Some of the early leaders of the Chinese Republic like Sun Yes-men were converts to Christianity. Following the Communist Revolution of 1949 led by Mao, all religious activities were banned as religion was considered an opiate of the people. Cultural Revolution saw persecution of its activists. But, many Christians still kept their faith alive despite all the difficulties and disadvantages. With the economic liberalization and assumption of power by Deng Xiao Ping, activities again picked up and the strengths of believers have been going up. Religious practices are still often tightly controlled by government authorities. Chinese over age 18 are only permitted to be involved in religious activities and that too through officially approved Christian organizations like "Chinese Catholic Patriotic Association". But, majority of believers follow Catholic Church headed by Pope and Unregistered Protestant Churches despite the difficulties faced by them. Most of the recent growth has taken place in the unofficial Chinese house church movement.

**Islam** dates back to a mission in 651, only eighteen years after Prophet Muhammad's death. Muslims went to China to trade and virtually dominated the import and export trade. Larger immigration began when hundreds of thousands of Muslims were relocated to administer China during the Yuan Dynasty. A Muslim contractor led the construction of the Yuan capital of Beijing. During the Ming Dynasty, Muslims continued their influence on government. Six trusted generals of the founder of Ming Dynasty were Muslims. Muslim immigrants began to assimilate by speaking Chinese dialects and by adopting Chinese names and culture. This era is considered the Golden Age of Islam in China. It saw Nanjing become an important center of Islamic study. Qing Dynasty prohibited construction of new mosques and pilgrimage and adopted repressive policies. The period saw five bloody rebellions by Muslims and virtual genocide of Muslims in the efforts to suppress rebellions resulting in the death of several millions. In 1911, the provinces of Qinghai, Gansu and Ningxia fell to Muslim warlords. During the Cultural Revolution, mosques were often defaced, destroyed or closed and copies of the Quran were destroyed along with temples, churches, monasteries, and cemeteries.

There is an upsurge in Islamic expression and many nation-wide Islamic associations have come up to co-ordinate inter-ethnic activities among Muslims. Muslims are found in every province in China. Of China's 55 officially recognized minorities, ten groups are predominately Muslim. Most estimates of the number of Muslims in China today put the figure between 20 to 30 million (1.5 to 2%) though the governmental figure is about 20 million. In 2006, the number of Chinese who traveled to Mecca for the hajj was 40 percent higher than that of the previous year.

**Bon** is the oldest tradition of Tibet. After Buddhism came, it adopted some of the Buddhist features to become Tibetan Buddhism. Dongbaism is the primary religion of the 'Nakhi' people near Tibet. About two-thirds of Nakhis (200.000 or 300.000) are Dongbas. Although it has remained exclusive to the Nakhis, deep similarities exist between Dongba and the Bonpo practices. Bonpos are said to have settled among the Nakhis spreading their religion. Dongbaism originated from the combination of Bon with Nakhi native beliefs. Elements drawn from Taoism are also identifiable. Dongbas worship nature, personified by human-snake like creatures 'Shu'.

**Xiantianism and Falun Gong** are characterized by syncretism, messianic and millenarian attitudes. These movements are currently banned in Mainland China due to their involvement in political issues. Falun Gong is a mind-body cultivation system related to Buddhism. It is sometimes described as a religion, spirituality or a metaphysical system. It was spread by Li Hongzhi since 1992. A 1998 figure from the Chinese government suggested that there were 70 million practitioners in China at the time the Chinese authorities banned it. Xiantianism is referred to have roots in the 13th century doctrine of the 'White Lotus'. It was formally founded in the 17th century as a unified religion, but in 1828 it split into many sub-groups. Xiantian religions claimed 5 million adherents before the crackdown in 1949.

More people these days openly show their religious inclinations despite the possible unfavorable consequences for them. Many local and foreign visitors are seen, esp. in Buddhist Temples. A lot of rural people can be seen praying in old Buddhist temples despite the possible risks of exclusion from the Communist Party and positions of power. In villages where vast majority of the Chinese live, a lot of superstitions, belief in miracles and symbols for good luck as in India, blind beliefs in 'Fengshui' and other old belief systems are still in existence. Earlier practices of prayer to Dragon God to escape from floods (which used to play havoc) and evil, to get long life, etc. have not disappeared from villages. Pictures or symbols of Dragons, dragon horses, dragon gods, etc. are visible at many places. Though Dragon originally represented royal power and higher classes, today it is proudly accepted as a symbol of China/Chinese culture. Boats are seen in dragon shape and dresses with pictures of dragon etc. are also common. Though party positions are not meant for religious people, today atleast 25% of the party members in rural areas are said to be followers of religions, mainly traditional or folk religions. According to an April 2002 government white paper, there were more than 200 million religious adherents (increased since then), representing a great variety of beliefs and practices. Most religious adherents profess eastern faiths. When those for Taoism, folk religions and other belief systems are also accounted for, the percentage is quite substantial demonstrating the impact of liberalization on increase in religiosity despite possible adverse career prospects. This could be one of the reasons why the CPC and the Government are less hostile to religious groups other than who are believed to pose a threat to CPC's power or national integrity, or are banned or considered subversive.

**'Suppression' of Religious freedom'**: After the revised Criminal Law came into effect in 1997, membership in unapproved cult or religious group is a crime of 'disturbing the social order'. Repression of groups called "cults" in general and of the Falun Gong in particular persist. State decrees 144 and 145 limit the practice of religion by foreign nationals to state-sanctioned places of worship against the UN Declaration on the Elimination of All Forms of Intolerance and of Discrimination Based on Religion or Belief. Religious freedom only means the freedom to evangelize, share or preach the faith in the government approved places of worship. The state reserves the right to register and there are only five officially recognized religions: Catholicism, Protestantism, Buddhism, Islam, and Taoism. These exist without tensions. The following factors are being highlighted by those who criticize lack of religious freedom in China.

a. Each recognized or registered religion is supervised by a government-affiliated association like the State Council's Religious Affairs Bureau (RAB) and the CCP's United Front Work Department (UFWD). They provide policy "guidance and supervision" on the implementation of government regulations.

b. According to a report of the International Religious Freedom issued by the US State Department in September, 2008, the government tried to limit the participation of Muslims in the Hajj and also pursued the forcible return of several Muslims living abroad.

c. Participants of unregistered groups were allegedly arrested, detained, placed under close police surveillance or internal exile, fined, in some cases tortured and religious literature and church property confiscated. Laws restricting contact with foreign co-religionists, laws prohibiting parents from exposing children under 18 to religion, etc. are other issues.

d. It is alleged that Government tries to control the growth and scope of activities of religious groups. "Patriotic education" campaigns in the Tibetan Autonomous Region and other Tibetan areas require monks and nuns to sign statements denouncing the Dalai Lama. Placing under surveillance prominent religious activists and leaders, including attorneys, restricting them to their homes, or forcing them to leave Beijing during the visit of foreign delegations, repressing the Roman Catholic clergy for their loyalty to the Vatican, etc. are some instances.

e. The Government allegedly tries to prevent the rise of groups that could constitute sources of authority outside its control and cracks down on groups which it perceives may pose a threat. In some areas, "underground" religious leaders face increasing pressure to register with the RAB.

f. Thousands of Falun Gong adherents have been arrested, detained, and imprisoned, and several hundred or more have died in detention since 1999. Imprisonment of 3 to 7 years for "cult" members, those who distribute publications, etc. and 7 years or more to leaders or recruiters is the norm. Thousands of Falun Gong practitioners are serving extrajudicial administrative sentences in reeducation-through-labor camps. Hundreds have been confined to psychiatric institutions and forced to take medications or undergo electric shock treatment. Party and PLA military personnel have been expelled for adhering to Falun Gong.

g. Advocacy of Tibetan independence or any form of separatism is forcibly suppressed. As Tibetan Buddhists generally recognize the boy identified by the Dalai Lama as the Panchen Lama, they are allegedly forced to sign statements pledging allegiance to the boy selected by the Government as the Panchen Lama. Impositions of limits on the number of monks in major monasteries using power to disapprove any individual's application, demolition of the houses of monks in big monasteries, overseeing the daily operations of major monasteries, etc. take place.

h. In 1999, the Party's C C allegedly directed authorities to tighten control over the official Catholic Church and to eliminate the underground Catholic Church if it did not bend to government control The Government also arbitrarily reorganized some dioceses without consulting church leaders. Some foreign teachers at the official Catholic seminary in Xian were forced to leave the country after the head of the seminary criticized the Government's position in its dispute with the Vatican.

i. Where ethnic unrest has occurred, especially among the Uighurs in Xinjiang, officials allegedly continue to restrict the building of mosques and prohibit teaching of Islam to children. Authorities also initiated a campaign to discourage overt religious attire such as veils and religious marriage ceremonies. They also began to conduct monthly political study sessions for religious personnel and to implement more vigorous restrictions on the religious education of youth under 18. Muslims have, allegedly been fired from government posts for praying during working hours.

j. Citizens may be sentenced by a non-judicial panel of police and local authorities up to 3 years in prison-like facilities called reeducation-through-labor camps. In Hebei Province, where an estimated half of the country's Catholics reside, friction between unofficial Catholics and local authorities continue. Bishops have been detained to pressurize them to join the Chinese Catholic Patriotic Association.

Some **positive aspects** were also reportedly seen. These were:

1. Some steps to show respect for the country's Muslims, including by offering congratulations on major Islamic holidays and permits, and in some cases subsidies, to muslims to go for Hajj (pilgrimage) to Mecca are reported. The major limiting factors for participation in the Hajj are said to be the cost and controls on passport.
2. In Tibetan areas outside of the Tibetan Autonomous Region, abbots and monks have greater freedom to worship and conduct religious training. Pictures of a number of Tibetan religious figures, including the Dalai Lama, are openly displayed in parts of Sichuan, Qinghai, and Gansu provinces. Foreign nationals are allowed to preach to other foreigners, to bring in religious materials for personal use, and to preach to Chinese citizens at churches, mosques, and temples at the invitation of registered religious organizations.
3. A lot of improvements have taken place compared with the situation 10, 20 years or even five years ago. Religious freedom is much better now as the government is trying to open up in different ways to Christians. Many Christian groups throughout the country have developed close ties with local officials, in some cases operating schools and homes for the care of the aged.
4. In Hong Kong and Macau, there is more freedom.Falun Gong is not banned. There is no need for registration of religious groups. Catholic Church under Pope is active. Both have large numbers of Buddhist and Taoist believers.

## References


a. http://en.wikipedia.org/wiki/Chinese_Patriotic_Catholic_Association (Dec. 16, 2009)
b. http://en.wikipedia.org/wiki/Religion_in_China (Dec. 16, 2009)
c. http://en.wikipedia.org/wiki/Chinese_folk_religion (Dec. 16, 2009)

d. http://en.wikipedia.org/wiki/Human_rights_in_the_People%27s_Republic_of_China (Dec. 16, 2009)
e. http://en.wikipedia.org/wiki/Freedom_of_religion_in_the_People%27s_Republic_of_China (Dec. 16, 2009)
f. http://historyforkids.org/learn/china/religion/
g. http://blue.butler.edu/~jfmcgrat/china/religion1.htm
h. http://asia.isp.msu.edu/wbwoa/east_asia/china/religion.htm
i. http://www.religiousfreedom.com/wrpt/Chinarpt.htm
j. http://www.state.gov/g/drl/rls/irf/2002/13870.htm
k. http://www.onenewsnow.com/Persecution/Default.aspx?id=68469
l. http://www.voanews.com/uspolicy/2008-10-03-voa5.cfm
m. 2008 U.S. State Department International
n. http://www.state.gov/g/drl/rls/irf/2003/23826.htm
o. http://www.religiousfreedom.com/index.php?option=com_content&view=article&id=163&Itemid=29
p. http://www.china-embassy.org/eng/zt/zjxy/t36496. htm
q. http://news.xinhuanet.com/english/2009-03/28/content_11088062.htm

## LINGUISTIC SCENE

Chinese language evolved from 'Proto-Sino-Tibetan'/Sino-Tibetan family, the source of all languages common to China, Tibet and Burma. The Chinese, vast majority of whom are Hans, perhaps had spoken and written languages for about 4000 years. Ninety five percent of the Chinese population speaks Chinese and the remaining Tibetan, Mongolian, Miao, Tai, etc. In 1955, Chinese government officially recognized 'Mandarin', the dialect being used in Beijing area and by over 70% of the Han-ethnic group, as the official spoken form of Chinese. Mandarin is now the fundamental means of communication among Chinese people.

Though speaking evolved over time, the written form of Chinese has not changed much over the years. The Chinese script emerged from carved symbols perhaps about 6000 years ago. The earliest known examples are 'shell bone writings' used for divination (on scapulae and turtle shells) dating back to about 1500–900 B.C. during the Shang Dynasty days. Print characters emerged from symbols used on bones and tortoise shells and from bronze inscriptions. Drawn figures were gradually reduced to patterned strokes, pictographs were reduced to symbols and complicated graphs became simpler. Earlier pictographs and ideographs were joined by picto-phonetic characters. Pictures of people, animals, etc., over a long period of time, became stylized no longer resembling the things they originally represented. Some have continued as such. Roughly 600 of about 6000/7000 commonly used Chinese characters are pictograms—stylized drawings of the objects they represent. These are generally among the oldest characters. Ideograms express an abstract idea in an iconic form. It may include modification of pictographic characters.

Chinese orthography centers around 'Hanze' written in imaginary blocks traditionally arranged in vertical columns and read from top to bottom and right to left across columns. About 3000 characters taught in schools are enough to read 99 percent of the writings. However, dictionaries, classical literature, etc. have a lot more most of which are archaic.

12 basic strokes[1] given below are involved in making the Chinese characters. A character may have 1 to 64 strokes which are written in the same direction. There is a set order to write the strokes of each character.

Most Chinese characters have phonetic parts. Modern Chinese has 400 spoken mono-syllables. In classical Chinese, each idea had one syllable and one character. 'Chinese' has no tenses, no voices and no numbers, but only a few articles. Nouns, adjectives and verbs are generally di-syllabic. There are several hundred pictographs for common words like man, horse, axe, and also compound pictographs. For e.g., a man carrying grain means a harvest.

For modern concepts, inventions are made from native stocks of meaningful syllables or these are rendered in terms of phonetic spelling. For e.g., Chemistry is expressed as study of transformation. Loan words from other cultures are also used. Many came along the Silk Road. For e.g. Lion, grape, pomegranate, Buddha, Bodhisattva, hutong, etc. are such loan words accepted in Chinese. The examples given below show how new words for modern terms emerged.

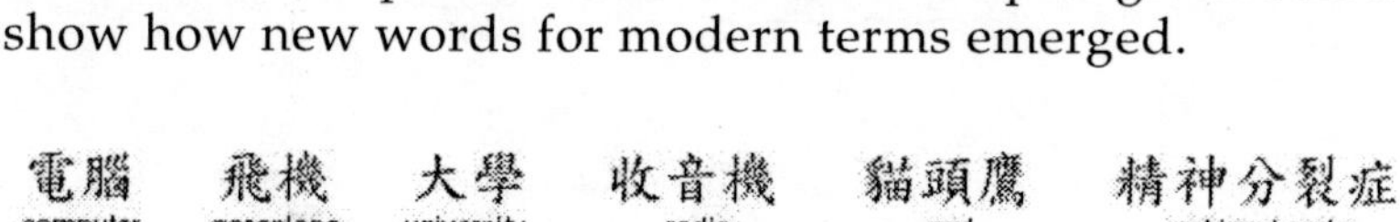


(Source: omniglot.com)

Modern Chinese language never changes in sound to indicate grammatical differences. Not all characters are pronounced with the same tone and so to the Chinese, they sound different, but are distinguished by the context.

About 1 bn. Chinese speak Chinese and its dialects; but, there is a high level of internal diversity for all spoken varieties. Mandarin is used in Government schools, media, etc. Chinese generally understand two or three dialects. For e.g., in Hong Kong, people know English, Mandarin and Cantonese. Cantonese is used informally in chit-chat, instant messaging and less formally. Chinese was in use in Japan, Korea and Vietnam till the Europeans came. Its simplified form is used in Singapore too.

Chinese government, in its efforts to increase literacy, simplified many Chinese characters. Simplification was done by decreasing the number of strokes and simplifying the forms of a number of characters. Some characters were simplified irregularly. Some simplified characters are very different from the traditional ones being replaced. Many characters were left untouched. Two examples of traditional and simplified forms[2] are given below.

Standard Romanization in Pinyin/Hanyu Pinyin was introduced from 1956 for teaching sounds and tones to children, telegrams, etc. Wades-Giles is anther phonetic spelling system for people with English speaking background.

| 漢 | 汉 |
|---|---|
| 字 | 字 |
| Traditional | Simplified |

The following examples will help to understand the differences between Pinyin and Wades-Giles.

| *Item* | *Pinyin* | *Wade-Giles* |
|---|---|---|
| Capital of China | Beijing | Pei-Ching |
| Confucius | Kongzi | Kung Tsu |
| Chairman Mao | Mao Zedong | Mao-Tsetung |

Since 1982, in the English speaking world, Chinese characters have been transliterated according to Wade-Giles romanisation. Personal names are romanized according to individual wishes. Place names follow the systematic spelling of Chinese Post Office.

## Endnotes

[1] Source: omniglot.com. permission granted by Simon Alger.

[2] As given in a US weekly/People's Daily.

## References


a. http://en.wikipedia.org/wiki/Chinese_language (Dec. 20, 2009)
b. http://omniglot.com/writing/chinese.htm
c. http://chinapage.com/learnchinese.html
d. http://en.wikipedia.org/wiki/File:Map_of_sinitic_languages-en.svg (Dec. 20, 2009)
e. http://en.wikipedia.org/wiki/Chinese_character_classification (Dec. 20, 2009)
f. http://en.wikipedia.org/wiki/Chinese_character (Dec. 20, 2009)

CHAPTER 3

# Political System

The Chinese polity operates virtually in a single party socialist republican mode. There are a few subordinate parties called "democratic parties" which participate in political consultative conferences. They generally endorse the policies of the CPC. There are some banned groups like China Democratic Party and Falun Gong (a controversial spiritual cult). Still, some progress towards democratization is seen in the open elections at village and town levels. Legislatures have shown some debates.

Though there are 8 political parties functioning since 1950, they virtually accept the control exercised by the CPC and their activities are directed by the United Front Department of the CPC. Their original role was to show that China was being ruled by a United Front and was not a one party dictatorship. They now serve, it is alleged, to attract and subsequently muzzle those with political tendencies like the academia. Members of these parties are also found in policy making organizations. The coordination between these and CPC is done through the Chinese People's Political Consultative Conference which meets in Beijing at about the time of the meeting of the National People's Congress (NPC), the Chinese Parliament.

**List of political parties and their memberships**[1]

Communist Party of China (CPC)—More than 70 million
The eight registered minor parties under CCP's direction are:

- Revolutionary Committee of the Kuomintang (Formed by leftist members of the Kuomintang who did not escape to Taiwan.-53,000 members. It is considered "second" in status to the Communist Party of China. It has 30% of the seats in the People's Political Consultative Conference)
- China Democratic League (Originally a league of pro-democracy parties.-144,000 members, mainly middle-level and senior intellectuals).
- China Democratic National Construction Association (Entrepreneurs from the manufacturing, financial or commercial industries, in both private and state sectors).
- China Association for Promoting Democracy (Intellectuals, mostly in the education, technology and publishing sectors.-117,500 members).
- Chinese Peasants' and Workers' Democratic Party (65,000 members work in the fields of public health, education and culture, science and technology, etc.).
- China Zhi Gong Party (Returned overseas Chinese, relatives of overseas Chinese, and noted figures and scholars who have overseas ties).
- September 3 Society (Most of its 68,000 members are high- and medium level intellectuals in the fields of science, technology, education, culture and medicine).
- Taiwan Democratic Self-Government League (1,600 people, most of whom are prominent people that are from Taiwan or are of Taiwanese heritage, but now reside on the Mainland).

(The figures are approx. and for purposes of comparison only.)

CPC with over 70 million members continues to dominate the Government. It controls learning, housing, T.V., no of children, etc. and suppresses dissent. Its members are mostly government officials, army officers, model workers, etc. These days, even businessmen are allowed in. As membership means privileges, influence, better information, housing, better schooling, jobs, relationship with decision makers, etc., its membership is highly coveted. To join CPC, backing of existing members, vigorous screening and examination by local party units, etc. are needed. Members are given training about their roles. In periods of relative liberalization, influence of non-CPC people shows increase, esp. on the economic front. Every State Owned Enterprise (SOE) has a party committee. With the intro-duction of the market reforms, in economic institutions, the party has limited power. But, in all governmental institutions, the party committees at all levels play important roles. The party control is tightest in the central government offices and in urban, economic, industrial and cultural settings. It is milder over government and party organizations in rural areas where the silent majority live. The most important role is in the selection and promotion of the officers and other senior functionaries. The aim is to see that the party policy guidance is followed and non-party members through autonomous organizations do not challenge the party rule. Small core party groups coordinate activities of different agencies. There is a convention that government committees contain at least one non-party member. Party membership is a definite aid in promotion and in being in crucial policy setting meetings. There are about 100,0000 units of the party spread over the whole country. Only about 20% of CPC members are women and 30% are degree holders. Nearly 77% are above 55 years.

Under a dual leadership system, each local bureau or office is under the theoretically equal authority of the local leader and the leader of the corresponding office or bureau at the next higher level. The will of the people is expressed through the legislative bodies of the people's congress system. Its members at the county level are elected by people. The county level congress has the responsibility of oversight of the local government and also election of members to the provincial/municipal people's congress. The provincial people's congress in turn elects members to the NPC which meets every year in Beijing. The CPC plays a key role in the selection of candidates to the local congress and higher levels.

In a recent article in 'Time', the power structure in China was represented as given below: The major organs of power in China are represented by block diagrams and CPC comes above all. The dotted lines represent informal power. The P.B., The Party leaders, Disciplinary system, etc. all have informal powers over the NPC which is the Parliament. In fact, the NPC and other organs like The State Council and Central Military Commission (CMC) created by the NPC are really creations of the CPC and its organs like P.B., senior party leaders, etc. These days, the effort is to arrive at a consensus though personalities still dominate even when not in positions of power as in the case of Deng Xiao Ping.

CPC has supreme political authority guaranteed by the Chinese constitution and it is exercised through its control over the state apparatus. Founded in 1921, it now stands for 'socialism with Chinese characteristics' as defined by Deng Xiao Ping. The highest political body is the NPC, selected

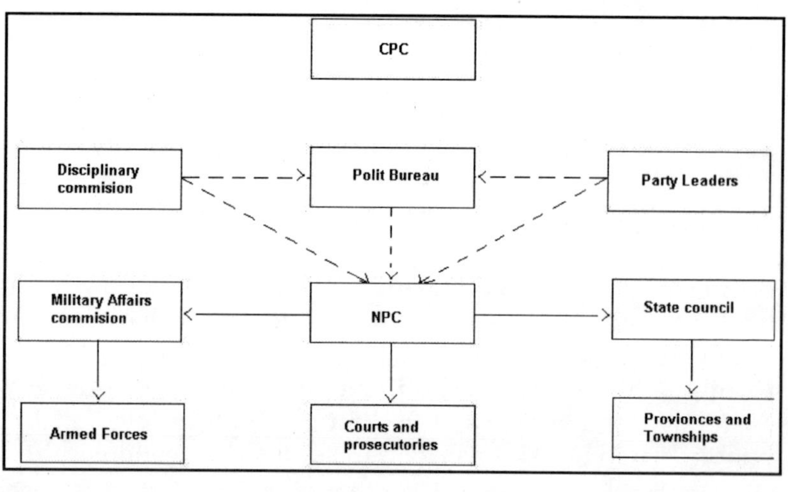

Chinese Leadership now[2] (PBM-Polit Bureau Member)
1. Hu Jintao, President, Gen. Secy, CPC and Chairman, CMC
2. Wen Jiabao, Prime Minister 3.Li Changchun (PBM)
4. Wu Bangguo (PBM) 5. Xi Jinping (PBM) 6. Jia Qinglin (PBM)
7. Li Keqiang (PBM) 8. He Goqiang (PBM) 9. Zhou Yongkang (PBM)

for 5 years and meeting once a year to approve changes in Party constitution and elect a New Central Committee with 300 members. The Polit Bureau (24+1 alternate member now), its Standing Committee (9), the Secretariat headed by the Gen. Secy, CMC (a parallel organization of the Government org. of the same name) and a Central Discipline Inspection Commission (at the same level as the C.C.) are its main bodies. There are also various commissions and leading groups for various purposes. It is said that there are two groups viz. 'Shanghai group' consisting of leaders from more prosperous regions and a 'youth league group' dominated by those from rural areas. Their interactions are said to be complementary and a balance is always kept on various issues.

According to Susan L. Shirk (Author, 'China: Fragile Superpower'), at the highest level there are two types of powers—'full' and 'weak'. The CPC acting through its General Secretary exercises full authority over the

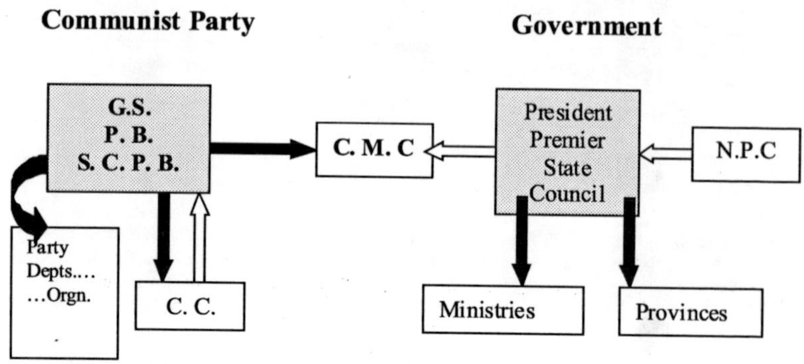


CMC-Central Military Commission.NPC-National People's Congress. CC-Central Committee.GS-General Secretary. PB-Polit Bureau. SCPB-Standing Committee of Polit Bureau. Party Departments include those for organization, propaganda, United Front and Liaison.

Central Committee, party organization and the Central Military Commission. The diagram below tries to represent the power system depicted by her. The Black lines represent 'full' authority and white lines 'weak' authority.

The Central Committee's authority over the General Secretary is weak. At the Government level, The President, Prime Minister and the State Council have full authority over Ministries and Provinces. But, their authority as governmental functionaries is weak over the Central Military Commission which controls the Defense Forces. Similarly, the authority of the National People's Congress over the President, Prime Minister and state Council is also weak. It is obvious that the Party Chief, General Secretary of the CPC, who selects the Prime Minister too for approval by the National people's Congress, is the focus of authorities in the Chinese power structure.

The Power lies with the Polit Bureau (24), esp. it's Standing Committee (9), a group of most influential leaders who work as an inner cabinet. It has the General Secretary of the CPC, P.M., Chairman of the NPC, Head of the National Disciplinary Commission, etc. as members. A lot of blunt speaking and disagreements are said to take place here. Normally, decisions are taken by a consensus and at times by majority. Once a decision is taken, it is binding on all. New members are selected after intense review only. To reach there, one needs strong records of achievements in working for the party, right patrons, should avoid making powerful enemies and dodge certain serious mistakes.

The CPC maintains effective control over all appointments. It has been clamping down on all dissidents and trying to reduce dissent by improving the economy and allowing public expression of grievances if they are not within the agenda of any organization. As national elections are always CPC dominated, its actual influence among the people is not known. The independent candidates are too scattered and disorganized to challenge the CPC. A survey in Hong Kong where there is more political freedom showed that the current mainland leaders enjoy sufficient support when the residents were asked to rank their favourite leaders from the mainland.

One of the main jobs of the NPC is to elect the CC with about 200 full-time and about 150 'alternate' members. In practice, these are greed upon in advance. It also elects a 24-member Polit Bureau and its 9-member Standing committee, the Secretariat headed by the General Secretary, the CMC and the Central Discipline Inspection Commission (to sort out corruption and malfeasance among party cadres). The Standing Committee of the PB is headed by Hu Jintao as Gen. Secy. In addition, there are 25 more members in the PB in-charge of different areas and roles like Hong Kong, Macao, Beijing, propaganda, Premier and Vice-Premiers, party chiefs of prominent areas, etc.

Its meetings were irregular during the Cultural Revolution, but are regular now. All the party organs of power are only parts of the C.C. During 1980s, an attempt was made to separate party and state functions with the party laying down the policy and the state council carrying it out. It was abandoned in the 1990s and the new leadership of the state are also leaders of the party creating a single central power structure. But, at lower levels, party and state offices are separated. It is meant to prevent either from becoming too dominant. Conflict has been known to exist between the chief executive and the party secretary. In Hong Kong and Macao, the party does not function as part of the Government. In autonomous regions, the chief executive is a member of the local ethnic group and the party secretary a non-local, usually Hans Chinese.

NPC is the highest organ of the state and the only legislative one. It meets every year along with the People's consultative conference whose members are from a broader background. It has authority over all state organizations for supervisory role on behalf of the people. It has the power to amend the Constitution, supervise its enforcement, enact and amend laws about offences, civil affairs, and state agencies, approve the choice and selection of leaders of the People's republic of China in the executive branch of the Government, State Council, CMC, statutory organizations, etc. It approves the budget. It can establish new Provinces, Municipalities, Administrative Regions and Special Administrative Regions. It oversees the Standing Committee of the NPC, State Council, CMC, People's Court and Supreme People's Procuratorate.

The members of the NPC about (3000) representing different provinces, Municipalities, Autonomous Regions and Armed Forces and organizations are elected for 5 years and meet once a year for 2 weeks. In between such meetings, major national legislations are adopted by the Standing Committee of the NPC.Most new initiatives are presented to the NPC by the State Council after previous endorsement by the Polite Bureau's Standing Committee. Although the NPC normally approves the state council policy and personnel changes, the NPC and its standing committee occasionally assert their roles. For example, the State Council has not been able to secure passage of a fuel tax to finance the free ways. Though called Parliament, it is generally seen as a rubber stamp body by the west. 70% of its members are from the Party, and the remaining from different services. The loyalty to the party comes first and then to the NPC. Hence, the party drafts laws and get them approved by the NPC. Its power is with its standing committee with 153 members which meets every couple of months.

NPC has one Chairman, Eight Dy. Chairmen and one Secy. Gen. It's Standing Committee can assume, administrative, judicial, or procuratorial powers, interpret the Constitution, enact, and amend laws except those reserved for the full NPC.Since 1979, more than 300 laws have been passed by it and over 3000 rules and regulations have been approved. It has eight Special Committees on ethnic groups, legal, and educational, scientific, financial and economic, culture and public health related, foreign affairs, over seas Chinese, internal and judicial affairs, Environment and resource protection, etc. The CPC has full control over the Standing Committee though nearly 1/3 delegates are non-CPC members like technical personnel, members of allied parties, etc. Delegates to NPC are elected by the provincial congresses based on a quota system proportionate to their sizes. Members to the provincial congresses are in turn elected by their lower levels which go upto the lowest level where direct election is held. The CPC which is well organized has a decisive say in all elections, esp. as at the highest level. Only 10% excess candidates are allowed to contest which goes up to 50% or more at the lowest level.

Some debates are seen in the NPC over issues on which the party or Government has no specific stand to assert. Proposals are sent for approval only when it is clear that there would not be any significant opposition. To ensure more and more unanimity of views, at least three reviews by the special committees are done before bringing the issue before the NPC. The process starts with a small technical committee which examines an issue and comes with a view which is then discussed at larger forums involving more and more people and building a larger consensus. The Property law passed some time back was debated for a long time before sending for approval. Review of the performance of the elite in power including top officials, approvals of work reports, etc.are also done by the NPC. If 70% approval is not received, it is considered a discredit and hence a lot of whetting is done before reports are presented for approval.

The structure and committees of the NPC[3] are given below:

**NPC.** Deputies to the NPC are members forming the highest organ of state power. They are elected from the provinces, autonomous regions, municipalities directly under the Central Government and the armed forces. The Standing Committee of the NPC consists of the chairman, vice-chairmen, secretary-general and members (who shall not assume any posts in the state administrative organ, judicial or prosecuting organs) with a term of five years. The chairman and vice-chairmen shall not serve more than two consecutive terms. Normally the Standing Committee is convened once every 2 months. The Meeting of the Chairmen of the Standing Committee: Participated by the chairman, vice-chairmen and secretary-general deals with major routine work of the Standing Committee. Special committees. Chairman, vice-chairmen and members. Under the leadership of the NPC, special committees are guided by the members of the Standing Committee of the NPC. Deputy Credential Examination Committee: permanent organ of the NPC Standing Committee for examining the credentials of NPC deputies emerging from by-elections of the present session and the newly elected deputies for the coming session. Composed of the chairman, vice-chairmen and members all nominated from among the members of the Standing Committee and by the Meeting of the Chairman of the Standing Committee, to be agreed upon by the plenary session of the Standing Committee for a term of five years. The General Affairs Office, Legislative Work Committee and Budget Committee. Permanent organs of the NPC Standing Committee for serving the plenary session of the NPC, meetings of the Standing Committee and sessions of the Meeting of the Chairmen of the Standing Committee; for serving the deputies of the NPC and members of the Standing Committee in their execution of functions and powers according to law and for serving the development of socialist democracy and improvement of the socialist legal system.

The state Council is the cabinet, a bureaucracy of Ministries and Commissions entrusted with the task of implementing decisions. The members of the State Council include The Prime Minister, a variable number of Vice-Premiers (now four), five state councillors (protocol equal of vice-premier, but with narrow portfolios), and 29 ministers and heads of state council commissions. It is answerable to the NPC. It drafts and manages the state budget, law and order, etc. The full council meets once a month only while it's standing committee headed by the P.M meets regularly.

Party elders who have left real direct decision making positions have come to acquire more importance after Deng Xiao Ping. Deng continued to be the real source of power even after he left all positions. Deng and other retired leaders were the real decision makers about the Tiananmen square actions. The patron–protégé relationship also gives them power. They manouvre their people into the P.B. The burning anxiety about reversal of their decisions and verdict on their performance, their effect on the future of their children, etc. are relevant issues. They are given body guards, drivers, secretaries, special housing, access to information, etc. too.

The People's Liberation Army (PLA) was created by the CPC to defend the party and also the borders of China. Though it is China's military, it upholds the party's absolute leadership. It is led by the CMC jointly established the Party and the Central Government Initially, all members of CMC had military background because of the civil war, but now it is more of a professional body headed by the President of China who is also the General Secretary of the CPC. It has 11 members now and senior appointments, troop deployments and spending on army are controlled by it. Most of the members now are senior generals. In practice, the chairmanship of the CMC goes to the most important leader of the party who also controls people's government and police which guards government buildings. Mao, and Deng and Jiang Zemin were political figures who headed the Military. Present Chairman Hu Jintao also has no military background.

PLA needs party's support for modernization. The 1954 PRC constitution provides that the State President would direct the armed forces and hence made the President, the Chairman of the Defense Services, an advisory body. In Sept. 1954, the CC of the CPC restructured the CMC as head of the PLA and people's armed forces. Then on the dual leadership of the party and the state military leadership was established. The Central Committee of the CPC leads in all military matters. The State President directs the Military Forces and the State Council (Cabinet) manages their development. The chairman of the CMC is chosen by the full NPC while other members are chosen by the standing committee of the NPC. The CPC after discussions proposes the names of the state CMC members so that they can be elected by the NPC to the Central Military Commission. The CMC of the CC and CMC of the state are one group and one organization. Organisationally, the two CMCs subscribe to two different systems—the party system and the state system. The armed forces are thus under the dual control of the state and the CPC. The present leaders are the Chairman, The President (Hu Jintao), Vice-President, Chairman of the Standing Committee of the CPC, Premier of the State Council, and 4 Vice-Premiers.

The Discipline Commission deals with cases of corruption, bad management and violation of the party line. As in all liberalized systems, the corrupt practices have increased. Hence, the commission has a very significant role. Top leaders can influence it and its decisions are given high publicity. It has a net work of informers, information and Personal Files on people making it a feared set up.

Autonomy is given to ethnic minorities. Relaxations in respect of population control measures, preference in school admissions, employment, military recruitment, etc. are also available to them. 'Hans's chauvinism' is condemned and equal rights for all minorities are asserted. Independent movements exist in Tibet, Xinjiang and to a lesser extent in Inner Mangolia. Many Tibetans and Uyghurs resent Chinese chauvinism. Hans Chinese have been moving into Tibet and Xinjiang for 50 years. Market liberalization has also resulted in large influx of migrants. The Government also moves people from overcrowded areas into thinly populated areas. Cadres and professionals are also enticed with financial incentives in the western parts. In Xinjiang, Hans's people have considerably increased in the recent past. Hans Chinese in these regions resent special treatments being given to local people.

## Endnotes

[1] http://en.wikipedia.org/wiki/List_of_political_parties_in_the_People's_Republic_of_China

[2] As given in a US weekly/People's Daily.

[3] http://www.china.org.cn/english/features/state_structure/64763.htm

## References


a. http://en.wikipedia.org/wiki/Politics_of_the_People%27s_Republic_of_China (Dec. 22, 2009)

b. http://en.wikipedia.org/wiki/Communist_Party_of_China (Dec. 22, 2009)

c. http://en.wikipedia.org/wiki/National_People's_Congress (Dec. 22, 2009)

d. http://en.wikipedia.org/wiki/Government_of_the_People's_Republic_of_China(Dec. 22, 2009)

e. http://www.china.org.cn/english/news/231852.htm

f. http://www.china.org.cn/english/features/state_ structure/64763.htm

g. http://en.wikipedia.org/wiki/List_of_political_parties_in_the_People's_Republic_of_China (Dec. 22, 2009)

h. a large number of other references from Wikipedia, articles in 'Time' and 'Newsweek' weeklies, etc.

## PEOPLE'S RIGHTS—SOME AREAS OF CONCERN AND CRITICISM

Just as the consistent and unprecedented economic growth has received universal praise and acclamation, certain features of the Chinese system have raised eyebrows and received fairly wide spread criticism from the democratic world. This is perhaps natural as once a system becomes the cynosure of attention, areas which are considered deficient or subnormal also get highlighted. In China's case, these are broadly violations of Human Rights on issues like Suppression of Religious freedom, Arbitrary Detentions, Torture and Ill-treatment of Prisoners, Absence of Freedom of the Press and Individual Trade Union Rights, Lack of Judicial Independence and Due Process, Inadequate Efforts to stop ill-treatment, One Child policy, abduction and trafficking of women, Forced Evictions, Environmental Damage, Increasing inequalities in Income and Development, Lowering of Water Table and Arms Sales and Support to Some Controversial Regimes. While some of these are systemic and relate generally to all communist systems, others are more specific for China. A brief account of the issues involved and criticisms or allegations are given below. The Chinese government has described reports of Human Rights groups from US and other democratic countries as 'unfounded and unreasonable allegaions'and has asserted that legal actions were only taken against certain separatist activities which would not be tolerated by any country. It also argues that the notion of human rights should include economic standards of living and measures of health and economic prosperity where China has made a lot of progress.

The Chinese Constitution guarantees freedoms of association and assembly, but national regulations severely limit these and give the authorities absolute discretion to deny applications for public gatherings or demonstrations. Human Rights associations allege that people are detained without due process for exercising their rights to freedom of association, freedom of religion and freedom of expression, including the right to impart and receive information. The total number detained, sentenced administratively to reeducation or reform camps, or held by other means, is not known, but is allegedly much higher than acknowledged for imprisoning for "counter-revolutionary" or political crimes. It is alleged the detention is often without charge or trial and depriving defendants of access to legal counsel. As only organizations that are approved by the authorities are permitted to exist, all not registered are considered "illegal." Thus independent advocacy of labour or human rights, environ-mental, development or political issues is effectively outlawed. Unofficial labour groups have been a particular target for suppression. In December 1994, the Beijing Intermediate People's Court imposed severe sentences of between 15 and 20 years' imprisonment, the harshest delivered to political dissidents in recent years, on three prisoners of conscience, convicted of "leading counter-revolutionary organizations" basically for formation of unapproved organizations. A 1993 State Security Law threatens the few legal means of operation for democracy and human rights activists, independent religious adherents and other independent voices, by criminalizing any contact with and funding from foreign organizations defined as "hostile", publication or dissemination of "written or verbal speeches" or "using religion" to carry out activities "which endanger state security" or create "national disputes." It gives state security officials unlimited power to detain individuals, confiscate property and determine what constitutes a "hostile" organization.

The Constitution guarantees citizens freedom of expression and of the press subject to "four basic principles" of CCP's leadership, socialism, dictatorship of the proletariat and Marxism-Leninism—Mao Zedong Thought. In practice, there is a wide range of severe restrictions on contacts between foreign news media and Chinese viewed by the government as critical of the regime, extensive censorship whereby bureaucracy licenses all media outlets and publishing houses and approves all books before publication violates the right to free expression and interferes with independent media. The practice of 'Self-censorship' to be followed allegedly means conforming to CCP Propaganda Department guidelines which say news must be 80% positive and only 20% negative. Sanctions for violations range from official criticism, demotion, firing or imprisonment of the individuals responsible and closing or banning of the publication. Dissidents who contact foreign media are subject to threats, detention, harassment, intensive surveillance or imprisonment. Even foreign correspondents have been detained, interrogated, telecasts banned, etc. for contacting dissidents.

Among the main areas of concern and criticism mentioned in the first Para above, allegations of suppression of religion, Absence of Individual Trade Union Rights, Environmental Damage and Increasing Inequalities in Income and Development have already been covered elsewhere (under Religious and Economic Scenes). Only the others are briefly covered here.

**Arbitrary Detentions:** Arbitrary Detentions are detentions basically through administrative procedures where the detainees are not charged or brought before a judge thereby denying them access to a lawyer and the right to defend themselves. A large number of suspect followers of Dalai Lama and Tibetan Buddhism, banned groups like Falun Gong and Xiantinism, unregistered churches, Muslim groups in Xinjiang who have been raising their voice against unjust discrimination or on religious grounds and suspected as separatists, activists of Human, democratic and workers rights, groups who organize people on issues like unjust evictions, suspects and their followers about the Tiananmen square protests of June 4, 1989, etc. are allegedly detained each year and sentenced administratively. These do not follow a uniform pattern and the intensity of arbitrariness varies from region or place to place with Tibet, Xinjiang and Hebei regions heading the list. There is a tendency to deal harshly with any group which questions the authority of the CPC.

The common forms of administrative detention are: (1) "reeducation through labor," under which police, without trial, can send individuals to labour camps for periods up to four years and (2) "shelter and investigation," under which police can detain people without charge or trial for periods up to three months, a time limit allegedly often ignored. The UN Working Group on Arbitrary Detention has determined that the practice of "reeducation through labor" is "inherently arbitrary" when intended for "political and cultural rehabilitation". 100,000 people are allegedly sent to "reeducation through labor" camps and one million are "sheltered" each year. When such detainees are released before the completion of their periods of detention due to international pressure, they are forced into exile or subjected to continuing police surveillance and harassment or detained again for alleged violations of the restrictive conditions of parole or new "crimes" of free expression. Many are not granted the identity cards necessary to gain employment or travel without express official permission. Recently, there have been allegations that Chinese authorities are incarcerating drug users in compulsory drug detention centers that deny them access to treatment for drug dependency and put them at risk of physical abuse and unpaid forced labor.

**Torture and Ill-treatment of Prisoners:** Though China is a signatory to the UN Convention against Torture in 1988, it has not taken effective measures to diminish the risk of prisoners being tortured or ill-treated. It had refused to release autopsy results to families or to initiate investigations in many cases of deaths. Beatings, inadequate food and poor hygiene are allegedly a routine part of the process of eliciting confessions and compliance from detainees.

Despite continuing efforts by the UN Special Rapporteur on Torture, the International Committee of the Red Cross and other humanitarian organizations, PRC officials have not agreed to allow open and unannounced visits to prisoners. In Tibet, many were incarcerated for peacefully expressing their political and religious beliefs. Allegations of torture and ill-treatment, violent acts against Tibetan women in detention centers and prisons, degrading and inhuman treatment like rape and sexual abuse, etc. too exist.

**Absence of Freedom of the Press and wide Censorship:** Majority of Censorship (suppressing or limiting of the publishing, dissemination, and viewing of certain information) is implemented or mandated by the Communist Party of China (CPC). The self-governing special administrative regions of Hong Kong and Macau have their own legal systems and hence are not termed as 'censorship'. Censored media consists of television, print media, radio, film, theatre, text messaging, instant messaging, video games, literature and the Internet. 'Reporters without borders', an organization partly financed by the Taiwan Foundation for Democracy, which is funded by the Taiwanese Ministry of Foreign Affairs, ranks China's press situation as "Very serious", the worst ranking on their five-point scale. The following area-wise details will facilitate a better understanding.

The objective of political censorship is to maintain the rule of the CPC, prevent unapproved reformist, separatist, counter revolutionary or religious ideas, peaceful or otherwise, from organizing themselves and spreading and to prevent Chinese citizens from discovering or learning more about past and current failures of the Communist Party that could create or inflame anti-government sentiments. Blocking of foreign governments' websites may be intended to prevent citizens from learning about alternative systems of governance and demanding similar systems. The guidelines issued to the local media before 2008 Olympics on reporting during the Games wanted playing down of political issues not directly related to the games and not reporting on topics like Pro-Tibetan independence and East Turkistan movements. Subsequently announced rules and regulations to 'strengthen oversight and administration of news professionals and reporting activities' included a "full database of people who engage in unhealthy professional conduct" who would be excluded from engaging in news reporting and editing work. Although these controls were ostensibly to "resolutely halt fake news", it was criticized as censorship. Communist Party's Propaganda Department micro-manages what newspapers and other media do and do not report as the government remains concerned about unrest amid the economic slowdown.

Though greater cultural freedom exists today, continuing crackdowns on pornography, the 2006 banning of foreign cartoons from Chinese prime time TV, and limits on screenings for foreign films are seen as a continuation of cultural censorship. Moral censorship includes limitations on pornography and violence in films.

A number of religious texts, publications, and materials are banned or have their distributions artificially limited. Foreign citizens are prohibited from proselytizing in China. The Falun Gong spiritual movement (labeled an "evil cult") has virtually all religious texts, publications, and websites under ban. Bibles are allowed to be printed only in limited numbers and that too in a single press. In 2007, "Year of the Pig" in the Chinese calendar, depictions of pigs were banned from CCTV "to avoid conflicts with ethnic minorities" as 20 million Muslims consider pig as "unclean".

In February 2007, the website of the French organization 'Observatories International des Crises' was banned after it posted an article on the risks of trading with China.

On the twentieth anniversary of the pro-democracy protests in Tiananmen Square (June 4), tremendous pressure was exerted to screen out any related content from newspapers. Some newspapers therefore instructed their editors to refrain from using the numbers '6' and '4' in their reports, especially in headlines, during this sensitive period. TV, CNN, BBC World Service, and Bloomberg Television are occasionally censored by being "blacked out". During the Summer

Olympics in Beijing, all Chinese TV stations were ordered to delay live broadcasts by 10 seconds to give censors time to react in case free-Tibet demonstrators or others staged political protests. In January 2009, during a television report of the inauguration of U.S. President Barrack Obama, the state-run China Central Television abruptly cut away its coverage of Obama's address when he spoke of how "earlier generations faced down fascism and communism."

No motion picture rating system exists and hence films must be suitable for all audiences to be allowed to be screened. Only twenty foreign films a year are cleared for shows within the country. Works dealing with "serious topics" such as the Cultural Revolution must be registered before distribution on the mainland. Films by PRC nationals cannot be submitted to foreign film festivals without government approval.

General Administration of Press and Publication has the legal authority to screen, censor, and ban any print, electronic, or Internet publication in China, deny people the right to publish, and completely shut down any publisher who fails to follow its dictates.

The album 'Chinese Democracy' by American rock band Guns N' Roses is banned in China, reportedly due to 'criticism' in its title track about the government and a reference to the Falun Gong. The album X by Australian pop singer Kylie Minogue was released as a 10-track edition of the album by EMI Records, but three tracks "Nudity", "Speakerphone" and "Like a Drug" were banned.

Internet censorship in China is regarded as the most pervasive and sophisticated. At least 18,000 websites are blocked including Wikipedia, Google, You Tube, Face book, Fleck, and the BBC. Certain search engine terms are also blocked. 52 cyber dissidents are imprisoned in China for their online communications. Recently Wikipedia, Google and You Tube have been opened up for public viewing with restrictions. Instead of Google.com, it is 'Google.cn' which China will see. Searches and clearance may be a means of forcing mainland Chinese users to rely on China's own e-commerce industry.

The government imposes a strict licensing scheme on news and information media that include oversight by government agencies with discretion to grant, deny, and rescind licenses based on political and economic criteria. The Censorship allegedly is pervasive and highly effective and denies Chinese citizens the freedom of speech and of the press guaranteed by their Constitution. Instances imprisoning journalists who provided news to foreigners are mentioned. Editors of Yang Bin of the Beijing News and Li Datong of the China Youth Daily were dismissed. In 2005, the government banned dozens of newspapers and confiscated almost one million "illegal" political publications.

**Lack of Due Process and Judicial Independence:** Due Process is a basic principle of fairness meant to safeguard private and public rights applied in all legal matters in courts, both criminal and civil. It is the system that constitutes the fundamental, procedural and legal safeguards of every citizen when a state or court purports to take a decision that could affect any of his rights. Due process involves both procedural and substantive aspects. In order for prejudicial or unequal treatment not to occur, all legal procedures set by statute and court practice must be followed for each individual. Procedural due process requires fairness in the methods used to deprive a person of life, liberty or property, while substantive due process requires valid governmental justification for taking a person's life, liberty or property. A person is entitled to notice and opportunity to be heard at a hearing when life, liberty, or property is at stake. Laws should be applied to persons equally, without discrimination based on gender, nationality, handicap, or age. In criminal cases, fair procedures help to ensure that an accused person will not be subjected to cruel and unusual punishment, which occurs when an innocent person is wrongly convicted. Due process requirements apply to trials, parole hearings, and administrative hearings involving benefits.

Judicial independence refers to the ability of the courts to act without influence from non-judicial powers (say, the CCP in China). It is alleged that there are few legal safeguards to ensure fair trials as the judicial system is controlled at every level by CCP and political-legal committees that may determine the outcome of a case before the court hears evidence presented at trial. In the case of situations of "verdict first, trial second", detainees are highly unlikely to receive fair and impartial hearings free from official manipulation. Though criminal Procedure Law in China provides for detainees to have access to lawyers no later than one week before trial, it is allegedly not always observed. Prisoners typically cannot call witnesses for the defense or question witnesses against them. In politically sensitive cases, lawyers are allegedly instructed that they may enter a not-guilty plea only if they get approval from the judicial administration. It is alleged that even in death-penalty cases, appeals are usually cursory, and defendants may have only a few days to file an appeal.

Communist Party authorities and local governments allegedly limit the independence of China's courts. Internal administrative practices of Chinese courts also compromise judicial efficacy and independence. Since the early 1990s, local people's congresses have exercised increasing influence over court decisions. Public opinion is an increasing source of pressure on Chinese courts, through sensational media reporting on cases.

According to an analysis by an expert, causes of interference in judiciary are both social and institutional and include the following:

1. The participation of the CCP committees in handling and even deciding some specific cases. The political-legal committees responsible for coordinating the relationships among the organs of public security, courts, and procuratorates are also meant to "supervise" the work of the various legal organs in "major and complex" cases. Supervision is often equated with adjudication.

2. Where senior CCP leaders are charged with economic crimes like corruption, litigation commences only after investigation by the Discipline Inspection Committee. In some cases, the Discipline Inspection Committee may itself decide the case.
3. Local CCP committees may appoint, dismiss, or rotate leading cadres in courts and they may intervene on behalf of the local government in cases that affect local economic interests.
4. Some CCP members do not understand the proper meaning of leadership and think that intervening in specific cases is appropriate. The society also at times considers CCP interference as reasonable and beneficial, providing opportunities to "right the wrongs". There are no provisions in the constitution, laws, or CCP Charter punishing CCP members for interfering in judicial work.
5. Local governments and local CCP committees control the personnel and financial arrangements of the local courts. Appointment and dismissal of judges and provision of salaries are determined by local government and CCP committees and the judiciary is managed like an administrative agency. Junior judges must listen to the opinions of chief judges and presidents of courts.
6. Where the existing law does not suitably address an issue, judges may suspend the case to wait for the National People's Congress to enact a new legislation or seek comments or instructions from the Supreme People's Court. The policies of the CCP viz. "Three Conducives"of society's productivity, strengthening the state's power, and improving people's standard of living may be used for guidance. All these become sources of interference and affect judicial independence.

Steps suggested to improve the independence of the Judiciary are: (a) punishments of CCP members who interfere in the judiciary by making them criminally liable, (b) redesign of the jurisdiction of courts to limit the ability of local CCP and government officials to interfere in the judicial system, (c) redesign of jurisdictions of High Courts to span multiple provinces, (d) merger of intermediate courts with District Courts with jurisdiction over multiple cities, (e) empowering of the Supreme People's Court to send teams of experienced judges to establish "circuit tribunals" to adjudicate particularly difficult disputes that require special handling, (f) nomination of the judges of district courts and circuit tribunals by the Supreme People's Court and appointment by the National People's Congress, (g) leading of the Court system by the Central Political-legal Committee, better legal education and training for high-rank party members, check on media's negative coverage of cases influencing outcome of trials in some cases, etc.

Judicial independence and impartiality have to be seen differently too as they mean different things. Independence refers to the ability of judges to act without interference from non-judicial authorities. Impartiality is acting neutrally and going by rules. One aspect of impartiality is 'judicial oppositionism' meaning that the judiciary should develop into an independent branch of government reducing the power of the executive, legislature, and thc Party. In China, for eg. holding a demonstration for the overthrow of the Communist Party is clearly 'subversion'. Under the theory of 'judicial impartiality', a judge would have no real choice but to send the indicted person to jail. Under the 'judicial oppositionist' meaning, there is perhaps a hope that the judiciary would challenge and limit the rule of the Party as the judiciary in England limits the power of the king. The criticism about judicial oppositionism is "if the judiciary does not apply the laws as written, then what laws does it apply." There is no historical 'Fundamental Laws of England' for the judiciary to fall back on as the appeal can only be to the 'natural and scientific laws of Marxist-Leninist-Maoism'. Judicial Independence in China will develop better if the judiciary sticks to interpreting the law as written than trying to appeal to some higher law as ultimately, the problem of bad laws is a problem that should be solved in the legislature.

Resistance to administrative power and bribes are of primary importance as the biggest influence on China's judicial system is allegedly abuse of administrative power. If judges are professional and transparent, their rulings cannot be influenced by anyone else. The media's responsibility is to tell the public the truth and accurate media reporting will be beneficial to judicial independence in the long run.

**Inadequate Efforts to stop ill-treatment, abduction, trafficking of women and other issues adversely affecting women's and children's rights:** When women's rights or interests conflict with those of the CCP or government policy, the latter take precedence. Abuses related to the family planning policy are not reported in the media or discussed publicly. Information on extent of domestic violence, trafficking in women or abuses directed at lesbians, is also effectively prevented by the CCP's injunction that most news should be positive. The controls on freedom of expression and association, also adversely affect women's rights. Though spousal abuse is common, data on this too is not available. Shelters and other resources are also not easily available to affected women. Women are under considerable social pressure to keep families together. Legal action is not taken against batterers unless the victim initiates it, and, if she withdraws her testimony, it is closed.

Tens of thousands of women are bought and sold in China each year with the poor areas of Yunnan, Sichuan and Guizhou as the most popular areas for abduction of girls/ women. China is also said to be a destination for trafficked women from Ukraine and Russia. The pre-revolutionary custom of bride selling has returned to rural villages in some parts of China.

Shangchuandao Island off Guangdong is a tourist spot offering drugs and sex casinos including allegedly about 300 women from all over China. Until recently, men who purchase women as wives were not prosecuted and hence the trade continued unabated. Even now, action to rescue victims of trafficking is generally initiated only if a complaint is made by the woman or her family. Local officials often turn a blind eye, even formally registering a marriage into which the woman is sold.

Women's wages average 77% of men's, and they are mostly in low-skill and low-paying jobs. 70 to 80% of laid off have been women, although women constitute only 38% of the work force. They are 60% of the unemployed. In some areas, employment discrimination too is allegedly justified on grounds of lack of facilities for the pregnant and feeding women, infants, etc.On the educational front, proportion of women to men declines at each educational tier. In subjects which are very popular with women, sometimes higher entrance examination grades are required from women. About 70% of illiterates in China are girls.

**One Child Policy:** Implemented since 1979 to alleviate the overpopulation problem, it is credited by the Chinese government with prevention of 250 million births. It made having more than one child illegal and punishable by fines. Critics argue that it contributes to forced abortions, human rights violations, female infanticide, etc. Sex-selective abortions are believed to be relatively commonplace in some areas of the country and is said to have contributed to the gender imbalance of 118 to 100 ratio of male to female children. Forced abortions and sterilizations have also been reported.

There are complaints about forced abortion of pregnant women who already have one child. In Zheijang Province, for example, the family planning ordinance states that "fertile couples must use reliable birth control according to the provisions. In case of pregnancies in default of the plan, measures must be taken to terminate them." As a minority community, though Tibetans can have more than one child, allegations of forced abortions and sterilizations of Tibetan women with one child are heard. Widespread sterilization of certain categories of women suffering from mental illness, retardation and communicable or hereditary diseases, etc. are also alleged. Such sterilization was mandatory in certain provinces. Under the new law too, certain categories of people may still be prevented from bearing children. Female infanticide, concealment of female births and abandonment of female infants also take place, particularly in rural areas and among communities who prefer male children. Female children whose births are not registered do not have any legal existence and face difficulty in going to school and receiving medical care and other state services. The overwhelming majority of children in orphanages are females and/or mentally or physically handicapped. Though the use of ultrasound machines for sex determination is outlawed, physicians continue the practice, especially in rural areas. The problem of female child infanticide in China can be understood from the fact that while the worldwide ratio of male to female newborns is 105/100, in China it is 114/100.

**Forced Evictions:** The International Federation for Human Rights (FIDH) published a report documenting widespread violations of human rights caused by house demolitions and forced evictions in Chongqing. It highlighted the price paid by its inhabitants, in particular the poorest, that do not benefit from the fast development changing the face of the city. Urban modernization is a consequence of the economic boom. It also promoted China's image abroad before the 2008 Olympic Games in Beijing. It was used to promote the 2010 Shanghai Universal Exhibition. However, modernization often becomes an excuse for profit-oriented or even speculative projects that result in house demolitions and forced evictions of citizens. No reliable statistics exist on this sensitive issue, even though it results in major social transformations. It is alleged that very few citizens are informed or consulted about the projects involving their eviction in a timely manner and most of them receive no adequate compensation either in terms of payment or new housing.

In theory, the Chinese legal framework concerning demolitions and forced evictions provides guarantees to evictees. However, the administrative reforms in the 1980s and the booming real estate market encouraged the local governments to ignore public interest and pursue lucrative projects, in collusion with real estate companies. Local authorities allegedly do not abide by the guarantees provided to evictees by the national regulations. The law on property rights, which was adopted by The National People's Congress in March 2007 reinforced legal security and regulated property rights. Unfortunately, it included no significant step on matters of forced evictions, as it does not establish additional protection for victims, and does not define the notion of 'public interest' which appears to be the main justification for a great number of evictions. The report of the Human rights group appeals to the Chinese government, to the United Nations, European Union, international financial institutions, and companies investing in China to put an end to arbitrary forced evictions and related human rights violations. According to the BBC correspondent, in this report, it is alleged that more than 1 million people were evicted from their homes to construct new buildings for the Olympics.

**Arms Sales and Support to Some Controversial Regimes:** China has a significant arms trade with Africa. Some of these arms reach African conflict zones. Arms sales to ill-reputed African regimes as business by China is partly because they may be the only customers left after the United States, the United Kingdom, France, and Russia have carved up the global weapons market. China is emerging as the supplier of last resort for those who cannot afford better quality products, or those who are unable to access other sources. Many of these are small arms and light weapons like Chinese model AR-56 assault rifle. The damage done by such weapons is more because of the character of the clients like Sudan, Robert Mugabe regime in Zimbabwe, the military junta in Myanmar and rebel groups involved in Congo's civil war.

Some African governments have transferred Chinese weapons to rebel groups that either serve their interests in neighboring countries or they transfer them to groups within their own country as Sudan did when it supplied weapons to the Janjaweed in Darfur. Some of the Chinese weapons found in African conflict zones were purchased on the open market by organizations active in African conflict zones. Between 2000 and 2003, China delivered by value about 13 percent of all arms to Sub-Saharan Africa and it increased to 18 percent between 2004 and 2007. Transfers of small arms and light weapons are especially hard to track and statistics are suspect and probably all countries understate their accounts for these. Since 2000, China, it is said, delivered SALW to at least twenty-seven of Africa's fifty-three countries. Three of the largest recipients— Sudan, Nigeria and Cote d'Ivoire—have experienced significant internal conflicts. China had sold a large quantity of weapons to both Ethiopia and Eritrea during their 1998–2000 war. Ethiopia had purchased ammunition, light mortars, AK-47s and vehicles. The ammunition was one-third the cost of its Russian equivalent and just as good. Chinese mortars were light and easily deployed by two soldiers in rugged terrain making them more appropriate than their American counterparts. Because its small arms and ammunition are relatively inexpensive, China is becoming the provider of choice for the generic version of the AK-47.

China's most controversial military sales concern Sudan where there have been two major conflicts—the North-South civil war and the crisis in Darfur. China provided up to 90 percent of the SALW delivered to Sudan between 2004 and 2006. It also delivered more sophisticated equipment. In terms of all armament deliveries to Sudan, however, China said it is providing only 8 percent of the total. The government of Sudan reportedly transferred some of these weapons to the Janjaweed militia in contravention of the UN arms embargo. China also joined other countries in helping Sudan to develop its own weapons manufacturing capacity. Most ammunition used by all parties in Darfur is manufactured by Sudan or China. The recent charges of genocide and crimes against humanity by Sudanese President Omar Hassan al-Bashir underscore the moral bankruptcy of China's arms transfer policy.

China is not alone in transferring arms that are used in African conflicts. Arms from many countries, including the United States, have shown up in these conflicts. China is, however, the largest provider of SALW to Africa.

China's engagements in Africa also include peace- keeping and anti-piracy operations and de-mining assistance. Chinese units were in Liberia, southern Sudan, Darfur and the DRC. These are meant to project an image that it is supporting the building of a "harmonious society" and also to balance western influence. It can also learn important lessons that may improve their responsiveness, especially in riot-control capabilities, coordination of military emergency command systems and ability to conduct non-combat missions at home. China also deployed early in 2009 two destroyers and a supply ship to help combat piracy in the Gulf of Aden. The ships have about 800 crew and seventy special operations troops. This naval experience gives the PLA Navy valuable experience far from its shores and permits China to project power in an area that is important to its trade. The Chinese naval contingent has performed well and coordinated effectively with other navies in the region. In addition, involvement in Africa and other underdeveloped regions gives it access to valuable raw materials and resources which would help in its faster economic growth when resources could become a constraint. It also expands its role as a super power and a major global player at times counter balancing the might of US and other countries.

**Death Penalty:** There was a dramatic increase in death penalty in China in the recent years when generally in most of the other nations the effort is to abolish it or reduce it to the rarest of rare cases. It may be partly due to the anti-crime campaigns in the country. Criminals can be put to death for criminal offenses, including theft, embezzlement and forgery. In 1993, 77% of all executions worldwide, it is said, were carried out in China. On 9 January 1993, 356 death sentences were given by Chinese courts and 62 were executed that day. During 1993, 2,564 were sentenced to death and at least 1,419 were executed. China is the world leader in the use of the death penalty. Amnesty International documented some 1,700 judicial killings in China last year, but, it is said, the true total could be three times the figure. The recent international furor over China's recent execution of a British man convicted of heroin-trafficking has drawn attention to the country's harsh criminal-justice system. The execution had sparked a diplomatic row between China and the U.K., but global condemnation will do little to provoke reform. In a statement issued after the execution, a Chinese court said drug crimes were "serious criminal offenses" demanding harsh punishment. But, there are signs that the rapidly modernizing country is curbing its use of the death penalty of its own accord. There are reports to show that the Supreme People's Court has lately asked other courts to ensure that death penalty is awarded only in serious cases. Thus, though the reforms are modest, observers see them as rare bright spots for human rights in China.

The primary motive force for change and progress in the area of capital punishment is internal. In 2007 China's Supreme People's Court resumed reviewing all death-penalty cases following public anger at a number of questionable convictions including the case of a man sentenced to 15 years in prison for murdering his wife who later turned up alive. In the first half of 2008, the Supreme People's Court overturned about 15% of the death sentences. The number of prisoners executed annually, it is estimated, may have fallen by half from the 10,000 believed to be cited by a National People's Congress delegate in 2004. Even with such a decline, China still puts to death more people than the rest of the world combined—about 70% of the global total in 2008, according to Amnesty International. But China's willingness to at least discuss and review the death penalty cases offers hope that in the future it will become lesser.

In short, damage to environment, lowering of water table, etc. are common in many developing countries including India. Some aspects of Women's rights are also issues in many other countries. Arbitrary detentions also take place in countries facing terrorism, insurgency, and emergency conditions. In a communist country which is a dictatorship of the proletariat, many of these are inherent. Some of these are serious concerns for the Chinese Government and society too. In view of the fast changes taking place in Chinese economy and society, some of these have been accentuated. Many of these perhaps have to be tackled better at the earliest in China's quest to emerge as a developed country. Human rights issues have great relevance in getting acceptance as a country which values finer aspects of culture. The Chinese government has cited the need for deterrence and public support of the death penalty to justify its broad use of capital punishment.

(Also see 'Suppression of religious freedom' under the 'Religious Scene' (pages 85–88) and 'Environmental Damage', 'Lowering of Water Table', 'Increasing Inequalities in Income and Development' and 'Absence of Individual Trade Union Rights' under the 'Economic scene' (pages 140–144) for a more comprehensive view of the topic.)

## References


a. http://en.wikipedia.org/wiki/Human_rights_in_the_People%27s_Republic_of_China (July 29, 2009)
b. http://www.onenewsnow.com/Persecution/Default.aspx?id=68469
c. http://www.cecc.gov/pages/virtualAcad/exp/
d. http://books.google.co.in/books?id=iurkg0CsdowC&pg
e. http://www.economist.com/displaystory.cfmstory_id=11848496
f. http://chinaview.wordpress.com/category/social/law/forced-Evictions/(July 26, 2009)
g. http://nationalexpositor.com/News/1165.html (July 26, 2009)
h. http://www.christusrex.org/www1/sdc/hr_facts.html
i. http://allafrica.com/stories/200805061078.html (July 26, 2009)

j. www.newamerica.net/files/080606PBChinaArmsTrade.pdf (July 26, 2009)

k. http://sites.google.com/site/davidhshinn/china-s-involvement-in-African-conflict-zones (July 26, 2009)

l. http://www.catwinternational.org/factbook/China%20and%20Hong%20Kong.php

m. http://www.onenewsnow.com/Persecution/Default.aspx?id=68469

n. http://www.catwinternational.org/factbook/China%20and%20Hong%20Kong.php

o. ICRF Report on Tibet

CHAPTER 4

# Economic Scene

The Chinese economy is the second largest today and it could overtake the US economy in size after a few decades if the growth in the recent past is sustained. Its growth at about 10% p.a. during the last nearly three decades following liberalization of the economy has been one of the most remarkable developments of the last centuary. Its nominal GDP in 2009 is estimated to be 4.91 Trillion US $. The Income p.c.during the last three decades has grown at about 8% p.a. According to estimates of the IMF, it reached 3187 US $ and 5943 US $ (nominal and ppp basis respectively) in 2008. The recent (Oct., 2010) meeting of the CPC leadership to prepare targets for China's next Five years based its current

**China GDP growth**

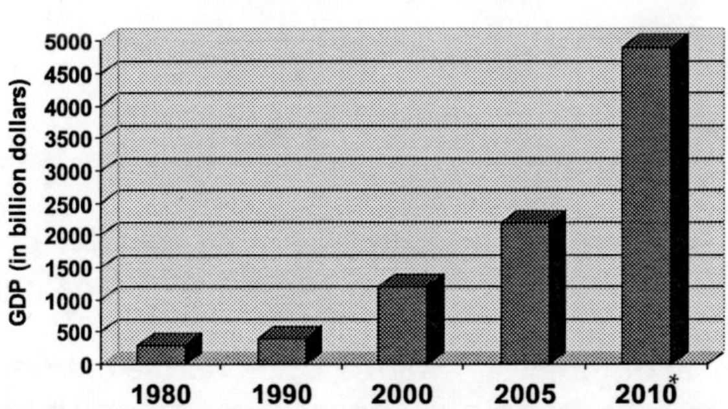


* Comments: *Data for 1980 to 2005 from* Sandra Polanski and Li Shantong reports *and for 2010 from CIA Fact Book, China.*

GDP per capita at 3600 US $ and the plan is to raise it to 5000 US $. in five years. The bar diagrams, according to Sandra Polanski, Carnegie Endowment for International Peace[1], show the rapid growth in GDP after 1990 (till 2005).

The growth of China in two phases, 1990–98 and 1998–2006 either separately or jointly, is unmatched by any other country, big or small, developed, developing or underdeveloped. Other countries, which have made substantial progress, are perhaps Ireland, Singapore, India, Korea and Taiwan. In the post 2005 situation too China has done well despite the economic slow down.

To get a good understanding of its current situation, it is worthwhile to appreciate the context in which this has happened.

**Post-1949 Revolutionary phase.** The economic strategy of the pre-1949 Imperial (Qing) period was to encourage heavy industries, reduce consumption and rapidly industrialize. Foreign trade was a state monopoly. After the revolution in 1949, which brought Mao to power, the strategy was again rapid industrialization. All industries were also state-owned. Prices for key commodities, investments, energy resources, wages, employment rights, whole and retail sales, finances and banking, cropping patterns, price levels, output targets, etc. were fixed by the state or state controlled. There were regular campaigns against small and big business men and from 1951–52, capitalists were also targeted. Coal, iron and steel, electric power, building materials, heavy engineering and basic chemicals received maximum investments. Soviet assistance for industrialization was fairly liberal. Agriculture, which employed 78.6% of people, got neglected. In the second Plan (1958–62), 'Great Leap Forward' was the theme with focus on people's communes, abolition of private plots, small scale industries, etc. A massive auxiliary network of small scale industries was built up and managed locally. Enormous quantities of low quality products, esp. steel, were produced. The peasantry was neglected and agricultural suffered serious decline. The differences with the USSR on the boundary issue resulted in the withdrawal of soviet experts and technicians. By 1960, China was on the throes of an economic disaster.

Mao began to lose importance on the economic front and Liu Shao Qui became the President. In an about-turn of policies, he restored private plots, reduced the size of the communes and gave greater independence to various production teams.

**Cultural Revolutionary Phase.** In 1966, Mao started the Cultural Revolution to take back power from Liu, eliminate bourgeois, etc., but without any economic rationale. During the Cultural Revolution, industrial production was seriously affected and many units stopped working. On the agricultural front, per capita out put in 1977 was in no way higher than that of 1957. Industry grew by only 17% in 1960s compared to 70% in 1970s. Wages were frozen and bonuses were cancelled. Over employment and cancellation of incentives hit production. Technicians and mangers had no effective role. Inefficiency prevailed and outputs declined.

**Post liberalization Phase.** Accordintog a BBC analysis[2], the following are the highlights of the changes in the Chinese economic scene after Deng Xiaoping wrested power from Hua Guofeng and in 1978 outlined an ambitious program of economic reforms.

**1980–1984:** Special Economic Zones (SEZs) allow China to accept foreign capital and adopt foreign technologies in controlled phases. In 1978 itself, FDI in coastal special economic zones had been allowed with out much red tape and increase in FDI in areas where it was already possible was allowed.14 coastal cities and areas were opened for FDI with favoured tax treatments. Steps were taken to create legal and commercial infrastructure.

**1985–1987:** Inefficient State-Owned Enterprises (SOEs) were heavily subsidized by central government exploiting the agricultural output reducing profits for farmers. Rural unemployment increased as factories could not absorb the population freed from collective farming. The economy entered a period of high-speed growth, with rampant inflation and corruption.

**1988–1989:** Workers in SOEs used to an "iron rice bowl" of jobs, housing, and benefits for life were encouraged to become entrepreneurs, but few dared. Workers watched inflation eat into their fixed wages, becoming angered by government profiteering and corruption. Deng's plans for price reform plans ignited a run on banks and panic buying. Changing course, he advocated economic stabilization, not reform.

**1990–1991:** The Shanghai Stock Exchange was allowed to open, although it was described as an experiment. The Shenzhen exchange followed soon after.

**1992:** Deng pushed SEZs to accelerate their reforms. China's economy boomed, yet problems mounted. Urban SOEs were losing money and draining capital from the state budget. Foreign companies did not invest inland, creating a large disparity in income between coastal regions and the rest of China. Millions were unemployed, and village factories often could not pay their workers.

**1993–1996:** Zhu Rongji took charge of the economy, heading the Central Bank and tightening regulatory controls over the stock and other markets. He tried to stem rising inflation after price rises soared more than 21 percent in 1994.

**1997:** On July 1 Hong Kong was handed back to China after 150 years of British colonial rule. Beijing inherited one of the world's most vibrant capitalist economies and an international financial center. In September Jiang Zemin consolidated his power following Deng Xiaoping's death. The Party began to focus on reform of SOEs through mergers, acquisitions, bankruptcies, and share issues.

**1998–2000:** By 1999, with 1.25 billion people and a GDP of $ 3,800 per capita, China is the fastest growing economy in the world, and also the second largest after the U.S. But the country remains poor, lacking the monetary and fiscal controls to manage its vast economy. The government turned to banks to provide failing SOEs loans, but they were not repaid. The banking system was threatened.

**2001–2003:** After China joins the WTO, foreign investment surged to a record high. Strong growth masked internal disparities between cities and rural areas, coastal and interior regions. Cuts in tariffs and rules streamlined business, but the huge state-owned sector remained deeply troubled and extremely hard to reform. In 2003 the spread of the deadly SARS virus had a severe impact on China's economy.

**Agriculture:** Agricultural reforms began with major price increases for products following dismantling of most of the collective farms by 1984. These gave greater scope for decision making by peasants. Sizes of plots were increased and restrictions on sale of products in private markets were removed. Long-term contracts and sub-leasing of land were allowed. Planned procurement was mostly eliminated. State-allocated products quota was made less stringent.

Private ownership of articles of production was legalized. After liberalization began in1978, tremendous gains in production were seen mainly due to sharp rise in the procurement price and family responsibility system that motivated farmers. Agricultural output in total GDP rose from 30% in 1980 to 33% three years later. But, by 2002, it accounted for only 15.4% of GDP and 20% of the Gross National Product. Most of the agricultural production is restricted to the east though more than half of the population depends on agriculture for living.

**Industry:** Village enterprises and self-management of state owned ones were allowed. Competition was encouraged. Direct contact between foreign and Chinese traders was legalized. Joint ventures with foreign companies were allowed. Foreign funding and foreign trade/imports were liberalized. State enterprises were made responsible for profits and losses. Private industries were allowed to compete with state owned ones in a number of sectors like infrastructure and construction. Investments in high tech and light industries were liberalized. A consumer ethics was created.

The share of industrial production in GDP went up to 52.3% of GDP in 2003 drastically reducing the share of agriculture to 15.4% (in 2002).Earlier, industrial output was dominated by large state-owned enterprises. But, their share in gross industrial output value shrank and in 2002 it was around 41%.Purely state owned enterprises now contribute only about 16% of industrial output as a large number of them are not 100% state-owned. The large numbers of light industries that produce consumer goods in special economic zones mainly account for the large exports, growth of GDP and economic advancement. The share of the services sector has remained nearly steady (33% in 2003).

**Employment:** Individuals were given jobs based on their skills, talents, training, etc. From 1990 to 2005, productivity of Chinese worker grew at an impressive rate of 9 percent per year due to capital investment, increasing openness to trade, strengthening of the educational system, shift from central planning toward a greater reliance on markets, particularly for allocating capital investment and continuation of strong economic growth.

**Systemic changes:** Managerial authority was strengthened giving powers to hire and de-hire based on needs, suspend or discharge workers, etc. Light industries, which produced high quality items, were given incentives like power at lower rates. The pricing situation was restructured. Products above the quota could be sold in open markets thus bringing in a 2-tier pricing system.

Through the mid-1980s, the Chinese economy had grown at around 10% annually, doubling in size every seven and a half years. China's rebirth stunned the world with its speed and breadth, propelling what was an isolated, near "pariah" state into the forefront of world powers.

According to the studies Prof. Sandra Polanski, Carnegie Endowment for International peace, the following data will show how the role of trade in China's economy increased between 1980 and 2005.

**China's Exports and Imports, 1980–2010**

| *Measure* | *1980* | *1990* | *2000* | *2005* | *2010* |
|---|---|---|---|---|---|
| Average annual export growth rate (percent) | | 13.2 | 14.8 | 25.1 | 24.25* |
| Average annual import growth rate (percent) | | 10.4 | 15.4 | 24.1 | 11.39* |
| Trade dependence ratio | 0.13 | 0.30 | 0.40 | 0.64 | 0.69* |

* *Source:* Nationmaster.com

Trade represents a significant share though value added in China is less.

The percentage changes in the composition of the economy[3] between 1952 and 1997 can be seen from the diagram given below. While the contribution of Agriculture has continuously declined, that of Industry has consistently increased. There was only marginal increase in the per-centage contribution of services though in terms of actual figures the increase was substantial even here.

According to the results of the Sandra Polanski studies, in all scenarios (optimistic, pessimistic and base line) the share of agriculture in employment and output will fall. Employment and output of secondary sector will grow through 2010 and then decline as growth in service industries begins to pull in larger numbers of workers. Pace of this transformation will depend on level of domestic

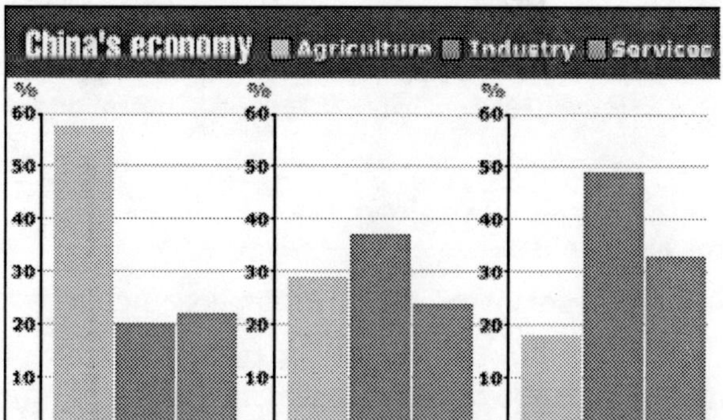

SOURCE: World Bank, Riskin: China's Political Economy and Research Centre

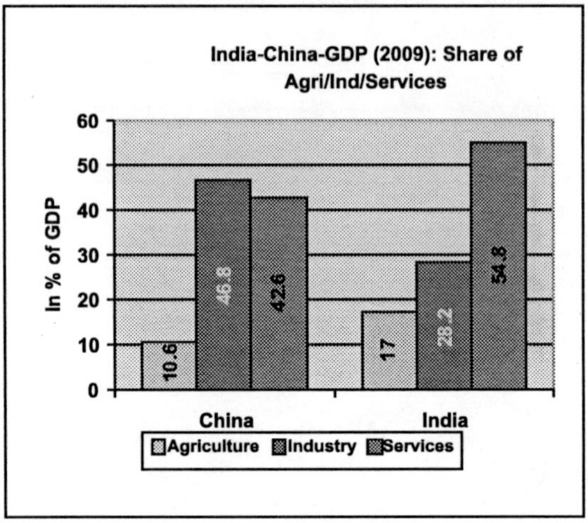


investment in human capital and growth in the technologically advanced service industries that serve manufacturing industries. 'The studies concluded that the percentage change in the returns to labour in 2020 relative to 2002 may be as given in the bar diagrams 'below' (in the three scenarios of optimistic,pessimistic and average/baseline results).

Other conclusions of the study were:

Agricultural workers stand to gain the most, but also face greatest losses relative to baseline if risk scenario materializes.

Costs of adverse developments in international environment and/or domestic policy missteps will be borne dispropor-tionately by the rural poor Trade can play only a limited role in creating employment opportunities.

Broad-based domestic demand will be required to sustain growth; additional advantage that it relieves international pressures and risks

Labor-intensive service sector industries, such as education and health care, represent promising sources of new jobs

Demographic structure of China means demand for health care by aging population will grow.

Moving up the technology ladder means China will need

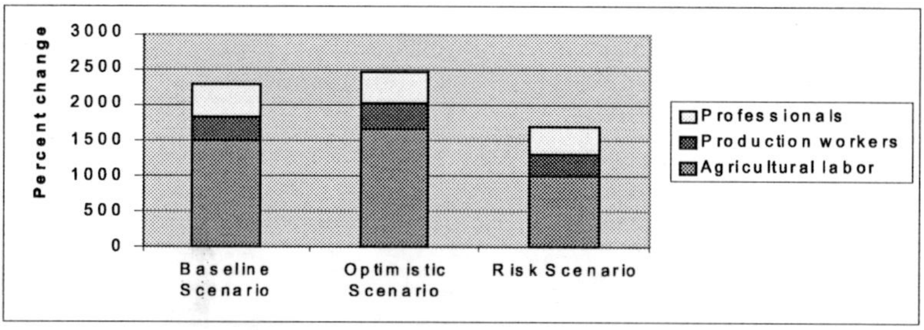


more and changing mix of skills—more educational services would be needed.

Four factors can be seen now in respect of inter-regional comparison in a huge country like China. These are (a) a Wealthy East Coast, (b) Rising central China-Shaanxi, Henan, Anhui, Hubei, Hunan, and Jianxi, (c) need to revitalize North-East China-Lei long, Jiang, Leaoning, etc. and (d) need to develop western China. To meet the above needs and achieve balanced development, a 3-step development strategy is being followed: 1. double the 1980 GNP (which was achieved by 1980s itself.) 2. Quadruple the 1980 GNP (which was achieved by 1990s, ahead of schedule.) 3. Increase per capita income to the level of developed countries by 2050 when people will be fairly well-off. The Key national projects being pursued now for this purpose are West to East Electric Transmission using coal and hydel resources. This is in full swing now. South to North water Transfer Project launched in 2003 and the first phase is to be completed by 2010. Rational distribution of waters of Yangtze, Yellow, Huaihe, and Haibe rivers is sought to be achieved. West to East Gas Transmission. Hong Kong and Macao are in one country, two systems mode with freedom to negotiate with foreign countries, WTO, APEC, etc.

The data on different economic indicators in the table below shows the superb performance of the Chinese economy in the recent past.

| *Economic Indicators* | *Data* |
|---|---|
| GDP (official exc.rate/2009) | 4.909Trillion US $* |
| " PPP (09) | 8.748 " " * |
| " " (08) | 8.019 " " * |
| " " (07) | 7.357* |
| " " P.C.(09) | 6600 US $* |
| P.C.(08) | 6100 US $* |
| P.C.(07) | 5600 US $* |
| Real Growth Rate | 9.1% (09), 9%(08), 13%(07)* |
| Contribution of Agri/Ind./ Serv. to GDP | 10.6/46.8/42.6 % of GDP* respectively. |
| Ind. Prodn.Growth Rate | 9.5%(09)* |
| Labour Force | 813.5 million* |
| Share of Agri/Ind/Serv in Labour Force | 39.5, 27.2 and 23.2% respectively* |
| Investment | 45.2% of GDP* |
| Gross Savings | 50.41of G N I** |
| Exports | 1.204 Tn US $(09),37.46%of GDP 1.435 Tn US $ (08) |
| Current A/C Bal | 297.1 bn US $ (09)*426.1 bn US $ (08)* |
| Stock of MoneyStock of Quick Money | 2.434 Tn US $ (08),2.09 Tn US $ (07)* 4.523 Tn (09),3.437 Tn (08)* |
| Stock of Domestic Credit | 5.555 Tn US $ (09)* |
| Market Value of Publicly Traded Shares | 5.011 Tn US $ (09)* |
| For. Exc & Gold | 2.422 Tn US $ (09)* |
| FDI at home | 456.3 Bn (09), 378.1Bn (07)* |
| Ext.Debt | 347.1Bn(09), 400.6 Bn (07)* |
| Unemployment | 4.3 %(09), 4.2%(08) for urban areas and about 9% if rural areas also included* |
| BPL | 2.8%(21.5 m below 90$ p.a., the official base and another 35.5 m below 125$ p.a income. |
| Revenue | 1.002 Tn (09) |
| Expenditure | 1.111 Tn. (09) |
| Public Debt | 16.9% of GDP |
| Income Distribution | Lowest 10%-3.5%, Highest 10%-15% of GDP* |
| NPA Banks | 9.8% ** |
| GDP Growth 1980–2000 | 382%** |

* *Source*: CIA Fact Book. China. ** Nationmaster.com. China

**Systemic Problems.** Economic changes have created social tensions. Corruption, economic crises, etc are also facts. About 210 million workers are adrift between towns and villages on part time wages. As of 2006, 50% of the GDP was limited to 7% of land along the coast between Shandong in the East to Guangdong in the South. Regional disparities and income variations have been high with the coastal regions progressing faster.

Central planning was strengthened when the actual progress was found to be lower. At times, restrictions were tightened due to inflation. The state council still guides the economic plan. The state budget is still a top-down chain of command exercise with 100 Ministers, administrators, bureaus, academia and corporations controlling the affairs. The People's Budget, National Development and Reforms Commission, Ministry of Finance, etc. control various sectors though gradually interactions with all concerned have been growing. Directive planning, Indicative planning and market focus are still the controlling features. Operational supervision is, however, increasingly left to provinces/municipalities and county governments.

Shortages of skilled labour and rising export costs because of factors like increasing labour rates are problems. Labour charges in some cases have reached 150 US $/week. One child policy is also a contributory factor. Preference for higher education among youth is another reason. Chinese youth going to US for education, jobs, etc. have also been adding to the problem. Hence, some foreign firms think of relocation to countries like Vietnam and Bangladesh with cheaper labour. Inflation also has its adverse impact.

Renminbi (RMB-people's currency) called 'Yuan', divided into 10 Jiao and 100 fens, is China's currency. It is issued by People's bank of China. Outsiders consider it to be under valued by about 30%. It is allowed to fluctuate upto ½ % a day against a basket of currencies. It grew from 8.35 RMB per US dollar in 1995 to 7.4 RMB in mid 2007. There are demands from US, Japan and European countries that are adversely affected by its lower value contributing to the competitiveness of China's products that the value of Yuan should be raised to more realistic levels. There are legislative moves in US to impose tariff restrictions on Chinese exports to US in case the demand is not met. But, China argues that any such step would be against the norms of WTO and would be legally fought. Chinese leaders like Wen Jiabao, Prime Minister, point out how millions in China would face unemployment in case the vale of Yuan is raised. As high level of unemployment in US is the major problem faced by the US Government, China may have to at least marginally increase the value of Yuan vis-a-vis US $.

Some of the problem areas or issues on the economic front on which China is being criticized in the democratic world are given below.

**Environmental Damage[4].** While no country has emerged as a major industrial power without some damage to environment, China's unprecedented rise is matched by unprecedented damage to its environment with serious repercussions for the whole world too. It would have major long-term burdens for the Chinese public and pose acute political challenges to the communist party. Pollution has already made cancer China's leading cause of death. Ambient air pollution alone is blamed for hundreds of thousands of deaths. In many cities, people rarely see the sun and children are falling sick and even killed by lead poisoning or other local pollution. Coastlines are swamped by algal red tides with large parts of the ocean losing capacity to sustain marine life.

China is 'choking on its own success' of double-digit growth rates and a staggering expansion of heavy industries. It requires colossal inputs of energy, almost all from coal, the most readily available, but most polluting. According to the Journal of Geophysical Research, Sulfur dioxide and nitrogen oxides coming from coal-fired power plants in China fall as acid rain on Seoul, South Korea, and Tokyo and much of the pollution over Los Angeles originates in China. Many believe that China has over-taken US as the leading producer of greenhouse gases. Meanwhile, nearly 500 million people lack access to safe drinking water. Only 1 percent of the country's 560 million city dwellers breathe the air considered safe. The authoritarian system is addicted to fast growth and increase in prosperity is placating the public and providing spoils for officials forestalling demands for political change. A major slowdown could incite social unrest, alienate business interests and threaten the party's rule. But, pollution, esp. about air and water has started creating thousands of cases of social unrest. Health care costs have climbed sharply. Severe water shortages could turn more farmland into desert and unconstrained expansion of energy intensive industries creates greater dependence on imported oil and dirty coal.

Recognizing the dangers involved leaders like Prime Minister Wen Jiabao, have been stressing on environmental protection, giving numerical targets for reducing emissions and conserving energy. Export subsidies for polluting industries have been phased out. Campaigns have been started to close illegal coalmines and shutter some heavily polluting factories. Clean energy sources like solar and wind power are getting priority. Environmental regulations in Beijing, Shanghai and other leading cities have been tightened. But, targets for energy efficiency, improvements in air and water quality, etc. are not being met. The leadership is unable or unwilling to make sacrifices to effect fundamental changes at the cost of reduced growth levels. Even heavy polluters get land, water, electricity, oil and bank loans at low rates. Beijing has declined to use the kind of tax policies and market-oriented incentives for conservation that have worked well in Japan and many European countries. Provincial officials, who enjoy substantial autonomy, often ignore environmental rules and help to reopen mines or closed factories. Enforcement is often marred by corruption. In 2003, when pollution was much lesser, it was estimated by western analysts that 3 lakhs/year died due to air pollution mostly from cancer. 1.5 lakhs/yr may be dying due to indoor air pollution. It is assessed that toxic fume may kill about 3.8 lakhs by 2010.and 5.5 lakhs by 2020. A World Bank study showed that 3.5–4 lakhs premature deaths may be due to air pollution and another 3 lakhs may be from indoor pollution. About a million may be dying due to cigarette smoking. Chinese experts feel the western estimates are on the lower side.

The current objective of quadrupling the size of the economy may need 20 more years of continuous growth. Energy heavy sectors may grow faster and efficiency gain targets may not be met. As a result of the recent economic recession, Government has given tax incentives for rapid industrialization.

**Lowering of Water Table.** Demand for water all over the world, which has tripled over the last half a century, has been consistently increasing. The need for hydroelectric power has grown even faster and dams and diversions of river water have drained many rivers dry. As water tables fall, springs that feed rivers also go dry. Nations are over pumping aquifers-both replenishable and non-replenishable (or fossil). Over pumping has largely depleted the replenishable shallow aquifer, forcing well drillers to turn to the regions non-replenishable deep fossil aquifer.

Falling water tables, the conversion of cropland to non-farm uses and the loss of farm labor in provinces that are rapidly industrializing combine to shrink China's grain harvest. Even with a worldwide grain crunch and climbing grain prices providing an incentive to boost production, it will be difficult for China to regain earlier grain production levels, given the loss of irrigation water.

If overproduction of groundwater continues at the same rate as at present, it should result in depletion or more lowering of water level, and may induce ground subsidence and water quality deterioration. To overcome these problems, it may be essential to use water more effectively for irrigation and recycle used water from industrial and domestic sources.

**Increasing Inequalities in Income and Development.** During the impressive growth over the last two decades, Chinese economy has experienced remarkable increases in inequalities. According to the World Bank (1997), China's Gini coefficient, which shows the extent of inequalities (from 0 to 1), rose from 0.288 in 1981 to 0.388 in 1995. It, is believed to have further gone up subsequently and reaching near 0.5. During the early stage of rural reforms (1978–84), the Household Responsibility System successfully released farmers' potential and significantly raised production efficiency. Along with improvements in agricultural productivity, increased agricultural prices also contributed to rural income growth over this period. As a result of egalitarian land distribution, the gains of rural reforms were widely shared among rural households. Thus, the rural Gini coefficient increased only slightly from 0.212 in 1978 to 0.244 in 1984. China witnessed significant changes in household income structure since 1985, due mainly to stagnant agricultural production and fall in their prices, unbalanced growth, and the rapid development of off-farm opportunities significantly accentuating the inequalities. It is noticed that the ratio of total rural loans to rural GDP, significantly contributes to the reduction of rural inequality in China. Thus, to lower China's rural inequality, the Chinese government should make greater efforts to strengthen rural financial systems, paying particular attention to development of viable credit markets in poor areas of rural China. Market reforms, financial decentralization, and economic globalization have greatly accentuated China's social and regional inequalities. The state policies have not sufficiently addressed inequitable practices. Hence, a new system of social stratification driven more by market forces than socialist principles is fast developing.

**Absence of Individual Trade Union Rights[5].** The All-China Federation of Trade Unions (ACFTU) is the sole national trade union federation of the People's Republic of China. It is the largest trade union in the world with 134 million members subdivided into 10 national trade unions, 31 regional federations and 1,713,000 primary trade union organizations. It has a monopoly on trade unionizing in China, as creation of competing unions is illegal.

Wal-Mart signed collective-bargaining agreements with workers in two provinces in July, 2009. Further agreements covering all 50,000 of its local employees in China are a foregone conclusion. With this, Wal-Mart now has a business partner in ACFTU, and if it wants to close stores, lay off employees, or change other aspects of its business like operating hours and work quotas (what employees are expected to accomplish), ACFTU must be consulted. There are allegations that China has emphasized growth and business investments at the expense of workers' rights. As China's labour laws include provisions requiring business firms to consult employees on "material" work-related issues, some companies responded by forming in-house workers' groups. The ACFTU objected claiming that it amounted to the creation of an alternative labour union, and hence was illegal. ACFTU plans to sign up 80% of the workers in large foreign companies in China.

## Endnotes

1. Sandra Polanski and Li Shantong, Sandra Polanski and Li Shantong reports, The Carnegieendowment. Paper No. 83, April, 2007. www.carnegieendowment.org.
2. Modified extracts from BBC.com on China's economic profile.
3. http://news.bbc.co.uk/2/hi/special_report/1999/09/99/China_50_years_of_communism/453330.stm
4. http://www.nytimes.com/2007/08/26/world/asia/26china.html?_r=1
5. http://en.wikipedia.org/wiki/All_China_Federation_of_Trade_Unions

## References

a. http://en.wikipedia.org/wiki/Economy_of_the_People's_Republic_of_China (Jan 29, 2010)
b. http://en.wikipedia.org/wiki/Economic_reform_in_the_People's_Republic_of_China (Dec. 2, 2009)
c. http://en.wikipedia.org/wiki/All_China_Federation_of_Trade_Unions (Dec. 2, 2009)
d. http://carnegieendowment.org/events/index.cfm?fa=eventDetail&id=980&&prog=zgp&proj=zed-SandraPolanski and Li Shantong reports
e. http://federalreserve.gov/newsevents/speech/bernanke20061215a.htm
f. http://economywatch.com/world_economy/china/ Structure-of-economy.html (Dec. 2, 2009)
g. http://news.bbc.co.uk/2/hi/special_report/1999/09/99/china_50_years_of_communism/453330.stm
h. http://adb.org/Documents/Speeches/2006/ms2006014.asp (July 26, 2009)
i. http://www.economist.com/displaystory.cfm?story_id=11848496
j. http://survey09.ituc-csi.org/survey.php?IDContinent=3&IDCountry=CHN&Lang=EN-2009
k. http://nytimes.com/1987/07/31/business/economic-scene-China-s-debate-on-reforms.html (Dec. 2, 2009)
l. http://books.google.co.in/books?id=iurkg0CsdowC&pg=PA116&lpg=PA116&dq=China+%2Blowering+of+the+water+table&source=bl&ots=D77PeZeuG8&sig=DayMyvkL-h9FuX3wScgH0xnEZkM&hl=en&ei=gKNkSqfeL8SGkQXe8sn1Dw&sa=X&oi=book_result&ct=result&resnum=2
m. http://survey09.ituc-csi.org/survey.php?IDContinent=3&IDCountry=CHN&Lang=EN
n. http://survey07.ituc-csi.org/getcountry.php?IDCountry=CHN&IDLang=EN
o. http://www.wider.unu.edu/publications/newsletter/ articles/.en_GB/18-12-feature-Article/(July 26, 2009)
p. http://www.fidh.org/Developing-at-the-Expense-of (July 26, 2009)
q. http://www.britannica.com/bps/additionalcontent/18/31474052/Water-Resources-Drying-Up (July 26, 2009)

r. http://www.eoearth.org/article/Aquifer_depletion (July26, 2009)
s. http://books.google.co.in/books?id=iurkg0CsdowC&printsec=Frontcover&source=gbs_v2_summary_r&cad=0#v=onepage&q=&f=false
t. http://www.worldwatch.org/node/4407
u. http://Business world
v. http://Business week
w. http://books.google.co.in/books?id=iurkg0CsdowC&pg
x. different issues of 'People's Daily'
y. Reports of Xinhua news

CHAPTER 5

# Tourism

## A—SEEN MARVELS

We first visited the main tourist attractions (Marvels) in Beijing and adjoining areas and then then went to the earlier capital Xian. From there, we went to Guilin and later to Shanghai. Below is an account of the places and sights we saw. It may be of interest to any one visiting China for the first time.

### *i. Beijing and adjoining areas*

Beijing had emerged as a city called 'Ji' as far back as the Western Zhou dynasty (1046–771 B.C.). It was called 'Jadu' too. It has been the capital of the country for about 600 years only. Earlier, for over 2000 years, Xian was the capital. It is located on the northern edge of the north central plain with mountains on the western and eastern sides and a plain on the southern side. It has a temperate continental climate with a short spring, rainy and humid summer, long and cold winter and a very pleasant autumn.

Beijing city and its suburbs now have a population of over 20 million, including a huge floating population. They have a web-like structure with 6 radial roads and a large number of arterial ones. Many attractive High ways and roads are decorated with greenery and flower beds. These and the smooth organized flow of traffic looked typical of what one would expect in developed countries. The modern sky rise buildings, decorative work on modern roads and parks, etc. even in older areas are quite attractive. The older parts of the city, though more orderly than the Indian ones, do not have such charms. The areas around the 6th ring road are only settled partially with people. As the government owns virtually all the land, development work and other improvements are fairly easy.

**a. The 'Summer Palace'.** 'Yi Le Yuan' in Chinese, meaning 'garden of natural harmony', located 15 km. away from central Beijing, was the first place we visited. It was built as a residence in the countryside for imperial rulers or a retreat from the 'Forbidden City', the imperial palace. Built during the Jin Dynasty (A.D. 1115–1234), it was extended by later emperors. Empress Cixi, the only female ruler in Chinese history, who spent most of her later years here, changed its name to 'Summer Palace'. It was started in 1750 as 'Garden of Clear Ripples' and its architects reproduced the architectural styles of various palaces in China. A lake was created by extending the boundary of an existing water body to imitate the West Lake in Hangzhou.In 1890, it was given the current name after rebuilding. It suffered serious attacks by the Anglo-French forces in 1860 and later by the eight Allied Forces in 1900.After the 1911 revolution, it was opened to the public.

It spans an area of 294 hectares, 3/4th of which is water. It is considered a museum of Chinese gardens that uses rocks, plants, pavilions, ponds, curved stone paths, and other garden styles to create a poetic effect. Called a 'garden of gardens', it represents harmony between man and nature with its, hills, pavilions, bridges, temples, Kunming Lake, Longevity Hill and 5 gardens blending harmoniously. It is dominated by Longevity Hill and Kunming Lake. South to South-west is the Kunming Lake, a man made one. Soil from its excavation was used to create the Longevity Hill. On the top of 'Longevity Hill' is the 'Duo Bao' pagoda which contains examples of ancient arts, graceful landscapes, and magnificent constructions.

The Marble Boat[1] at the Summer Palace in Beijing. The wooden structure was built in 1755 on a stone base and rebuilt in 1893 as a wooden lakeside pavilion in the shape of a paddle steamer.

Throne hall[2] in the emperor's administrative area close to the East Gate of the Summer Palace in Beijing.

'Marble Boat', a marble structure in the shape of a boat, is located near the South-west foothill. A 17-arch bridge with 500 engraved lions, Cloud dispelling hill, Tower of Buddhist Incense, Jade Belt Bridge, Bronze Quilin statue, etc. are among the other attractions.

The 'Long Corridor', 726 M long, (pl. see page 160) is famous for its decorations with more than 14000 paintings. The main hall in the complex is the Cloud dispelling hall where Empress Cixi used to celebrate her birthdays. The 'Cloud Dispelling Gate' marks the centre of the Corridor. Cross beams divide the corridor into 273 sections along the length. There are 4 octagonal pavilions with double eaves representing the four seasons. The paintings in the corridor are on the beams and ceilings. They depict episodes from classical literature, folk tales, historical and legendary figures, famous Chinese buildings and landscapes along with birds, fish, insects and flowers. In each of the four

Close up of one of the Long Corridor murals[3] at the Summer Palace in Beijing.

pavilions, there are two major paintings like The 'Tale of Beh-Blossom land', 'Sun Wukong's fight with nezha', 'Zhang Fei's fight with Ma Chao', 'The Battle of Zhuxian county','Yue Fei defeating Liang Gui with a spear', 'The seven sages of the Bamboo grove', 'Zhao Yun's fight at Changbau and 'Lu Bu's fight with Liu Bei Guan Yu and Zhang Fei' . It leads from the 'Gate for Meeting the Moon' in the east towards the northern shore of the Kunming Lake. The 'Marble Boat' comes at the western end of the Corridor. The middle section of the corridor passes in a southward bend around the central building complex on the lake side of the Longevity Hill.

**b. The 'Forbidden City'** is located in the 'Imperial City', which itself is inside the 'Inner City'. To the south of the 'Inner City' is the 'Outer City' where' where the public lived. Two lakhs men worked for 14 years to build the 75 buildings and 9999 rooms constituting the Forbidden City. Rectangular in shape, (960 meters long and 750 meters wide), it covers an area of 74 hectares. There is a 6 meters deep and 52 meters wide moat, all around. A 'golden water river' runs through it. The walls of the city (8.62 m to 6.6 m wide from bottom to top) were built to withstand cannon fire. At its corners, towers with intricate roof work are seen. All the gates were decorated with golden door nails. Thousands of halls and gates of the city are arranged symmetrically along a north-south axis at the centre of the Beijing city north of the Tiananmen Square.

The 'Forbidden City' was built (A.D. 1406–1428) by Ming Emperor Yougle, based on religious and philosophical principles, to reflect imperial power. It was the residence of 24 emperors of the Ming and Qing dynasties. The entourage of the imperial family and imperial officers stayed in it. The Qing dynasty maintained the original schemes of the Mings except for some changes in names of halls to emphasize words like 'peace' and 'harmony'. It was called 'Forbidden City' as the Emperor had supreme powers and his residence was a forbidden place for the common people.

The Emperor also wanted his city to be separate from the rest of the city to reflect its glory. It was forbidden to build higher buildings. It was also called the 'Purple Forbidden City' as purple was the symbolic colour of the North Star which was believed to be the centre of the Cosmos. Emperors believed that their residence was the centre of the universe and that the meridian went right through the city.

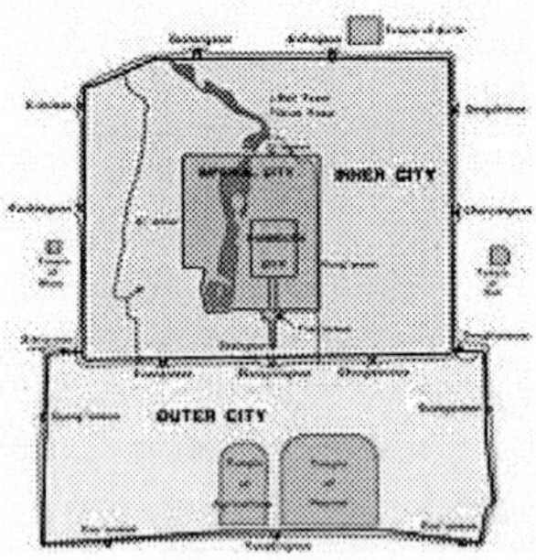

Layout[4] of the Forbidden City and the Gate of Heavenly Peace[5] leads to the former Imperial City

It is the world's largest and best imperial palace which boasts off over 1050,000 pieces of relics. Today, the palace is called the 'palace museum' showing ceramics, paintings, bronze ware, jade, palace artifacts, time pieces, etc. of the earlier periods. A lot of expensive relics were taken out by the last emperor 'Pu Yi'. Many were also lost while being moved to safer places during the Japanese invasion. The main entrance to the Forbidden City is the 'Meridian Gate' (page 160) in the south. It has five openings with the central one meant exclusively for the emperor. The next two on either side were for the royal family and high officials and the outer two were for petty officials. The Empress could enter the Forbidden City only on her wedding day and thereafter no exit was allowed. Inside the Forbidden City, buildings were arranged on three north-south axes with most of the buildings on the central axis. The inner court was used by the royal family and the outer one was for ceremonial purposes. The Inner court had three halls namely the 'Palace of Heavenly Purity' for the emperor, 'Hall of Earthly Tranquility' for the queen and the 'Hall of Union' where the 'yin' and 'yang' mixed to produce harmony. It was believed the emperor was representing 'yang' and heaven and the queen the 'yin' and earth. Perfect harmony between yin and yang was essential for success/luck. On the northern side of the premises are beautifully landscaped imperial gardens, inner palaces, Taoist shrines, etc. The 'Jingshan Park' located on the northern side was created from the excavations for the moats. On the eastern and western sides were imperial gardens. Now they are used as the headquarters of the communist party or for other similar purposes. On the southern side is the Tiananmen Square Gate (Gate of Supreme Harmony) with the Tiananmen Square further down. *(Pl. see pictures on pages 160)*

c. **Tiananmen Square** is the geographical centre of Beijing. It is the largest square in the world with a conglomeration of beautiful flowers and red flags fluttering around. It was built uring the Ming dynasty (A.D. 1368–1644). Spanning an area of 109 acres, it can accommodate 1 million people. It has the

The Hall of Supreme Harmony[6] as seen from the Inner Courtyard of theForbidden City in Beijing. *(pl. see page 161 for more pictures)*

The 'Monument to the People's Heroes' in Tiananmen Square in Beijing.* Constructed in 1958, it commemorates those who fought in revolutions from 1840 to 1949.

'Magnificent Tower' in the North, the solemn Mao Ze Dong's Memorial Hall in the south, National Museum in the East and the Great Hall of the People in the West. At the centre of the square is a beautiful memorial column viz. 'Monument to people's Heroes (Martyrs)', built in 1977 to honour 'People's Heroes'.

The 124 ft high monument made of granite is the tallest monument in the Chinese history. It has Mao's epigraph engraved on it. There are also eight reliefs depicting crucial events of the modern times. The remains of Mao are kept in a coffin in the main Hall of the Memorial Hall where silence is observed. There are two other halls to the north and south. Details from the lives of Mao, Chou–En–Lai and other leaders are exhibited in the northern hall.

**d. 'The Great Wall'** known as the "Wan Li Chang Cheng" or the "Ten Thousand Li Long Wall" in China earlier stretched for 7,350 km from the banks of the Yalu River in Liaoning Province in the east to Jiayuguan Pass in Gansu Province in the west. It is a symbol of ancient Chinese Culture and pride of the Chinese People. It passes by Beijing at a distance of

The National Museum of China on Tiananmen Square in Beijing. Completed in 1959, the museum's mission is to educate about the arts and history of China. *(Also pl. see more pictures on page 160–161)*

about 60 km. It now covers 6400 km from the Shanghai pass to the Hop Nur in the West. It had its origin in several walls built by local rulers between 7th and 5th cent. B.C. as a series of earthen and stone fortifications using rammed earth, stones and other local resources. In the 5th cent B.C. Qi, Yan and Zhao states had extensive fortifications to guard against nomads. These were given the present form between 220 and 200 B.C. by the First Emperor Qin Shi Huangdi by connecting the northern walls as a continuous one along the northern boundary of his empire mainly to protect his farming people against the cavalry of the northern tribes.

This was north of the present one built by the Ming dynasty. It had cart tracks in many areas with smoke signaling to warn of attacks. But, today hardly anything of this structure remains. Shi Huangdi believed in building large structures and also wanted to make his mark in history. Shi Huangdi ordered several defensive portions of a stone wall to be connected to form the "Great Wall". This northern boundary was fourteen feet high and forty feet thick. More than a million laborers died in its construction. It was said "each stone in the Great Wall cost a human life".

The majority of the labour force who went to build the "Great Wall" were convicts and other outcast groups. From Shi Huangdi's biography comes this description of the "Great Wall". "He... built a Great Wall, constructing its defiles and passes in accordance with the configurations of the terrain. It started at Lin-t'ao and extended to Liao-tung, reaching a distance of more than ten thousand lei. After crossing the Yellow River, it wound northward, touching the Yang Mountains". At its peak, it was guarded by a million men.

Qin Shi Huangdi had built the wall from east of Liaoning Province to Lintao, Gansu Province. When Hans became powerful during the Western Han dynasty, the wall was expanded along the western and northern sides. The 'Silk Route' was along the length of the Hans' wall. The Northern and Western Hans, Northern Qi and Northern Zhou dynasties also built some sections. Hans, Sui, Nui and Jin dynasties took care to repair damaged portions and also rebuilt and expanded some parts. Even double or multi-line walls had come up at some places. Granaries, watch towers, etc. were also built on the wall.

During the Ming period, threats from the North-West had increased. Following the Ming defeat by the Mongols in the battle of Tumu in 1449, the Mings made substantial changes on their northern boundary. The Ming construction was stronger and was mostly with stones and bricks. A lot of repair and fortification works were also undertaken, esp. near the capital. During the Ming dynasty, a general opposed to the dynasty had opened the doors to allow Manchus to come in thereby allowing the Manchus to seize Beijing and establish the Qing dynasty. During the Qing rule, China extended beyond the Wall to cover Mongolia and hence major repairs and maintenance works were not undertaken.

The section of the wall adjacent to Badaling Hills, 75 km north of Beijing, is typical of the wall of Mings. It has a height of 8.5 M and width of 5 M for 5 horses or 10 people to walk abreast. There are ramparts, embrasures, peep holes, and apertures on the top for action and galleries to drain away water. The watch towers are two-storied with the first floor for storage of grains and the other for fodder, gun powder, weapons and other equipments. Signal teams on high posts were meant to call for reinforcement during times of attack by enemies. The highest part which is like a ladder to heaven is reached only after a steep climb. The wall follows the contours and provides a good view of the neighborhood. The most impressive portions were built during the Ming rule in the 14th cent. 'Visibility of the Wall from moon is only in legends. It is barely visible 100 miles above and looks like a gigantic dragon winding up across deserts, grass lands, mountains and plateaus. It appeals because of its grandeur and historical significance. The noteworthy areas in the Wall are:

(a) The Northern Parts of Juyonguan Pass (Badaling high grounds). Bricks and stones cut in rectangular shapes were used to give a good appearance to the outer and inner faces and gateways. Battlements lined the upper portions. In many areas, the wall has disappeared. Graffiti and vandalism have damaged many repaired areas. About 60 km in the Jiansu Province may disappear in 20 years because of sandstorm erosion. The height has already been reduced to 2 M.

(b) The Mutianyu section of the wall in Huaisou county is south of the Juyonguan Pass. It winds along 72 km northeast of Beijing, opposite to the Badaling, for 2.25 km from southeast to northeast. Near Shauhai Mountain, the wall is on a bridge. The Juyonguan Pass, Zijingguan Pass and Daomaguan Pass of this section were the three main barriers North-East of Beijing during the Ming period. The areas adjoining these passes are like gardens with scenic spots. They are beautiful tourist attractions for those who want to enjoy the Chinese landscape.

(c) Shanhaiguan Pass is an important pass on the Eastern Great Wall. It was built by the Mings and connects the Yanshau Mountains with the sea and gives a good view of the sea.

(d) Jin Shauling, 130 km from Beijing in Hebei province, is an important door way to the North-East defence line. The area, like Badaling, is beautiful, but, it is yet to be opened to the public.

(e) Huangyaguan Pass, 20 km north-east of Tianjian, was also an important pass during the Ming days. There are a lot of precipitous cliffs here with the wall wandering across mountains and ridges. In this section, the watch towers are rectangular. A network of T shaped road junctions were built to confuse enemies and get them entangled in routes as part of the defence engineering

The Juyongguan section of the Great Wall close to Beijing.*

Multiple Watch Towers along a section of the Great Wall.*

A crenellated walkway on the Great Wall.*

Long corridor, the covered walkway, is famous for its great length (728 m) and elaborate decoration with more than 14,000 paintings.*

The Forbidden City[7], viewed from Jingshan Hill to the north.

The Meridian Gate—the largest gate in the Forbidden City with five arches—is the southern entrance to the Forbidden City in Beijing.*

In front of the Great Hall of the People in Tiananmen Square in Beijing.* Below: The Mao Zedong Mausoleum (or Chairman Mao Memorial Hall) was constructed in 1977 on Tiananmen Square in Beijing.*

A View of the Oriental TV Tower, Shanghai.*

A View of the Terra-Cotta Warriors.*

Shanghai Museum.*

Grand Theatre, Shanghai-a view.*

A close-up of the colorful architecture at the Temple of Confucius in Beijing.*

work. A lot of damage to the wall is visible here.

(f) Jiayu Pass, built 600 years ago, is the western terminus of the wall. Full of grandeur, it is majestic with a solid construction. It touches the Quilian Mountain and Gobi desert and is an imposing and strategic point in the Western wall. It is well preserved and has a magnificent castle with inner and outer sections.

(g) Yumen Pass is a point on the western Silk Road. It is also called the Jade gate as jades of Honan in Xingjian region were transported to central China through this pass.

**e. The Ming Tombs*** contain tombs of 13 Emperors, 7 concubines and a eunuch of the Ming Dynasty period covering an area of 120 sq. km. The tombs were built either by the Emperors or their successors from A.D. 1409 onwards. They are located 50 km away from Beijing at the foot of Mt.Yan between the Dagon and Tiger mountains

* From CIA Fact Book Photos—In public domain.

Each tomb has a forecourt where ceremonies, sacrifices, etc. were held. The most prominent one is of Emperor Changling completed in A.D. 1420. Here, housed in a building supported on 60 unpainted columns of the 'Nanmu' tree, are many articles used by the emperors and other objects of that period excavated from the tombs.

**f. Visit to a Modern Silk Factory.** On the way back from 'The Great Wall', we visited a Modern Silk Factory. It was impressive to watch the making of silk from the cocoon stage. Here we were shown the process of silk manufacture from the very beginning to the end. i.e. final packaging especially that of various high quality products meant for export. We were shown how the silk thread in a cocoon gets spread on to a fairly large table top in a single pull and stretch movement, to facilitate extraction of thread without breakage. In general, we found the silk to be quite fine, but, the prices were exorbitant too. Silk was also being utilized to make various works of art.

**g. Kungfu.** In Beijing, we had opportunities to watch 'Kungfu' and Chinese Acrobatics shows. 'Kungfu' is a traditional Chinese martial art with references dating back to the Zhou dynasty period (1100–221 B.C.). The modern 'Kungfu' covers the systems taught by the Five Elders/ Ancestors who emerged from the destruction of the Hinan and Fukies temples in the 17th century. It has both external and internal components with the external one involving use of muscular force. The internal component focuses on relaxing the muscles as much as possible, with stress on meditation and the use of "chi", the internal energy. The true essence of 'Kungfu' is to reject all offers of violence and if unavoidable, the combat is to be ended in one to four movements. The basic weapons are staff, spear, broad sword and straight sword. In the hand method, weapons are not used and only hand movements like forearm strikes, throws, locks, etc. are used. Kungfu can be divided into two types-Long hand and Short Hand. Normally, the technique starts with the Long Hand method and ends in Short hand. Internal Kungfu is more about development and is a path of faith and courage. Stamina, strength and co-ordination are built up first. The training includes meditation, unarmed combat, types of weapons, herbal medicines, etc. which work together to help in the path to enlightenment. Both offensive and defensive styles are taught.

**h. Chinese Acrobatics** is a system of performing arts, over 2000 years old, perhaps from the days of the Warring States period (475–221 B.C.). These techniques stemming from people's lives and involving the use of instruments like tri-

The Sacred Way* leading to the Ming Tombs in Beijing.

dents, tables, chairs, jars, plates and bowls acquired great improvements during the Tang dynasty period when Chinese culture was at its pinnacle. "Flying trident", "balance on chairs", "jar tricks", "hoop diving", "wushu and lion dance", etc. originated from folk sports and games. Though popular among the common people, these were looked down upon by the higher classes and hence were never performed in theatres. Nowadays, municipalities and cities are developing these arts and setting up their own troupes using harnesses, musical accompaniments, good costumes, props, and lighting. Above the county level, there are 120 acrobatic troupes and 1200 performers. Below is a short description of some popular performances:

Lion dance. Small and big lions portrayed by one and two people respectively perform movements like rolling and jumping to depict the lion's strength, agility and playful nature. Cycling feats using mono cycles and bi-cycles show various feats including that of a peacock fanning its feathers. Tight wire feats show vigor and skills using techniques like cart wheels, somersaults on a trembling wire, etc. Conjuring involves tricks like- using a big robe, some pieces of cotton cloth, and many bowls filled with water to produce water and fire without burning or wetting cloth. Other feats to be seen are Hoop diving using rings, Wushu gymnastics(showing somersault skills and various other postures), Spring board struts (leaps and somersaults in the air to show agility and grace), meteor juggling tricks involving throwing show glass bowls into the air to resemble meteors in the sky, revolving 2 glass bowls filled with water fastened to either ends of a rope, forward and backward rolls, catching them again and continuing to dance without spilling water, gymnastics on double and fixed poles(jumping from one to the other, swift descent, etc.), etc. Great alacrity, synchronization, etc. are visible as a result of professional training and practice from childhood. The artists have vigorous schedules, but hard work gets respect and admiration from people.

**i. Some interesting experiences** during our stay in Beijing will enable better understanding of the state of affairs:

(a) In a three or four star hotel where we were accommodated, one day I and my wife were locked out of our room because of our failure to keep the computerized key of the room with us. Our efforts to communicate our plight to the front desk of the hotel and get a duplicate key proved futile as none of the staff on duty could understand English. While we were going down in the lift to the restaurant, one English knowing Chinese gentleman in the lift understood our plight and told us to use three gestures. These consisted of signs for key, inside of the room and keeping our hands on the chest in crossed condition. When we went to the front desk after break fast and did as suggested, they laughed and in a minute produced a duplicate key.

(b) On the first day, those who were used to taking liquor regularly were picking up these from the fridges in rooms paying fairly high prices. The next evening when we were strolling in the near-by market from were local people purchase such items, it was found that they were being sold at about ten percent of the price we were paying. Thereafter,liquor was purchased from such shops only avoiding some waste of money.

(c) Initially we shopped with out taking help of the local guides most of who were teenage girls. We found that getting specific items was taking a lot of time though shops were in large numbers. To locate items difficult to find and to save time, we later used the services of guides who were very courteous and took us straight to the shops after checking up the specifics of the items needed, the price we were prepared to pay, quality, etc. Though we tipped them, it was found that there was an arrangement for them to get a commission from the shops concerned. Hence, they do not normally expect to be paid by the tourists. In big shopping centres, a large number of girls live on such jobs. When the time is short, they can quite useful as they know the correct prices, quality, reasonably priced shops, particular shops where special and rare items can be purchased, etc.

### *ii. Xian and adjoining areas*

Xian, capital of Shaanxi province, is the largest metropolis in north-west China. It has 3000 years history. Earlier called 'Changan', it is a centre of Chinese culture, unlike Beijing and Shanghai where traditional Chinese culture is dying. It was the capital of China for nearly 2000 years during the period of the Tang and twelve other dynasties. Xian has never seen external attacks or natural calamities and hence the name 'Xian', which means 'a place of eternal peace'.

The city is located between a mountain and a tributary of the Yangtze River which is considered an ideal location by the Chinese 'Fengshui' tradition. It was a window to the West and also the starting point of the Silk Route to Iran and further west. Through this route, in exchange for Chinese silk, came Iranian horses. The Chinese used these horses to defend the country from attacks by the northern tribes of Manchuria. Tea, spices, fruits, new vegetables, etc. also were sent to Iran and Europe. Spaghetti is said to have reached Europe from China. Marco polo visited China in the 13 the century following such trade. Apart from the Terra-cotta Warriors and Mausoleum of the Qin Shi Huangdi, The First Emperor, four ruins of Zhou, Qin, Han and Tang dynasties, the Bell Tower and the Forest of Steles, it has three national forest Parks as attractions.

**a. Mausoleum of the First Emperor Qin Shi Huangdi,** located 30 km from Xian, is of great archeological importance because of its sheer size and age. The whole complex covering an area of four sq.miles was designed as a city (with protecting walls, a palace, and even a cemetery) for his after-life. As the legend goes, it was carved out of a low mountain top, 700000 prisoners of war and slaves working for 36 years. Only a part of it which contained the terra-cotta warriors as a replica of his security system has been unearthed.Qin who came to power at the age of 13 in 246 B.C. began its construction immediately after he ascended the throne. It was completed by his son immediately after his death in 210 B.C. It is a symbol of the immense power and ego of Qin. Though a tyrannt and a despot, his reign was marked by progress on various fronts. Towards the end, he focused only on an immortality formula which would allow him to rule as a divine power.

He died a broken and insane man after a trip to Japan in search of his elixir of life. The centre piece of the mausoleum is the terra-cotta army of 8000 life size men and horses sculptured from three inches thick clay and buried underground. It formed the court guarding his tomb from the enemies he had vanquished who supposedly would come from the direction faced by the formation. All his needs and amenities were provided for including precious stones and metals, thus creating a scaled down model of his capital city. It even had a small river system depicting Yangtze, Yellow and other major rivers in which mercury was circulated. There was also a planetarium with constellations made of pearls. The burial chamber had all the interiors waterproofed with bronze. The emperor's tomb has not been opened as it is believed to have been sealed with mercury, and protected with poisonous arrows and other weaponry to bring havoc to any body who tries to do so.

**b. 'Terracotta Warriors'** located near Xian is an excellent representation in sculpture of the army which guarded Emperor Qin Shi Huangdi's capital in Xian. It is a collection of about 8000 real life-size Terracotta figurines, of army Officers and men, of different ranks and races in full battle formation complete with uniforms and insignia of distinctive ranks. The figurines were secretly buried underground, without a mention anywhere in history. To keep its secrecy, all men involved in its construction are believed to have been killed by the emperor. It was discovered by a General after the emperor was overthrown in a revolt. Nearly 2000 warriors, protected by wooden columns and a roof made of thick layers of bamboo reeds with soil over them were ransacked and burnt by the General. He could not reach the remaining about 6000 and these still remain underground. The damaged figurines have been rebuilt to a great extent using clay from the same region and also the traditional methods.

The emperor believed in life after death and in his after life wanted to see the soldiers as at the time of his death. He also had got two half size brass chariots made and

[8]Views of the excavation pits, Terra Cotta warriors scene.

A cavalry man with his mount[9].

A four horse war chariot with mounts[10].

kept before his tomb for his spirit and security man to go round and inspect the warriors in his 'after life' (The chariot found in pieces near his tomb was fully rebuilt and is displayed nearby). It shows how well developed brass work was nearly 2200 years ago in China. The museum opened to the public in 1994 covers 16300 sq. m. divided into three parts tagged in order of their discoveries. Three columns of soldiers in front and war chariots at the back can be seen in the first part. The second part has 1000 soldiers and 100 chariots of wood. The third part, 25 meters n-w of the first part, represents a command centre. It has 68 warriors, a war chariot and four horses. In total, about 7000 pottery soldiers, horses, chariots and weapons were unearthed. Most of them have been restored to their previous grandeur.

**c. Xian city wall,** built in A.D. 1374–79, is the best surviving city wall in China. It is said that the first Ming emperor was advised by a hermit to fortify the city and unify the states. So he modified the pre-existing wall of the Tang era to include large defense systems. The wall is 12 m in height and 12–14 m wide at the top and 15–18 m at the base. It is 13.7 miles long with a circular moat around. At every 120 meters, there is a rampart (total 98) and sentry buildings to defend against climbers. There are 5948 battlements on the outer face. In ancient times, as it was not possible to destroy the wall, the attack points were gates which were secured by armed guards. There are elaborate gates, watch towers, suspension bridges, etc. on all sides with three towers each guarded by army. Initially, the walls were made of dirt and lime. The wall was strengthened in 1568, 1784, and 1983.A circular park has now been built along the length of the wall and moat. Luxuriant trees and flowers decorate the classical architecture of the wall.

**d. Xian Bell and Drum Tower.** It was originally built in the Ming days (1368–1644). A large wall was set up at the centre of the city at a junction of roads. The bell is

36 m high and is on a base of 35.5 m long and 8.6 m height. As the original bell fell silent in Ming days, only a small bell is seen now. To the north-west, across from the Bell Tower square, a drum tower was set up at the end of a lively street. Xian was an important military town in Ming days and the construction of the tower is a reflection of that. It was built to be an imposing structure dominating the country side around it. It has three layers of eaves, but only two storeys and is typical of the Ming architectural style. It has 6 m high arched doors on each side. In 1582, the tower was shifted 1000 m to the east to bring it to the centre of the then city.

**e. Giant Wild/Big Goose Pagoda** located in southern Xian is an important tourist attraction. It was built in A.D. 652 during the Tang Dynasty and originally had only five stories. The pagoda was built to hold sutras and figurines of the Buddha that were brought to China by the Buddhist translator and traveller Xuan Zang, the first Chief Monk of the pagoda. In A.D. 704, the ruling Empress Wu Zetian had five stories added to it. However, later wars damaged the pagoda reducing it to its current height of seven stories. It is now 64 meters high and offers great views of the Xian city. The folklore holds that once while a monk of the place was very hungry and praying for food, from among a flock of wild geese flying by, a big goose dropped dead to provide food for him.

Statue of Xuan Zang

Wild Goose Pagoda

The pagoda is believed to have been built to commemorate the unusual event.

**f. Xian Museum** is located beside the wild Goose Pagoda and is the first museum there with modern facilties. It is in fact a combination of ancient architecture and modern technology. Construction began in 1983 and it was opened to the public in 1991. It has 70000 sq. m of space which mostly displays architectural designs. 11000 sq. m is used for permanent, special and temporary exhibitions.

**g. Tang dynasty Music and dance show.** In Xian, we watched a 'Tang dynasty show' of the song and dance forms of China when the Tang dynasty was at its pinnacle of power and Chinese culture at its zenith. It had an assembly of songs and dance forms of the past with clear essences from many ethnic groups and foreign cultures, reflecting the conditions and systems of the dynasty at the peak of its power. It was an excellent example of the progress the Chinese society had made during the Tang era and it was also a reflection of the peace and prosperity then.

During the Tang dynasty period, dance was performed by people as part of the rituals for a good harvest or a better life. Such dances, over thousands of years, had developed from a few simple postures or gestures to delicate and artistic levels and reached a peak in the Tang era. Tang society was open to outside influences and absorbed the best from the ethnic groups of the north-east and central and western Asia. By combining poetry with skilled playing of musical instruments, singing, dancing and also stunning costumes, these shows give an impressive insight into Chinese history, arts, customs and traditions. The programmes presented with exquisite grace and sophistication were titled 'Melody of the Longevity of the Emperor', 'The White Ramie cloth costume dance', 'Da Nuo Dance', Rain Bow Skirt and Feathered Coat dance', 'The spring oriole's singing', 'Dance in feathered clothing', 'The King of Qin breaks the battle array', 'the Quarrelling Ducks', 'The

Tiger guards its teeth' and the 'Ritual music of the Grand Tang dynasty', etc. The first was an instrumental ensemble representing the emperor holding court. By playing various Chinese instruments, esp. drums and bells, and showing hundreds of officials of various types paying homage to the emperor, the affluence and strength of the Tang empire was presented.' The White Ramie cloth costume dance' had its origin in the Jin Dynasty period (265–316). 'The Da Nua dance' created by Emperor Huangdi 2000 years back was first performed for good luck and to dispel evil spirits. All dancers wore masks and danced to mysterious classical music. 'Rain Bow Skirt and Feathered Coat dance', a brilliant form of singing and dance, is said to have been choreographed by Yangyuhuan, a favourite concubine of Emperor Xuanzong of the Tang dynasty. The Emperor was inspired by a dream of a dancing fairy that was wearing a rain bow skirt and a feathered coat. He created a melody for it which the concubine choreographed and won his favour. In another dance, a group of graceful and charming girls enter slowly and their gentle, beautiful, light dance and willowy figures together with the radiant and enchanting rural landscape formed a wonderful scene. All the programmes showed the tunes, dresses and instruments of the relevant period. A few were created by the emperors or depicted court scenes. Some showed the urge for peace in people's mind after long wars. Some depicted nature's beauty. All had the tenor and texture of the Tang and earlier periods.

**h. At the Huaqing hot springs** 30 km off Xian, we saw the bathing tubs and other facilities built for the emperors, their concubines, etc. to enjoy the 43°C water containing various minerals flowing down from the near-by Lishan Mountains. At the foot of the mountain is the Mausoleum of Emperor Qin Shi Huangdi famous for its jewels and other precious objects.

**i.** The **following experiences** during our stay at Xian are worth mentioning:

(a) After getting down near the site of the Terra–cotta warriors, our guide asked to use horse driven carriages to travel to the actual site which was about a km away from the parking site of our tourist bus. A particular rate was agreed upon for the to and fro trip. While we were proceeding to the site, conversation, suggestive of foul play was heard between the guide and the owner of the jhonga. For the return we found that jhongas were not available to us unless we paid again. We all felt cheated by the guide whom we had trusted. It showed us that sharp practices of the kind we see in Delhi or some other Indian cities are experienced in China too though generally the conduct of guides in China was courteous and above reproach.

(b) The driving of buses and other vehicles and the behaviour of their staff were found to be quite courteous and disciplined. Obedience to signals, observance of speed limits, disciplined parking, etc. were all done routinely unlike in India. The rule that no eatables are allowed in tourist buses was being strictly implemented.

### *iii. Guilin and adjoining areas*

Situated in south-eastern China in Guangxi province, Guilin was conquered by the first Chinese emperor Qin as it was the centre of high quality sea pearls. In its center is the beautiful Chuanshang park. It has a Buddhist pagoda of the Ming Dynasty days at the top of a hillock. Yangshou, 90 km south on the down-stream side of the Lijiang River (on whose bank Guilin is also situated), is popular for trekking, cycling to interior areas and to get an insight into the local rural life. Local people lining up on roads to sell fruits, flowers, pickles (even of insects), etc. can be seen en-route.

**a. Lijiang River,** flowing from Guchin to Yangshou, is the biggest attraction in Guanxi Province. Its breath-taking beauty attracts millions every year. It has a large number of gorgeous karst peaks on either side. These are supposed to have been formed 360 million years ago by lime stone deposits at the bottom of the sea. Cormorant fishing is associated with the river. Water buffaloes, fishermen on boats, peasants reaping paddy, etc. are regular sites for tourists on the 80 km cruise in the river. Various types of love stories associated with the hills are prevalent among the local people. The breath taking scenery and taste of life far from the city with school children and fishermen floating on bamboo rafts, karst peaks with surprise peaks at each bend, water buffaloes in the fields, ducks paddling in water, peasants reaping paddy and fishermen catching fish using cormorant birds (which dive into water, catch the fish and bring to the fisherman without swallowing as there is a cord around its neck to prevent swallowing) are all refreshing sights. According to a legend, a group of seven beautiful hills in the locality were originally seven fairies from heaven who came there to take bath, but got enthralled by the local scenery and stayed on to become peaks.

Lijiang River scenery.[11]

**b. Elephant Trunk Hill.** This is on the western bank of the Lijiang river scenery. A semi-circular karst formation on the river bank resembles an elephant sucking water and hence the hill is popularly called Elephant Trunk Hill. Inverted reflection of the semi-circular cave in water gives the appearance of a moon. On the top of the hill is a two storied pagoda of the Ming era surrounded by green trees. The pagoda, when seen from a distance, looks like a Flower Vase on the top of the elephant. The hill is the symbol of Guilin and is also the most beautiful scenic spot of the area. The Elephant Trunk Hill has a monastery too. On another side of the hill is a cave considered as eyes of the elephant.

Author and wife near Elephant Trunk Hill.

Tiger Leaping Gorge, Lijiang River[12], beautiful scenery.

**c. 'Reed Flute' cave** is situated about 5 km away from Guilin city at a concealed spot on Guang hill. It is called 'Reed Flute' cave as in earlier days reeds for making pipes and flutes used to grow in plenty here. It is 790 ft deep and involves a 550 yards walk on a zigzag path of stalactites and stalagmites. Dazzling colours in the shape of bamboo shoots, pillars, curtains and flowers form a visual treat. Described as a 'palace of natural arts', with imagination flying, one can see any picture—birds, plants and animals. There are 30 scenic sights in the karst caverns variously called "crystal palace", "Lion forest facing the sun" and "primitive forests". With backlighting producing different colours and resonant sounds, it makes a very impressive 'art palace of nature'. One Grotto called 'Crystal palace of the dragon King' resembles a miniature garden. Over 70 wall inscriptions of the Tang dynasty period are also visible there. Naturally, one is overwhelmed by surprises and a feeling of paradise.

**d. Seven stars Park** is on the eastern bank of the Lijiang River and covers 120 hectares. It is the largest park in the Guilin area and is 1.5 km from the down town. Seven peaks (four of Putuo and three of crescent mountains) resemble the 'Big Dipper' constellation. This park has been popular since Sui (581–618) and Tang (618–907) days because of elegant mountains, clear water, stone inscriptions, forests, deep serene valleys, valued cultural relics and plenty of plants and animals. The main sights here are the Flower Bridge, Putuo Mountain, Seven stars cave, Camel hill, Crescent Mountain, Guilin stele forest and light of China square.

The Flower Bridge is the oldest bridge in Guilin and is from the Song era (960–1279). In spring and summer, it is full of blooming flowers and beautiful streams and hence the name. The arch of the bridge and its inverted reflection look like a full moon. In the main body of the park, there are a lot of caves and pavilions. At the west belly of the mountain is the seven stars/Qixia/Bixu cave, with a lot of stalactites and stalagmites. A number of pavilions, tablets and also some tombs of local heroes are seen here. Behind the Putuo mountain is the Camel hill. It is so called as its back looks like a squatting camel. A lot of plum trees, Bonsai plants, etc. are the other points of interest here. South of the Putuo Mountain is the Crescent Mountain with a lot of murals, stone carvings, etc. epitomizing 5000 years of Chinese civilization.

**e. Mount of Unique Beauty (Duxiu Feng).** In the town centre, a steep path of 306 steps takes us to the top of a mountain (ht. 152 m) from where a magnificent view of the town is possible. An anchored edifice called 'Southern Gate way to Heaven'is seen here.On the slopes of the mountain, are a number of caves with inner and outer walls covered with inscriptions from Tang to Qing era. South of the mountain was the residence of the king of Jingjiang, the local ruler of yester years.

**f. Visit to a Pearl Factory.** As mentioned earlier, Qin Shi Huangdi, the First Emperor, was motivated to conquer Guilin area because of its pearls. Hepu, the centre of pearls from South China Sea, is located near it. Pearls from the region are known for their fine quality of colour, size, luster and weight. Sea pearls are highly valued as only one pearl is there in an oyster unlike fresh water oysters where the number could be 20 though 10 to 12 are more common.

The special minerals in the sea water result in deposits inside the oyster's shells forming pearls which are then taken out after they acquire a desirable size. In artificial pearl culture, incisions are made inside the oyster's body and small pearl shells are deposited for mineral deposits to form over them. These are later extracted after attaining sufficient size in a couple of years. Today golden and black coloured ones are in high demand. From places like Hyderabad where most of Indian pearl industry is located, whole-sale merchants regularly import both natural and artificial pearls from this region. We visited a pearl factory-cum-sales unit located close to Guilin where the basics of pearl culture was explained to us. We had opportunities to purchase pearls of quality though the prices were generally high as per Indian standards.

**g. The following experiences** in Guilin and adjoining areas may give a better under standing about the nature of the region:

(a) The scenery in this area is superb with nearly vertical limestone hills in large numbers visible on both sides of the Lijiang River. During a four hour river cruise, we could see cormorant fishing where the bird goes under water catches the fish and brings it back to its owner. Life in village areas, fishing habits of villagers, etc. could also seen first hand.

(b) While passing through a village we found that villagers had displayed their products on the road side for sale. To our surprise, these included, besides local fruits and vegetables, some of which we could not name, pickles of worms, ants and small snakes to the horror of many vegetarians in the group.

(c) At a tourist site we found vendors selling CDs containing pictures of places of tourist interest. Though the initial demand was 10 Yuan (about Rs. 75) per CD, when no body was interested, the price was halved. As there were still no takers from our group, he was prepared to reduce the price further. When we were about to leave, he sold the item@ one Yuan per CD showing the variability of prices.

### *iv. Shanghai and adjoining areas*

Also called "Hu" or "Shen", Shanghai was originally a fishing village on the banks of the river 'wangpu'. Foreigners accessed China through this port for trade and foreign settlements gradually came up after the Opium War when foreign powers like U.K., France, and US imposed unilateral terms on defeated China. The city, divided into two by Wangpu River, now has about 22 million people including about 5 million floating population. 'Pudong' on the east is a tariff free zone and the city today has over 130 buildings above 130 meters ht. Maglev/Magnetic suspended train running at upto 430 km/hour between Long yang road station and Pudong International Airport takes only eight minutes. It is the headquarters of the Far eastern Economic Zone in China, which extends from Dalian in the north to Hainan in the south. It is now the leading port and gate way to China for foreigners. Yangtze River empties into the sea here.

This region has been witnessing unprecedented growth

through Foreign Direct Investments (FDI) by the Chinese Diaspora and US and Other foreign companies who want to benefit from China's low man-power cost. Shanghai today is an important centre for metallurgy, machine-building, shipping, chemical and electrical industries, textiles, Ocean shipping, banking, etc. With Pudong as an export oriented district, Shanghai is getting transformed into an international economic, banking, and trading centre and a modern metropolis. A number of festivals like International Tea Festival, Orange festival, and Shanghai town festival attract a large number of tourists from all over the world, especially US and European countries. As the biggest city in China, in terms of not only population but also economic and industrial activities and as a tourist centre, it is a source of great attraction for the Chinese youth too.

It is well connected to other parts of the country and world with two international airports of Podong and Hongqiao. The major attractions are People's Square, Nanjing Road, the Bund, Shanghai Museum, Old Town Shanghai, Oriental TV Tower, JinMao mansion (tallest building in the country-office complex, commercial, sight seeing and residential areas), ancient water side town of Zhujiajiao (Venice of Shanghai/a waterside town), etc.

a. **People's Square** is in fact a large public area of about 14000 sq. m just off the Nanjing road in the Huangpu dist. of Shanghai. It is now a vast green area with plants and trees and spectacular buildings on all sides. It has the municipal government mansion on the north, the Shanghai Grand Theatre on the north-west and Exhibition Hall on the east. It is the central place of the city used as a standard for measuring distances. Till 1949, it was a part of the Shanghai race course. Part of the race course has been converted into a public park and club house buildings have become the Art museum.

Grand theatre and Workers Planning and Exhibition Hall are new additions.

b. **Oriental TV Tower.** The design of the tower is based on a verse of a Tang Dynasty poem about the wonderful sprinkling sound of pearls falling on a jade plate of a pipa instrument. The tower features 11 spheres, big and small. The two biggest spheres, along the length of the tower, have diameters of 50 m for the lower and 45 m for the upper. They are linked by three columns, each 9 m in diameter. The highest sphere is 14 m in diameter. The entire building is supported by three enormous columns that start underground. The tower has fifteen observation levels. The highest known as the 'Space Module' is at 350 m ht. The lower levels are at 90 m (Sightseeing Floor) and 263 m (Space City). There is a revolving restaurant at the 267 m. The tower also contains exhibition facilities, restaurants and a shopping mall. There is also a 20-room hotel called the 'Space Hotel' between the two large spheres. A broadcasting TV and radio antenna extends the ht. by another 118 m to a total height of 468 m. *(pl. see Pict on page 162)*

c. **Nanjing Road,** the first commercial road of Shanghai, stems off the Huangpu River at right angles and links the city's main commercial and residential districts. This is the main shopping area today. A good part of it is pedestrian zed and in the evenings, the road looks its best with neon lights and advanced bill-boards illuminating the glazed buildings along the road. The river bund, 4 km long, is the most famous landmark of Shanghai, with rows of buildings, housing complexes, financial and commercial centers and world's greatest banks and trading enterprises centered there. At Sunshine, people of all ages fill up the boulevard.

In the evening, couples wander around enjoying the spectacular city lights, buildings and atmosphere of the area which reminds people that Shanghai was, and in many ways is, a foreign invention. Many hotels, bars, theatres, buildings of Gothic, Baroque and Romanesque styles are visible. Formerly, British, Russian and Japanese embassies were there and places like 'British Public Park' were forbidden to the Chinese.

d. **The Bund.** Bund is derived from the word 'band' meaning an embankment or dam. The area was initially a British settlement, generally international in nature and was also a major financial hub of East Asia. After the Chinese revolution, many financial institutions moved out, hotels, clubs etc. were closed and statues of colonial figures were removed.

e. **Shanghai Museum,** located in the centre of the 'People's Square', contains 120000 pieces of ancient Chinese artifacts. These are of bronze, ceramics, paintings, calligraphy, sculpture, jade, coins, Ming and Qing furniture, seals and art pieces of minorities of China. It is in an impressive building resembling a Chinese cooking pot with two

View of The Bund[13] area in Shanghai. Most of the buildings were built in the early 20th century in a neoclassical style by European and American businesses.

handles on either side. A number of international exhibitions are also regularly held here. View from here is particularly spectacular at night when steam appears to seep out of the roof of the museum and light bounces off the glass walls of the fully glazed 'Grand Theatre' nearby. The square offers an unusual and impressive view on all sides by mammoth and over-shooting constructions and new buildings overlooking from all sides.

Bronze ware of Shang and Zhou dynasties helps to understand the ancient civilization. The ceramic collection (500) of various dynasties include painted and grey pottery from Neolithic age, primitive celadon from Shang, Zhou, and warring states, mature celadon from East Han, Tri-coloured glazed pottery from Tang, blue, white glazed as well as painted porcelain from the Song period, brilliant works from Jingdezhen, Jiaanxi, the centre of the industry during Yuan, Ming and Qing periods.

The ancient sculpture focuses mainly on Buddhist themes. Jade in ancient China was used for decoration and represented wealth and power. The wood patterns and crystal colours proclaim their elegance. Qing and Ming period furniture show the hey days of Chinese furniture. The gallery of seals shows the importance of seals between Zhou and Qing periods. The 7000 pieces of coins show the development of coinage and currency and economic exchange between China and foreign countries. The clothes, textiles, metal ware, sculpture, pottery, bamboo work etc. of the ethnic minorities show their creativity. It enables the people, as the Chinese saying goes, to see directly and experience their country's culture rather than read about it many times over. *(pl. see pict. on page 163)*

f. **Old Town Shanghai** (called Nanshi) is south-east of the city centre (Yuyuan) and is centered between Renmin road and Zhongshan road. South-west of the Bund, this was the first settlement. In olden days, the city had a wall which came down in 1911. During the colonial days, only the Chinese used to come here as westerners had their own enclaves. Nowadays, a lot of foreigners come here to have a feel of the old Chinese culture. Of late, entire sections are being pulled down to make way for modern multi storied structures.

The interesting places here are Shanghai old street, fuyou antiques market, Temple of the Town God (Taoist), curio stores, Bridge of nine turnings, Huxington tea house, Yuyuan garden, a maze of ponds, bridges, pavilions, small gardens, small commodities streets, white closed Taoist temple with thousands of statues of Taoist deities, 50 m of the original city wall built in 1553, Yunnan Lu food street, etc. Traditional Chinese arts and sorceries, chop sticks, Chinese medicines, walking sticks, umbrellas, fans, bamboo, gold fish, pottery, dumplings, spicy cold noodles, etc. are the common items on sale here.

**g.** **The 'Jade Buddha'** temple is located in a very prosperous area of western Shanghai. It was built in 1882 to accommodate 2 Jade Buddha statues brought here from Burma. The temple is still used and a lot of monks stay here. There are two Buddha statues—one sitting and one reclining—the former showing Buddha in a moment of meditation and the other showing the powerful mood of 'shakya muni' when he renounced the world. A recumbent Buddha brought from Singapore subsequently is also located here. Many ancient carvings and Buddhist sculptures are also seen here.

**h.** We also visited **a Jade factory** here which gave us the chance to select a few jade pieces as memoirs though the prices, again bargainable, were quite high by Indian standards. The word 'jade' has a Spanish origin where it is reputed for efficiency in curing diseases of loin and kidneys. Jade, infact is an ornamental silicate stone with the hardness of quartz in blue, lavender, emerald, green and pink colours, which can be beautifully carved and delicately shaped to make axes, knives, weapons and works of art like statues and ornaments. The most priced jade is emerald green jadeite. Sale of various jade/

pearl items to foreign tourists was found to be a major objective of such arranged visits to factories.

The **following experiences** could be mentioned to give a better account of Shanghai and adjoining areas:

(a) My wife was interested in purchasing a green jade statue from the above factory as a momento. When we enquired about the price of an item we liked, it was quoted as 1000 Yuan (about Rs. 7500). We found it to be very high and decided to try elsewhere. Seeing that she was really interested in it, even after we left the counter, the sales manager of the section, kept track of our movements and came to us on a couple of times to assess at what price we would take it. As we had decided not to take it for a price beyond 250 Yuan, we kept on telling her that we could not afford it. When we were leaving the place, she asked for our last price and we mentioned the amount. After trying to raise it by another 50 Yuan, to our surprise, she offered it at our price on the plea that she wanted to satisfy the need of a genuine customer. In fact, it was found later that prices in such shops are flexible above a lowest price fixed and for sales above it, there was a profit sharing arrangement. We had perhaps offered a price slightly above the lowest fixed for it.

(b) Shanghai is China's Mumbai, may be 10 to 15 years ahead in time. The skyscrapers remind us of Brooklyn. It is a mixture of modern and traditional Chinese life which is fast disappearing from the city. The Maglev/ Levitation train running at about 430 km per hour to take people from the city to the airport is a major attraction. Many of us traveled by it before leaving for Delhi.

(c) At the Jade Buddha temple, one interesting item was the presence of a large number of different varieties of very old, but well-kept bonsai plants. From their sizes and thickness of their stems, we could see that some of them were perhaps 75 to 100 years old. Their complicated shapes and quality of maintenance were worth noting.

## B—OTHER MARVELS

As the duration of our organized tour was rather limited especially for a country three times the size of India, we could visit only a few prominent places primarily in the four major tourist centres of Beijing, Shanghai, Xian and Guilin. There are a number of other places and sights worth seeing for those who want to know more about the country and its tourist attractions. Some basic facts about these are given below.

### i. Beijing and adjoining areas

**a. Behai Park.** Beihai literally means Northern Sea. The Park, initially built in the 10th century, is an imperial garden to the northwest of the Forbidden City in Beijing. It was built to imitate renowned scenic spots and architecture from various regions of China like the Taihu Lake, pavilions and canals in Hang Zhou and Yang Zhou and garden structures in Suzhou. Many emperors believed that the positions of hills and water conditions had different effects on their longevity. There are stories of three image mountains whose gods had a herbal medicine which could help attain immortality. Many emperors sought this and tried to imitate the conditions given in the legend. Behai Park is one such imitation where an emperor tried to create a garden with three hills and a pool layout. Half of Behai garden is a lake with a Jade Flowery Islet in the middle topped by an imposing white Dagoda Pagoda, the land mark of the park. The park has four scenic areas which are the Eastern shore, the Northern shore, a botanical garden and a circular city near the north gate. In front of the Dagoda Pagoda, on a slope on the Qionghua islet is a white Taoist temple and a number of other beautiful buildings. The Eastern shore area has many important gardens. Hao Pu Crek garden is one such garden made in 1757 by Emperor Qianlong to relax and to feel as 'free as a fish in water'. On the northern shore area, the

Quintet Heart studio is an independent garden with many pavilions, natural and artificial hills, palaces and corridors. To the North-West of the park is the well-known 9 'Dragon Screen' built in 1757 with numerous dragons on both sides. It is 27 meters long, 6.65 meters high and 1.42 meters thick. It depicts numerous dragons, big and small, in different colours coiling in different postures giving the illusion of 635 dragons. To the south-west is the Five Dragon pavilion built in 1602, half of which is over water. Many carvings and paintings present here attract royal visitors.

At the south-west corner, is the circular city with a circumference of 276 meters and height of 4.6 meters. It has many pavilions, hills, towers, and the Chengguang Hall. The Hall has a white jade Buddha statue brought from Burma. In front of the hall is a grand urn of dark jade used by emperor Kublai Khan for storing wine. Exhibitions of water lilies, water plants, paintings, etc. are held here.

**b. Temple of Heaven** is a complex of buildings in eastern Beijing where emperors of the Ming and Qing dynasties worshipped Heaven for good harvest. It was really the altar to worship Heaven. It is considered a Taoist temple though Heaven Worship pre-dates Taoism. The temple was constructed between 1406 and 1420 during the reign of Yougle emperor who also constructed the Forbidden City. The temple construction had a great influence on the architects of the Far East for many centuries. It was recently renovated, as a popular place for exercising.

As emperor was regarded a son of Heaven administering the earth on behalf of Heaven with heavenly authority, prayer by the emperor to Heaven was considered a mark of respect to a higher authority. Twice a year, emperors, wearing operational robes, visited the temple with their entire retinue in a procession. No ordinary person was to see the ceremony or the procession. The high part of the ceremony on winter solstice was performed by the emperor on the earthly mount.

Earth was represented by a square and Heaven by a circle. Several features of the complex show the connection between

Earth and Heaven. The whole procession had a taller semi-circular northern end and a rectangular southern end. Both altars were round and stood within squares. No. 9 was used to represent the emperor and is evident in the design of the mound altar. Administration buildings had dark blue tiles representing authority.

c. **Hutongs** are dwelling places of native Beijing residents. Older hutongs give a glimpse of earlier life in the city. Each hutong is in turn connected to another. They were arranged as per social classes. At the centre was the Forbidden City where the emperor and his closest circles lived. Then came the Inner and Outer cities. Aristocrats lived in the eastern and western wings of the imperial palace. The residences of high ranking officials and wealthy merchants had beautiful beams, roofs, and landscaped gardens. Such hutongs had spacious houses and walled gardens. In the north and south were commoners, merchants, artisans and labourers lined. Most of them had their main buildings and gates facing south for better lighting and the hutongs ran from north to south. Almost all the main buildings in a hutong were quadrangles—a building complex formed by four houses around a quadrangular courtyard. The quadrangles varied in size and design according to the social status of the residents.

The names of hutongs were often based on places, plants, directions, idioms, positive attributes, markets and business, names of people, etc. The largest administrative division in ancient Beijing was a 'fang' equivalent to current day precinct. Each fang was divided into communities or neighborhoods each of which had several hutongs. Hutong was the lowest administrative unit under the emperors. During the Ming dynasty, there were 36 fangs in Beijing. As the population increased and modern administration came in, other administrative approaches have taken over.

d. **Temple of Confucius** is a temple devoted to the memory of Confucius and to the sages and philosophers of Confucianism. It is located on Guozijian Street inside Anding

A Hutong in Beijing[14].

Front view of a street in a hutong, Beijing.*

Gate and was the place where people paid homage to Confucius during the Yuan Dynasty (1271–1368), Ming Dynasty (1368–1644) and Qing Dynasty (1644–1911). It was built in 1302. Now, the temple houses the Beijing Capital Museum.

The temple consists of four courtyards. The main structures include Xianshi Gate (Gate of the First Teacher), Dacheng Gate (Gate of Great Accomplishment), Dacheng Hall (Hall of Great Accomplishment) and Chongshengci (Worship Hall).

**e. The Yonghe Lamasery** is the largest and best-known lamasery in Beijing. Its principal components are three exquisite memorial archways and five major halls, all of which stand on a north-south axis. It was originally built by order of Emperor Kangxi in 1694 to serve as a residence for his son and successor to the Chinese throne-Yinzhen. When Yinzhen became Emperor Yongzheng after his father's death, a section of the residential grounds was maintained as a palace to be used by the emperor during short visits, while the other half was turned over to the Lamaists to serve as a place for the recitation of scriptures. Later, the palace section was razed by fire and in 1725 the section of the compound occupied by the Lamas was given the name Yonghe (Harmony and Peace) Lamasery.

The buildings are on a central axis rising progressively from south to north and a visitor entering in the south can see roof ridges rising impressively one above the next. The place is a treasury of Buddhist art. Calligraphy of Qing emperors in scrolls, bronze lions and incense burners, sculptured images of gods, demons and Buddhas, and a lot of Tibetan style murals are the other specialties.

**f. The Western Qing Tombs** are situated in Yixian County, Baoding City,120 km west of Beijing (and hence the name Western Qing Tombs). The reason for the laying out of two dynastic tomb sites was that the emperor Qianlong made a law according to which fathers and sons could not be buried in the same grave-yard. There were altogether 10 emperors in the Qing Dynasty (1644–1911) after they conquered central China in 1644. Buried in the fourteen tombs are four emperors and 72 members of the family including wives, concubines, sons and daughters.It is smaller than the Eastern Qing Tombs. The fourteen mausoleums and the temple buildings reflect the strict rules of the feudal hierarchy. The tombs of the emperors and empresses are larger than those of the concubines and princesses; the former have red roofs and the latter have green roofs. Baoding was the capital of Zhili Province (an ancient name for Hebei. Province) from 1730 to 1911. The Governor's Office here served as the governmental office of Hebei Province. Zhili Province was the only province that circled the capital, so each Qing Dynasty emperor thought highly of the governors in Baoding. Often the emperor would choose his favorite official to be the governor.

**g. The Eastern Qing Tombs** is a sacred burial ground near Beijing devoted to the emperors, empresses and imperial concubines of the Qing Dynasty (1644–1911), located along Changrui Mountain, Hebei Province. Along the southern side of Changrui Mountain are the tombs of five emperors, four empresses, five imperial concubines, and one princess arrayed based on the traditional concept of placing the most senior and most distinguished in the center. The centre of Eastern Qing Tombs is Xiaoling, the tomb of Emperor Shunzhi, the first Qing emperor to rule China and the first to be buried there in 1663. Xiaoling is aligned with the axis of the main apex of Changrui Mountain showing that the person buried there is the most exalted of the group. Other tombs lie on both sides of Xiaoling from east to west according to the position in the family hierarchy. Sacred ways connect the tombs of the women with those of their husbands, and the other emperors connect with Xiaoling. Xiaoling is the focal point of the entire structure and was the first sepulcher constructed for the Qing Dynasty. An example of the most exquisite architecture of the Eastern Qing Tombs is Dingdong ling, the tomb of Empress Dowager Cixi who handled affairs of state for more than 45 years without ascending the throne.

**h. Ancient observatory, Beijing.** This is a pretelescopic observatory and the tools originally used in the observatory were built in 1442 during the Ming Dynasty period. One of the oldest observatories in the world, in covers an area of 10,000 square meters. It is a museum of nature science displaying ancient Chinese astronomical equipments. The observatory itself is located on the rooftop of what is now an astronomy museum. Eight magnificent equipments made of bronze stand high on the black brick platform. They are celestial body equipments, equator theodolite, ecliptic theodolite, horizon longitude equipment, quadrant equipment, Simple Phenomena equipment, horizon theodolite and Jihenfuchen equipment made during the Qing Dynasty period.

The Observatory has 500 years successive astronomical observation history from the Zhen tong period in Ming Dynasty to the year 1929.

**i. The Niujie Mosque** is the biggest and oldest mosque in Beijing. It was built in 996 and was reconstructed and enlarged under the Qing Emperor Kangxi (1622–1722). The Mosque is located in Beijing's Xuanwu District, the spiritual centre for the 10,000 Muslims living in the vicinity. It is a mixture of Islamic and Chinese cultures. Its exterior architecture is of traditional Chinese style. The interior decorations are mostly of Islamic style. The mosque, built out of timber, is home to some important cultural relics and tablets such as the upright tablet of an emperor's decree proclaimed in 1694 during the Qing Dynasty. According to this decree, the local Muslim community was forbidden from constructing the mosque in a style other than traditional Chinese architecture with the exception that Arabic calligraphy was allowed.

The mosque has undergone three renovations since the founding of the People's Republic of China in 1949. The Beijing Municipal Government has started rebuilding the residential area. The work on the 35.9-hectare area around Niujie will involve moving 7,500 families, 58 percent of whom are Muslims. The project will turn Niujie into a Muslim-style commercial street. The area will be home to multi-storey buildings, schools, kindergartens and public facilities.

**j. Liulichang Street of Chinese culture.** Curios, calligraphy, painting and other artworks of China are the attractions of Liulichang Street located south of the Peace Gate of Xuanwu District, Beijing. During the period of the Yuan Dynasty (1271–1368) and Ming Dynasty (1368–1644), a colored glaze factory (Liuli Chang in Chinese) was in production here. Glazed tiles for palaces, temples and residences of officials were made here. During the Qing Dynasty (1644–1911), many businessmen and vendors began to sell curios and old books. Over the years, the factory has gradually been replaced by a market for calligraphy, painting, copybook, artifacts and the four treasures of study, i.e. writing brush, ink stick, ink slab and paper.

The most famous shop here is the Rongbaozhai Bookshop, built in the early years of Qing Dynasty. It now sells authentic calligraphy and paintings of both ancient and modern artists of China. It is also well-known for an expert copying technique which cannot be easily distinguished from the original. In China Bookshop, block-printed editions and hand-copied books of the ancient times are available.Guanfu Classic Art Museum opened in 1997, displays about 50 porcelains from the late Ming Dynasty as well as old-fashioned furniture, carpets, costumes and other articles of the Ming and Qing Dynasties. The street has often been selected as the platform for the performance of the Beijing Opera.

**k. Happy Valley** is an amusement park located in the south-east corner of Sifang Bridge in Chaoyang District, Beijing. It is a Disneyland in Mainland China, completed and opened to the public in July, 2006. With six theme zones and 120 attractions, there are exciting performance like 'Maya disaster', challenging entertainment games like 'Snow Phoenix', 'Energy Collector' and also 'Ant kingdom'. These offer a rare opportunity to experience the charm of various civilizations regardless of the distance of space and time.

As the core of the park, Atlantis recreates pictures of the lost empire. We can feel the mysterious culture of the distant past by the flying tracks, transparent balls, steel framework and huge mountains. There are several interesting outdoor play areas, such as Crystal Wing, Water Play, and Magic Theater. Crystal Wing is the only flying roller coaster in Asia. The Aegean Sea is made up of three parts: a deserted town destroyed by volcano, a new gulf, and cultural relics.

**l. Prince Gong's mansion in Beijing** is the largest and the best preserved Qing Dynasty (1644–1911) princely mansion. It is located at Qianhai Xijie to the north of Shichahai. It is a fine example of ancient Chinese architecture. The mansion was constructed around the year 1777 as the private residence of a member of the imperial guard who was promoted to positions normally occupied by the most experienced officials by the Emperor. He gradually acquired great wealth by corrupt means. The aging Qinglong did nothing to curb his corruption. His successor, Emperor Jiaqing (1796–1820), had him executed and his property was confiscated. The mansion was later transferred to Prince Gong and thus it acquired its current name.

**m. Great Bell Temple.** The Bell complex was one of the three projects Emperor Yongle started in 1403 after re-establishing Beijing as the capital. Initially called 'Juesheng si', it was often chosen by emperors to pray for rain and for blessings for people. In the temple complex, there are many buildings like the Mountain gate, Bell and Drum tower, 16 Scripture collection pavilion, Great Bell tower, etc. The Bell and Drum tower is the main building here. It has a circular shape at the top and is square below. According to Chinese beliefs, the sky is circular and earth is square. It is also called 'King of the ancient bells' as it sounds crisp and sweet when rung lightly and deep and resounding when struck forcibly.

**n. Fragrant Hills Park.** It is a park of hills and forests covering 160 hectares located in the eastern part of the western hills, 28 km north-west of Beijing. It was built in 1186 during the Jin dynasty and later extended by Yuan and Ming dynasties. In 1745, Emperor Qianlong built new halls, pavilions, gardens, and gave it a new name of 'Garden of Tranquility and Pleasure'. A lot of relics were damaged by foreign troops in 1860 and after 1900 when foreign armies set ablaze some of the buildings.

Xianghu peak is the highest in the park. The most spectacular natural scenery is the red smoke tree leaves over the mountains. When autumn comes, fiery red leaves blanket the whole mountain. Cable cars are used today to see the beautiful scenery. There is a large Tibetan style lamasery complex here, built in 1780 as residence of the 6th Panchen Lama during his visits to Emperor Qianlong. Another point of interest is the villa used by Chairman Mao as his residence and also the hqrs.of the CCP.

**o. Olympics park and Bird's Nest Stadium.** The Olympics Park is located on the northern part of Beijing. It is 68 sq. km in area and contains stadia, gymnasiums, Convention halls, exhibitions centres, sports complexes, shopping malls and other facilities created for various and sports. Stadium began in 2004 and was completed in 2007. With 204000 sq. m grass area out of a total area of 258000 sq. m, it can accommodate 100000 people and hence can host all important competitions.

### ii. Xian and adjoining areas

**a. Banpo village.** This is an archeological site on the outskirts of eastern Xian, between the Chanhe and Bahe rivers. Here, in 1921, evidences of China's ancient (about 6000 years old) Yangshao matrilineal culture which prevailed in the middle and lower valleys of the Yellow River were excavated in Mianche County (Hainan province).It was a prosperous Neolithic matrilineal society as women were found buried with more property and children were found to move with their mothers. Evidences of men concentrating on fishing and hunting and women on collecting wild fruits were also visible. Agriculture seems to have been the dominant occupation with fishing and rearing of animals also prevalent.

**b. Forest of stone steles[14].** Steles are stone structures rectangular in shape with their height more than their width.

The Forest of Stone Stelae museum in Xi'an

Steles were kept near tombs, to demarcate boundaries and to indicate other information of interest. Some are quite tall and many contain sculptures, artistic work, inscriptions and works of art in general. The forest of steles is a huge museum of stone steles and stone sculptures in Xian. It is housed in a 11th century Confucian temple. There are two groups of steles of the Tang era. When a rebel attacked the city in 904, these were moved to the inner city.

During the Song period in 1087, a separate cell was built to display the steles. They suffered some damage during the Ming days and also in 1556 in the Shaanxi earth quake. There are 3000 steles, most of Tang vintage.

c. **Afang palace** is one of the most famous palaces, built in 212 B.C. and rebuilt in 1995 on the ruins. It has the Front wall, Orchid Pond palace, palace halls of six states, Long corridor, Pengshi gate, Shangtian Terrace, Presenting sacrifices to the earth Terrace, and other magnificent buildings. There is a mosque, nearly 1250 years old, built in the Tang Period with 6000 sq. m of prayer space where 1000 people can pray together.

d. **Lishan Forest Park** is an ancient attraction. It was imperial garden of Zhou, Qin, Han, Tang and later days. It has many places of interest like Bacon tower, Old mother hall and Sunset glow pavilion. Spring dawn garden at Qujiang with an area of 40000 sq. m, and 17000 trees and flowering plants is east of the Wild Goose pagoda. Scenic spots are Dancing Horse with a ring in its mouth, stone Buddha, stone lanterns, white stone beach, etc.

### iii. Guilin and adjoining areas

The following places in and around Guilin are also frequented by tourists. Time permitting, they should also be seen.

**a. Cave of returned Pearls.** This is at the foot of a mountain called 'Mountain of gentle waves'. Legend goes that it was the lair of a dragon who owned a glowing string of pearls. A fisherman who came across these took them away, but later, pricked by conscience, returned these to the rightful owner. In the cave, touch stones on which swordsmen tested their weapons and other inscriptions can be seen.

**b. South creek Hill.** Two main points of interest here are a whirl pool hill and Zenpiyuan, where traces of a stone age settlement were found in 1965. The former is 300 meters east of the 'mountain of unique beauty' where an iron bell of 2.5 tonnes and a giant pot for 1000 men (from the Dingyue si temple of Diecaishan) from the Qing era can be seen. The latter, 10 km south of the foot of the Mt. of Dushan, is a cave 'zenpiyuan' where stone and bone tools,pottery,traces of fire, graves, etc. of the stone age can be seen.

### iv. Shanghai and adjoining areas

The following places in and around Shanghai are also worth seeing:

**a. The former residence of Sun Yat Sen,** a two storied European style building, is located at no. 7, Xian Shan Road. His wife Mrs. Soong Ching Ling and he had stayed here between 1918 and 1925. The building was donated by the

Chinese in Canada in support of the revolution. It was here that Sun Yat Sen. accomplished his doctrines of Sun Wen, China's development, three principles of people viz., nationalism, democracy and people's development. The cardinal principles of alliance with Russia, cooperation with the communists, and assistance to people's and workers movements were also finalized here.

**b. Yuyuan garden** was made in 1577 by a government officer for his parents. It was rebuilt after it suffered damages during the opium war. Rockeries, ponds, cloisters, etc. are the main attractions. It has 6 scenic areas viz. Sansui hall, Wanhua chamber, Dean Churn hall, Hoeing hall, Yuhua hall and an inner garden. Its 'great rockery' is fairly big.

**c. Tomb of Lu Xun.** Lu Xun was the greatest Chinese writer of the 20th century. He wrote with the pen name 'Zhou Shuren' and is considered to be the founder of the modern Chinese literature. As a short story writer, critic, editor, translator, essayist and poet, he wrote both in classical and vernacular styles.

**d.** There are **other worth seeing places** like Dianshan Hu Lake, Bridge of Gen. Well Bing and Pagoda for Pearls/Learning Pagoda. Dianshan Hu Lake extends to 50 km to the north of Shanghai and has an area of 60 sq. km. The main attractions here are a few gardens around it, a number of pagodas close by, 'Freedom bridge' built in 1571 as the longest stone bridge, etc. Bridge of Gen. Well Bing, built in 1265 as a single arch brick bridge, is located 54 km off Shanghai. It is a magnificent example of construction of the Song era. Pagoda for Pearls/Learning Pagoda is on the Tian Shan mountain and near the former residences of Sun Yat Sen and Lu Xun, Nanjing Lu, Bund, etc. There are also a few pagodas, parks, a Confucian temple, etc. near by.

### v. Some Prominent Attractions

In addition to the above places in and around Beijing, Xian, Guilin and Shanghai, there are a large number of places of historical, cultural and tourist interest in different parts of China. The most prominent among them are:

## 1. Potala Palace

Located in Lhasa, capital city of Tibet, an Autonomous region of China, it was the chief residence of Dalai Lama till the present one fled to India in 1959. Named after "Amalokiteswara", it is now a museum measuring 400 meters East to West and 350 meters North to South. It has slopping stone walls 3 meters thick at the top and 5 meters at the bottom. Copper had been poured at the base to guard against earth quakes. It has in 13 stories of buildings over 1000 rooms, 10000 shrines and 200,000 statues. It is located on the top of the "Red hill" and is 117 meters high. Three main hills of Lhasa represent three protectors of Tibet. These are "Chokpori"on the south representing "vajrapani", "pong man" representing "manjushi", and "morpori" representing "Amalokiteswara". It was a meditation retreat hall till A.D. 637 when a palace was built to meet the bride procession of Wen Cheng of Song dynasty. Potala was started in 1645 after an advisor told the 5th Dalai Lama that it was good to be a seat of the Government. It was completed in 1694 and was being used as a winter palace. A Red palace was added between 1690 and 1694. It got the present name from a hill in Cape Comorin rocky point said to be the God of mercy called "Amalokiteswara"worshipped as "Chenrezi" by Tibetans. Tibetans call it the 'Peak'. It suffered some damage in 1959, but escaped damage during the Cultural Revolution because of the intervention of Chou-en-lai. However, a lot of scriptures and other religious documents were damaged. The palace on the Red Hill is a 117 m high 13–storeyed building. It has mostly the Red and White Palaces. The political affairs are being handled from the White Palace.

## 2. Peking Man

'Peking man' refers to the man whose bones and other relics were found nears a village (Zhoukondian) 50 km south of Beijing in sedimentary strata estimated be 500000 years old. It is the most comprehensively and systematically studied site of 'Homo Erectus'. It also gave data about human

a. Peking man site at Zhoukoudian, near Beijing

b. Life of Peking man[15]

c. He knew use of fire

motivation and paleo-environment of human erectus than contemporary European and African sites.

In 1918, Johann Gunnar Anderson, a Swedish Geologist with the Chinese Government, was told about some fossils near a hill called "chicken bone hill". Detailed survey and investigation led by him resulted in the discovery of 2 human like teeth. In 1926, he announced discovery of 2 teeth of early man. An American Geologist A. William Graban, called it the "Peking Man". Systematic excavation in the area led to the discovery in 1928 of two lower jaws. In 1929, in red sandy clay, an almost skull cap was found. It led to more attention and coverage. Later, a skull cap was discovered in 1930 and in 1936, 3 more on a comprehensive search. Some skulls were lost during the war, but subsequently a female skull too was found.

Peking man was, however, a full man able to develop entire behaviour, develop culture, control fire, hunt big animals, etc. It was after evolution from ape to man. He made tools with quartz, flint, sand stones, etc. As time passed, the size of the tools got reduced and quality of materials used and tools improved.

### 3. Mogao Gaulois

Mogao caves are about 25 km of the Dun hang city at the foot of the Mingsha Mountain in a length of 1680 m South to North. It has 700 caves and in 492 caves alone there are 45000 murals and 2000 painted sculptures. There are 5 grottoes with wooden structures. There are 50000 scriptures and historical documents, textiles and other similar items. The caves contain ancient gallery of Buddhist art, mural paintings, and stucco pictures erected in situ over 1000 years. One cave contained a sealed library whose contents reflect the contacts with every part of Central Asia and the Chinese empire. It was originally a garrison centre of 111 B.C. Successive waves of invasions after the collapse of the Han Empire created upheavals. From Han days to Yuan days, the Silk Route was active. Dunhuang was an important place on the route which split here. The route to Mediterranean and Roman markets passed by it. Buddhist monks from China and Korea traveling in search of images and scriptures and Ambassadors from the West coming

Mogao Cave Paintings[16]

to China passed by this place. After Tangs, trade was curtailed and the place was left in isolation. With the decline of the Chinese power in the 19th cent., it lost its importance.

It is a consummate repository of Buddhist art. Many pavilions, towers, temples, pagodas, palaces, bridges, etc. are shown in murals providing plenty of materials for study of Chinese art and literature. Many paintings show musical performances, dancing and acrobatics. The cave for preserving scriptures discovered by a Taoist monk in A.D. 1900 contains 5000 sutras and documents/paintings from 4th to 11th centuries. It is thus one of China's most significant archeological findings.

Ruins of an old city on the Silk route[17].

**4. Yellow Mountains**

These are a group of peaks located in the southern part of Anhui Province extending across 4 counties of Shexian, Yixian, Taiping and Xining. It is said that a visit to these places results in special healing and brings luck. These Mountains came up because of the movement of earth's crust over a million years ago. As a result of erosion and glaciation, it is believed to have reached today's shape. It provides a scenic spot with wonderful sights across 154 sq. km. In spring, blooming flowers decorate the slopes in a riot of colours and fill the

A hub[18] on the Silk Route.

valleys with fragrance. In cloudy weather, the pinnacles are covered in mist. In summer, the peaks can be seen rising one above the other. In autumn, we see a range of red colours. In winter, frost, ice, silver boroughs and rocks are every where.

Plants of the glacial era–firs, ginkgoes, torreyas, nanmus, camphor woods, precious Mugua trees, etc.—are visible in plenty. It has a rich store of medical herbs too. It is also a natural habitat for a wide variety of fauna-monkeys, goats, deer-and rare birds like octave tone bird and oriole. Attractive love birds are exported from here.

**5. West Lake**

It was compared by a poet of the Song dynasty to Xizi, the most beautiful woman in ancient China. It is a traditional Chinese garden on a grand scale with three sides surrounded by hills. It was a favourite imperial retreat for centuries, with strangely shaped peaks, serene forests, springs, dense foliage and plenty of flowers in spring time. Sculptural and architectural features add to the exhilarating environment.

**6. The Grand Canal, Beijing**

Hang Zhou Grand Canal is the largest artificial river in the world. It passes through Beijing, Tianjin, Hebei, Shandong, Jiansu and Zhejiang provinces. Its oldest parts date back to 5th cent. B.C. Its various sections were combined into one in Sui dynasty (A.D. 581–681). It is 1770 km long with its greatest height in the Mountains of Shandong. It was used to flood troops downside during war times. Ship traffic was possible and this had facilitated growth of markets in urban centers.

West Lake, Hang Zhou, Zhejiang[19].

### vi. Other attractions

In this section, places and sites linking them to rivers, hills and mountains are first explained. First, the Yangtze River Basin is covered. This is followed by other regions. Holy Mountains' related to Taoism and Buddhism are briefly mentioned. It is followed by a fairly elaborate coverage of the 'Shangri-La Region' dividing it into groups of places based on their locations in Kamba region, Tibet, etc. This is followed by other mountainous regions. Later, other attractions including a few of international importance are gone into.

#### a. Yangtze River basin cities

Yangtze Basin is a golden tourist area with developed economies, good transport, rivers and lakes, long history, cultural sites, golden art, etc. It combines metropolitan flavors and ancient town styles. Taihu lake areas are quite charming and attractive with good tourist facilities. It is said the "flowers in the river bed are redder than fire and the river water in spring is as green as emerald." The "stone city" of Nanjing with Qinghai river passing though, historical and cultural city of Yang Zhou, Chan Zhou famous as city of Dinosaur,Wuxi famous as a pearl along Taihu lake, Suzhou and Hang Zhou famous as 'paradises on earth', ancient towns of Tongli, Zhouhuang, Luzhi, Xitiang, Nanxun (close to Huangzhou) with streets built along the river and houses with pink walls and grey tiles, small bridges over rivers, 100 year old styles and beautiful landscape, are the highlights of the area known as 'land of fish and silk'.

The tourist and other attractions of the region are mentioned below linking them to the cities close to them.

**Nanjing.** Nanjing, capital of Jianxi province, with a population of 5.62 millions, is on the lower reaches of Yangtze River. Quinhuai River, an important branch of the Yangtze River on the lower reaches, is like a moat of the city. It was the capital of China for 6 dynasties.

The most important attractions are the Xiaoling museum of Zhu Yuanzhang (founder of the Ming dynasty), city wall of the Ming dynasty, Mausoleum of SunYat-Sen, Sun Yat Sen useum, Imperial examination centre of A.D. 1146, and Nanjing bridge over Yangtze River with 6772 m for rails and 4589 m for road and double arches on northern and southern banks.

**Yanghzou.** The main scenic areas here are Shugang-slender West lake scenic area with 24 scenic spots, a five pavilion bridge and a white pagoda. The Tianning temple in which emperor Qianling stayed during inspection tours, Heyuan garden (a typical Qing garden), Museum of the site of the Tang city where emperor Yangdi of the Sui dynasty stayed during tours, Whenchan pavilion, a symbol of Yanghzou, memorial hall of the eight celebrities of Yang Zhou (depicting local customs of the nineteenth century), etc. are some of the other attractions.

**Zhenjiang.** One of the main tourist attractions here is Nan Shan mountains with a lot of cultural relics and important points in the Chinese history of literature, fine arts, religion, archeology and gardens. Ian Shan Buddhist temple (1600 years old) depicts the architectural style of temples in northern China and style of gardens in southern China. Some of the other attractions are statue of Confucius, ancient Ganhu Buddhist temple of the Three Kingdoms days, Jinshan hill (a famous scenic spot with a temple of the Eastern Jin dynasty), Jioshan hill in the middle of the Yangtze river, Mao Shan hill (famous as a natural resort and a sacred land of Taoism with beautiful sceneries, towering species of plum and cypress tress, bamboo forests and clean springs), etc.

**Chan Zhou,** also known as "the Dinosaur city", is located between Shanghai and Nanjing.Some of the main attractions here are Tianning Buddhist temple built in Tang dynasty (A.D. 627–655) considered the first temple in S.E. China, Yangcheng city with 3 rivers passing through and China Dinosaur park.

**Conxi** on the bank of Taihu Lake, 128 km from Shanghai and south of Yangtze River, has a history of 3000 years. Some of the main attractions here are the Taihu lake (the largest fresh water lake in China), Yuantosezhu and Liyuan Parks, Jichang garden, Grand Canal, Ling Shan scenic area (with a history of 900 years and a Buddhist temple with a great statue of Buddha, Huishan clay figurines, Yixing pottery and pearls of Taihu Lake), former residence of Xu Xialu, a traveler and geographer of 17th centuary (displaying many historical relics), Shan Juan caves and Wuxi CCTV and film city scenic areas.

**Suzhou** is a cultural city of 5.85 million people close to Taihu Lake. It has a history of 2500 years. It is located in the richest area in Yangtze delta. Its streets and downtown are of Song dynasty style. The other interesting places are Distance Fragrance Hill, Fragrance Islet, Lotus viewing pavilion and Pipa Garden. Pan Gate Scenic Area has a long history and is the only intact water–land gate in Suzhou with 2 water passages, 3 land passages and an outside gate. Pan gate,

Wumen bridge gate and auspicious Light pagoda provide a good view of the surrounding areas. Garden to Linger built in A.D. 1522–66 by the Ming dynasty is one of the famous gardens in China with a dozen court-yards, ponds, and woods in the styles of southern areas of Yangtze River. Pavilion of surging waves, built in A.D. 1041–48 during the northern song dynasty, is one of the oldest gardens in Suzhou.It is an open garden surrounded by streams, ancient trees, pavilions, platforms, etc. Tiger Hill, built in Spring and Autumn period 2500 years ago, is the oldest among the intact city gardens in China.

**Huangzhou,** one of the country's seven major capitals, is located on the southern part of Yangtze River delta at the southern end of Grand Canal bordering Shanghai in the north and Ningbou in the east. It is famous for its rice and fish. The main attractions include: (1) West Lake scenic area with the city on one side and mountains on the other sides. There are some famous temples, pagodas, museums of silk, tea and Chinese medicines. The city attracts people with different tastes in different seasons. (2) Bai cause way, built 1000 years ago in Tang dynasty, is famous for its spring views when its cause way is lined by green willow trees, red peach flowers, etc.and looks like a colourful band. Broken bridge is located at the eastern end of the Causeway. (3) Huqingyutang, traditional Chinese medical facility museum, built in 1874 based on late Qing style, houses 1000 samples of traditional Chinese medicines and details of their origin, development of pharmaceuticals, tools for making them and exchange of Chinese and foreign medicines. Three pools mirroring the moon has 3 stone pagodas built over 800 years ago as their theme. (4) Lingyin temple was built in 326 by an Indian monk who called it 'spirit's retreat'. It is one of the 10 most famous Buddhist temples in China and houses a gilded 24 m high statue of 'Sakya Muni' in the seated form. It is also the largest wooden statue in China. (5) Yaolin fairy land is a karst cave in Tonglu county with strangely shaped stalactites and stalagmites everywhere.

**Jiaxing** is famous for beautiful landscape, colourful local customs and rich mineral resources. South lake on the southern part of Jiaxing has charming landscape under mists.

**Xitang** town is a waterside town with houses reflected in water. It is famous for numerous bridges, lanes and corridors.

**Wuzhu** Town on the northern part of Zhejiang Province has many narrow rivers behind which people built their houses with covered corridors protruding into the rivers. It has the pure and natural landscape and beauty of a waterside town.

**Taihu Lake** has a history of 2300 years and is close to neighbouring Mogan Mountain, a summer resort. Feiying pagoda here is the only pagoda inside a pagoda. Iron Buddhist temple and Bamboo garden are famous scenic spots here. Nanxun town built 745 years ago is famous for its gardens. Xiaolian villa is a part of the garden built by a rich man in south west part of the town in late Qing period with unique architectural style.

**Shaoxing** in the eastern part of Zhejiang Province borders China Sea. It is famous for its landscape and many talented people. Main scenic spots are tomb of Yu the great, Lu Xun Memorial hall, and orchid pavilion. The orchid pavilion was a sacred place of poets and calligraphic scholars.

### b. Mountains, Hills and related attractions

For the sake of convenience, these are analyzed here under the categories of (1) sacred mountains, (2) those of Shangri-La region, and (3) interesting places in other cities.

#### *1. Sacred mountains*

Sacred mountains of China are the five great mountains considered sacred by Taoists and four by Buddhists. The five Sacred mountains of Taoism arranged according to the five (including the centre) cardinal directions are (1) for the East,

Tai Shan, Shandong (1545 meters), (2) for the west, Hua Shan/Splendid Mountain in Shanxi Province (1997 meters), (3) for the South, Heng Shan/Balancing Mountain in Hunan (1290 meters), (4) for the north, Heng Shan/Permanent Mountain in Shanxi Province and (5) for the Centre, Song Shan/Lofty mountain in Henan(1494 meters). They are also called East, West, North, South and Centre Great mountains. They are supposed to have originated from the head and limbs of Pangu, the first being and ancestor of the world. Tai Shan is associated with rising sun and signifies birth and renewal and is most sacred supposedly originating from the head of Pangu.

The Buddhist sacred mountains are (1) Wutai/Fine Terrace in Shanxi province (3058 Meters), (2) Emei Shan/ Delicate Eyebrow Mountain in Sichuan Province (3099 meters), (3) Jinhua Shan/Nine Glories Mountain in Anhui Province (1341 Meters), and (4) Putuo Shan/Potato Mountain in Zhejiang Province (284 meters). The holy mountains are supposedly supporting heaven to remain above. Sacred people who went to mountains are believed to have been buried there after living for 400 to 800 years on exotic herbs and elixirs. They are believed to be abode of magical spirits and powerful deities. In general, it maybe said that the most famous mountains are Taishan, Huashan, Song, Hengshan scenic spot (Hunan) and Hengshan (Shanxi).

### 2. Sights in 'Shangri-La Region'

Shaunbhala, a mysterious kingdom described in the scriptures of Taoism-Buddhism, is 'Shangrila'. It comprises of mountainous and highlands in Sichuan, Yunnan and Tibet regions. It is also a place of tranquil away from the turmoils of the world. Holy snow-capped mountains, precipitous glaciers, pure lakes, deep gorges, dense forests, blue skies, clear air, fertile grass lands, unique ethnic customs, sacred religions, simple and honest people, etc. are its basic features.

**a. Kangding** is the "door of Shangrila"and also the political and cultural centre of Kamba region. It has a large number of tourist attractions. The main ones are:

1. Moge Co is the largest alpine lake in the north-west Sichuan. Seven colour lakes has colours changing with climate and sunshine. Azaea gorge has 800 m long overlapping water fall starting from the end of the gorge to Moge Co.
2. Daocheng is in the south-western edge of Sichuan and 96% of people are Tibetans. It was the model Shangri-La in the novel "Lost Horizon".
3. Yading scenic area 128 km from Daocheng has three snow-capped mountains. Litang and Batang counties are important entrance and exit points to Tibet and are the main tourist attractions in the Kamba region.
4. Genian scenic zone has 8 mountains and its main peak (6204 m) is a renowned holy mountain. Presence of a large number of hot springs gave it the name "land of geothermal springs". Genian holy mountain has snow all around the year.
5. The nearby Copu scenic zone in Batang country has primitive forests, lakes, hot springs and Buddhist monasteries in an integrated way. Zagen Gyabo Sacred Mountain stands out prominently. It has many precipices of grotesque shapes and weird rocks.Copu lake is surrounded by primitive forests and grassy slopes. Many rare birds, animals and fishes are also seen here.
6. Luding is the east gate of Gorze.In the Qing dynasty (1644–1911), Emperor Kangxi in A.D. 1706 got the Luding Cable Bridge constructed to improve the communication between Sichuan and Tibet. Luding is known for the Couch Ditch Glazier and Forest Park which has glaziers at a low elevation, high temperature hot springs and primitive forests.
7. Jiulong is a transfer station on the western Sichuan ring route linking Liangshan prefecture, Yunnan Province and Daofu in the north. Its main attractions are Wuxu Lake, Wahui mountain, Ugly chicken, Yelong river valley, etc.

8. Liangshan in south-west of Sichuan area has Yi people living in compact communities. It has 10 scenic zones and 63 scenic spots including Qionghai Lake, Lishan Mountain and Luoji Mountain. The area is rich in mineral resources and is called China's "Ural". It is also called China's "kingdom of plants" because of varied natural and ecological types present here.
9. Luoji mountain has its main peak in the shape of a beautiful flying conch or a beautiful lady's hair coil and hence the name Luoji (conch and hair oil). Qalangdo'gye snow-capped mountain, always covered by snow, includes beautiful Baishui river, mysterious celestial water, serene Qagmi river, deep karst caves, etc.
10. Lugu lake, known as "pearl on the plateau", has its banks full of turns and twists. North of the lake is the Gemu mountain, personified god of the Masuo people, a branch of Naxi ethnic group. They adhere to matriarchal marriage and "walking marriage" with woman as head of the family. Yihai lake, also called fish lake (supin by local people), is like a shoe shaped gold in-got large in the south and small in the north and is home to a large number of ducks.
11. Panzhihua was an important communication hub and a distributing centre on the "south silk road." It is a rich tourist resource integrating mountains, forests, gorges, karst caves, towering trees, peaks enveloped by mist, spendid sunrise, Buddhaa's halo, oddly shaped rocks and elegant streams.
12. Ertan National forest park has a reservoir, a vast expanse of primitive forests, and 9 sub-scenes like Buddha rock, Serene Lake on the high Dam, scenic islet and Jinghe immortal's cave. The park area is home to many ethnic groups and a wide variety of animals and plants. It is an ideal resort both in winter and summer.
13. Dragon pond karst cave at Miyi is a "marginal cave" with bright and gorgeous colours, colourful and splendid stalactites and stalagmites, 2 palaces in one cave over

hanging waterfalls and running springs. It is 1800 m long with 7 halls, 9 ponds, 4 waterfalls, and 21 scenic spots which appeal to tourists.

14. Yanwa ecological tourism zone in the NW of Panzhihua has varied climates. People live in compact communities in yellow plank houses, eat Tuotuo meat, drink Shenzhen wine and adhere to their unique customs, costumes, architecture and culinary culture. Many Mosu people also live here. Their life style, languages, costumes, habits and customs are identical with those of Mosuos elsewhere.
15. Haita Scenic zone at the head Stream of Longdong River is a basin in the shape of a boat among mountains. Running streams, peaks rising one higher than the other, serene valley, etc. are other features. An "immortal cave" full of stone bamboos, walls with striking colours, small rivers rising in zig-zagway, etc. are other sights.
16. Deqen (meaning "auspicious treasured place)" is the only Tibetan prefecture in Yunnan Province. Disparities in elevation and low attitude have given it varied climatic environments and vegetation from sub-tropical to frigid zones.
17. Haba sow capped mountain nature reserve 120 km from Jiantang town has admirable vertical distribution of alpine forests which is a paradise of rare animals. Covered by snow and ice throughout the year and four minor peaks surrounding the main peak, it has moraine lakes scattered all over.
18. Meili snow capped mountain, 849 km away from Kunming, has 13 peaks, magnificence of the snowy plateau and elegance of south China. The climate here undergoes changes with the twinkling of an eye. In summer, various wild flowers like azaleas Gyaisang compete with each other for beauty. Kangpo Shongo monastery, constructed in 1729, combines the characteristics of both Han and Tibetan architecture and enshrines the statues of the Buddhas of the past, the

present and the future, the first king of the law, second king of the law and Master Padmasalbhava and some colourful murals.

19. Mingyong glacier at the foot of the Meili snow capped mountain is a low latitude and low elevation one with ice caves, ice bridges, elegant ice sprouts and shoots in various shapes. Glacier avalanche and explosion can be expended with smashed ice spreading all over with a thundering sound.
20. Qianhu mountain area has a large number of small lakes scattered all over like stars in the sky and stable water supplies and a variety of aquatic plants and animals.
21. Bita lake natural reserve 25 km away from the seat of the Shangri-La County is surrounded by pine and oak trees. It teems with fish.
22. Samage nature reserve and Cizhong churches are two other places of interest.

**b. Other interesting sites. 'Lijiang'** (meaning beautiful Jinsha River) is located at the junction of Yunnan, Sichuan and Tibet. It was a place of significance on the ancient "Tea and Horse Road".

Dali, located in the middle part of the Yunnan plateau, used to be an important transfer point on the narrow roads of Ancient Sichuan and Ancient Tea and Horse Road. It is now a communication hub and a collecting and distributing centre of west Yunnan.

In Cangshan mountain, a natural alpine botanic garden, 19 precipitous peaks forming a natural screen with a stream flowing between 2 nearby peaks, 18 rapid streams, etc. are the important attractions. As numerous rare flowers, grasses and trees grow in Congshan Mountains, it is known as a "natural alpine botanical garden". Erhal lake at its base is crescent shaped. It includes 3 islets, 4 shoals, 5 lakes and 9 twists. The mountain and lake are the birth place of the ancestors of Bai people who stay here.

Nujiang, named after a river, in the NW Yunnan, is an important thorough fare to Tibet and Myanmar. It has magnificent scenery with 4 large mountains and 3 major rivers. The snow-covered mountains have splendid canyons between them.

The Grand Canyon here is flanked by two steep precipices. Inhabited 7000 years ago, Lisu, Dulong, Nu and Pumi people live here now in compact communities. The place has the largest Mountain reserve in China with 6000 species of high class plants of different varieties and specifications.

**c. Tibet. Lhasa** (meaning holy land), capital of Tibet, also called 'Sunshine City', is situated in the Valley of Lhasa River. It is 1300 years old and has a population of 4.1 lakhs. Qinghai-Tibet and Chengdu-Lhasa are two prominent high ways to reach the place and it takes nearly $1^1/_2$ days to reach Lhasa by train from Qinghai. There are 30 ethnic groups though Tibetans constitute 87%. Sera Monastery, built in 1419, is one of the six main monasteries of the Gelug sect in China. On the 27th of the 12th month of the Tibetan calendar, Tibetans swarm the place for the Sera Bumchen festival.Gandan (meaning peace, happiness and satisfaction) Monastery, the first one of the Gelug sect, was built in early part of the 15th cent. by Zongkaba, founder of the sect.

Jokhang Monastery located in the centre of Lhasa is of the 7th cent. It combines the architectural features of Han, Tibet, India and Nepal and was constructed under the supervision of princes of Nepal and Tang Dynasty. The Sakyamuni hall is the quintessence of the Monastry. Its scripture hall symbolizes the core of the universe. Its main hall has a full sized golden statue of 'Sakya Muni' of 8 years brought from Nepal.

Ramoche Monastery, north of the old Lhasa, is of mid 7th cent. It was once burnt down, but was rebuilt. There are many murals and statues of Buddha and, Maitreya and Other Buddhist saints. The main hall has a golden full length of statue Sakya Muni of 8 years brought from Nepal. The monastery is the sutra institute of the Gulag sect. Around the monastery there is a shopping street called

Barkhor Street. where devotees move around turning their prayer wheels.

Drepung monastery, built in1416, is in Kainpe Muze Mountain five km from Lhasa. It is the largest of the 6 monasteries of the sect and has more than 10000 lamas. The 5th Dalai Lama had lived here before shifting to the Red Hill. A lot of sutras and a cultural classic are kept there. 'Sunning the Buddha' is an important religious activity here.Norbu Lingka, meaning precious park, in existence since 1740s, was the first palace of Dalai Lama, built by Qing officials. Now it consists of a large park and magnificent palaces. Tower museum at the south-eastern corner of Norbu Lingka has rich cultural relics, pre-historic items of cultural value, hand copied classics, musical instruments, handicrafts, pottery, etc.

Yangbajian Terrestrial Heat Hot springs is 90 km north-west of Lhasa and beside the Qinghai-Tibet highway. It is the largest (20000 sq. m) high temperature and moist hot fields of China. Swimming pools for surfing bath, fragrant bath, medicinal bath, etc. and varieties of good restaurants make it a famous tourist attraction and recuperation centre. Other interesting sites are Cosmic ray observation centre, Yangbajian temple and a Buddhist nunnery.

There are a number of other monasteries and places of interest. These include stupa halls of past Dalai Lamas and halls for worshipping Buddha. A number of cultural relics like imperial edicts and golden seals of the Qing Emperors giving titles to Lamas are of interest. Sera Monastery, built in 1419 by Zongkaba, founder of the sect, is one of the six main monasteries of the Gelug sect in China.

Nyingchi is reputed as south China in Tibet and is situated in south-east Tibet bordering India and Myanmar. It grows plants ranging from Snow lotus flowers in the Frigid Zone and bananas and Palm trees in the sub-tropical zone. It is inhabited by the Lhoba, Monba and other ethnic minorities who live by hunting and 'slash and burn' cultivation.

Qamdo (East Gate of Tibet) is an economic, cultural and communication center in the eastern part of Tibet with

Namco Lake, north of Lhasa, in Tibet[20]

5.5 Lakhs people, Jinsha, Lancang and Nujiang (three parallel rivers), complicated land forms, different climates and vegetation. It has over 80 high peaks including some sacred Mountains. At the foot-hills, a large number of lakes, hot springs and forests are home to many flora and fauna.

**d. Other Mountains.** Ling sham mountain, 2303 meters high, is in winter a world of ice and snow and in summer a charming place with constant change of cloud and rain.

Panshan Mountain 12 km away from Tianjin is a combination of natural scenery, Buddhist temples and imperial gardens. It is a scenic spot with highest rate of vegetation coverage .Five peaks here form a "unique feature of three terraces" with pine trees, grotesque rock formations, and clean waters. 72 temples, 13 pagodas and an imperial garden are other attractions.

Wutai Mountain (Shanxi province) is considered the first among Buddhist Mountains. It is the place where Manjushi (symbol of wisdom for Buddhists) performs Buddhist rites. The highest five peaks of Wutai Mountains stand in a ring with flat top in the shape of 5 terraces without a single tree. Wutai, in fact, means 5 mountains. The place is a sacred one for Buddhists and hence since the days of the Hans, many temples have been built here.

Hengshan Mountain, one of China's great five mountains, is located in Hunyuan County in Shanxi province. It is a well-known sacred place for Taoists. There are many ancient Buddhist and Taoist buildings of Importance. Yiwulu Mountains (Green Mountain in Manchu language) are in the city of Beining in Liaoning province. For thousands of years, Buddhist and Taoist disciples cultivated moral character and temperament and rulers offered sacrifices here to Mountain gods. It has a culture of attracting religious pilgrims. Changbai Mountains (Jilin Province) serve as a dividing line between China and Korea. It is one of the active volcano groups in China.

Huangshan Mountain (Anhui province) has, majestic and precipitous peaks, ever changing clouds, 6 scenic spots of hot springs, jade screens, with over 400 scenic spots, etc.It is famous for strangely shaped pines, grotesque rock formations, seas of clouds and hot springs called "wonderous Mountain under heaven". It is said that if you visit 5 great mountains, other mountains are not worth seeing and if you see Huangshan, the 5 great mountains are not worth seeing.

Jinhua Mountain (Chi Zhou city) is one of the 4 great Buddhist Mountains described as nine peaks in the shape of flowers. It is a place of Bodhisattva rites in addition to being home to 78 ancient temples, 1500 Buddha statues, 1300 cultural relics, jade seals, etc. One of the first temples of the Jin dynasty days is also here.

Taishan Mountain in Tai'an city (Shandong Province) has great scenic spots and cultural sites and temples and palaces in great numbers.

Laoshan Mountain in the south of Shandong Peninsula is close to the Yellow sea. It has since ancient days the reputation as "celestial residence of supernatural" and "fairy house".

Song Shan mountain (Shaolin temple area) has many high and precipitous mountains and historic sites. The Shaolin temple in dense jungle is the birth place of Shaolin Wushu. There is also a story of 13 Shaolin monks armed with rods rescuing an emperor and hence getting permission to have soldier monks. Shaolin Wushu with

An oblique view of the Himalayas[21], including the Mt. Everest and Makalu the highest and 5th highest mountains in the world respectively, as seen from the International Space Station, 360 km (225 mi) up

its own systems is a typical representative of Chinese Wushu. Main buildings here were built during the Ming and Qing periods.

Wangwu Mountain (35 km away from Jiyuan city) with 6 scenic spots, 24 ravines with special rocks and caves is a Taoist Mountain.

Jiugong Mountain in Tong Shan County (Hubei Province) has 27 natural karst caves, 170 ravines and 50 water falls. It is a sacred place for Taoists. Tianzi Mountain (Sangzhi County, Hunan Province) has more than 300 peaks pointing vertically upwards. Heng Danxia Mountain (Guangdong Province) is a representative of Danxia physiognomy and is considered a holy place of Buddhists. Baiyun Mountain (white cloud mountain, Guangdong Prov.) has a history of 1000 years. Wuzhi Mountain, also called Five Fingers Mountain, looks like five fingers pointing Upwards.Emei Mountain (Sichuan Province) is one of the 4 Buddhist Mountains. Four wonders of the Golden Summit sunrise, Sea of Clouds, Buddha's halo and Holy lantern are attractions here. Qing Cheng Mountain (63 km from Chengdu) is also called "green city mountain" because of the abundance of plants and flowers. It is considered the birth place of Chinese Taoism.

Cangshan Mountain (Yunnan Prov.) has 19 peaks and is precipitous like a wall. It looks like a vulture spreading its wings standing on the top of the Mountain.Kaebo Peak of Meiri Snow-capped Mountain (Deqin County, Yunnan pro.) is the highest of the peaks in this region with 6740 m. ht and is regarded as the "God of snow-capped mountain".

Quomolangma Mountain is located in Dingri County in Tibet in Sino-Nepal border. The mountain is regarded as "fortunate goodness" symbolizing supreme goodness and purity. Nyainqentanglha Mountain is a huge mountain range of 600 km with over 30 peaks higher than 6000 m. Gnyan-chen-thang-lha Mountain gives rise to 250 glaziers and sources of Indus, Ganges and Yarling Rivers are here. Maiji Mountain (Gansu Prov.) has one of the four largest rock cave groups in China. There are totally 194 caves starting from 4th cent., rock sculptures and murals. Mingsha Mountain (Gansu Prov.) is a mountain built with fine sand. Peaks look like knife edges and hence the Name. Kongtong Mountain (Pingliang city, Gansu Prov.) has five terraces and is known as "the first famous mountain of Taoist".

## 3. OTHER ATTRACTIONS

**Changchun,** capital of Jilin province, is also known as the 'spring city' of Northern China. It has 7.13 million people. The interesting places are (a) Puppet Manchuria palace (Important palace of former Puppet emperor Aisin Gioro Pu Yi), (b) Jing Skiing ground (the largest in Asia with 1800 m long course with gentle slope where 1000 people can ski at one time. Motor, dog and horse drawn sledges and horse are also available), and (c) Changchun film city (a famous film production centre with unique film and TV culture. New film tech exhibition zone, ancient arch zone, ethnic minority scene zone, amusement zone, and tourist facilities centre are also available).

**Changsha,** capital of Hunan province, has 5.96 million people. It has many cultural and historical sites with more than 300 ancient tombs of Spring and Autumn periods, 1800 of Warring states period and 800 of Han dynasty. There are 20000 well kept cultural relics and of these, the relics of Western Han are world famous.Yuchu Mountain, on the western bank of Xinjiang River with deep and serene gorges, tall and elegant peaks and lushly growing trees provide beautiful scenery.

**Changde,** an important city in the hinter land of the Yang Shan Mountains in North Hubei province, adjacent to Beijing and Tianjin, has a population of 3.59 million. Mountain resorts in the northern part of the city consist of an old palace and some garden areas.

**Chengdu,** capital of Sichuan province, has a history of 3000 years. It has 10.28 million people. It is a link to go the Three Gorges of the Yangtze River, Tibet and Xian. A lot of 5000 years old cultural relics can be seen in Sanxing. Qingyang palace of Tang dynasty is another attraction. Sichuan Provincial Museum too has a number of cultural relics.

**Chongqing,** with a population of 31.14 millions, is a municipality directly under the Beijing government. The city has waters on three sides and a mountain on the other. It has cultural sites of The Three Kingdoms period, rock carvings, Three Gorges on the Yangtze River (*pl. see page 231*), etc. as the main attractions.

**Shibazhai** on the bank of Yangtze River is a huge five coloured rock pointing to the sky. A 12-storied wooden tower on the body of the mountain was first built in Ming days, but perfected later in the Qing period. The Three Gorges of Qutang, Wuxia and Xiling cover 103 km. Qutang is the grandest as the precipes on either side are only 100 m apart.Baoding mountain stone carvings of the 12th Century are also interesting.

**Dalian** in Liaoding Peninsula, with a population of 5.58 million, borders yellow sea and hence is a seaside tourist centre. In the Bingyu Scenic zone, graceful mountains, stone forest, stone pillars and oddly shaped peaks attract a lot of tourists. Stary Sea Square with an area of 101 sq. km is the largest city square in Asia. It has a white marble ornamental column and a large fountain. Tiger Beach Sea Park is a very large sea side amusement park.

**Guangzhou** is the capital of the Guangdong Province. It has 7.2 million people and is known as a 'city of flowers'. It is a port and commercial city with modern amusement facilities and historical sites in plenty.

**Guiyang,** capital of Guizhou Province, with a population of 3.4 million, is located in the south-west China. 74 m high Huangguoshu waterfall is the largest in China and it produces a thunderous sound. There are 10 other waterfalls. There is a Hundred Flower Lake, with 100 islets, 22 km from the city.Qianling park, named after the Qianling Mountain, is in the north-west of the city. It has tall annual trees, limpid springs, oddly shaped rocks and towering mountains.

**Hang Zhou,** capital of Zhejiang Province and one of the seven capital cities of the country, is located beside the Qiantang River at the southern end of the Grand Canal. It has a population of 6.37 millions. West Lake Scenic Zone and Two Rivers and One Lake are interesting places. The Broken bridge view of the snow scenery possible from here is the best view of the snow scene in winter. A 'Three stone pagoda' constructed in 1621 in the lesser Yingzhou Islet Scene Area in the shape of the battle ground is a nice attraction.

**Harbin,** capital of Heilongjiang Province, is in the middle reaches of the Songhua River. It has 9.48 million people and is an important city in the north-east China. It is often called 'City of ice' with Ice lanterns, Sports on ice, and international Ice and snow festival. Sun Island on the northern bank of the river with lushly growing trees and flowers and serene and picturesque environment is attractive. St. Sophia Church of the Eastern Orthodox Church is in Byzantine style. Central Street, also called 'China Street' is of 1900 vintage. It is 1450 m long, 21.14 m wide and is the largest pedestrian street in

Asia. Yabuli Skiing ground, 195 km east of Harbin, has 4 skiing cable ways, 9 skiing courses and 7 cross country skiing courses. Jile Buddhist temple, built in 1920, is also of tourist interest.

**Huangshan** in southern Anhui Province has 10 key historical monuments. Old Street in Tunxi has many buildings of architectural style of Southern Song and Qing dynasties. Hongcun village of Northern Song days, in the shape of an Ox, is 1000 years old.Xidi village is in the architectural style of Anhui Province of Ming and Qing days.

**Hohhot,** meaning green city, is the capital of Inner Mongolia Autonomous Region. It has 2.13 million people- of Mongolian, Han, Hui, Manchu, Korean etc. ethnicities. It has many historical and cultural items of interest like temples and pagodas and Dazhao Lamasery of 1598 vintage. A tomb (of Wang Zhaojun) Han days, covered by a green slab, called 'Green Tomb', is famous.

**Kunming,** capital of Yunnan Province, is known as "city of spring" because of perpetual spring like weather. Pleasant climate, spectacular plateau scenery, time honored history, unique ethnic customs and unusual plateau and animals attract tourists all around the year.

**Luoyang** (population 6.32 million) is in west Henan province in the middle reaches of the Yangtze River. It was capital for 13 dynasties and is the oldest. Long man grottoes are one of the three treasure houses of stone inscriptions in China.

White horse temple here was the first temple to be constructed after Buddhism was introduced into China. Largest group of tombs of emperors after eastern Zhou (770–256 B.C.) in Mongshan mountain in the north and Zhongyue and Shoal temples have made the place world famous. Longmen grottoes, 12 km from Luoyang, started in 471–499 period of Northern Wei dynasty and continued for 400 years through Eastern wei, Western wei, Northern Qi, Sui, Tang and Northern Song have 2345 caves, 50 pagodas and 3600 inscriptions. The 'White Horse Temple' is 13 km east of the city and it was the first temple to be constructed after Buddhism came from India in Eastern Han days (25–220). Emperors used to send monks to India to bring scriptures and they used to be brought back on White horses and hence the name.

Guan Shan Mountain in Guanlin town is 8 km off Luoyang city in Guanlin town. It is the place where the head of Gen.Guan Yu of Shu state was buried during the Three Kingdoms period (220–280). Xiaolangdi Scenic zone in the Yellow River in Xiaolangdi town, 30 km from Luoyang city, is at the middle reaches of the Yellow River. It had a key water control project outstanding for water conservancy and control of the river.

**Matching,** capital city of Jiannxi Province, located adjacent to Poyang Lake, the largest fresh water lake, has a population of 4.49 million. It was first constructed in Western Han days (206 B.C.–A.D. 24). Prince Teng's pavilion is an attractive sight. It got a high reputation after a Tang poet wrote a poem over it. Another attractive site is 'Hundred Flower Islet' which got its name from a poem of the Song Period. Tianxing park has over 50000 birds of 32 species. Shengjin pagoda built in Tang days has typical South China architecture.

**Qixia mountain,** 22km north-east of Nanjing, was earlier called Sheshan mountain. Discovery of "Qixia cottages" of Northern and southern dynasties (A.D. 420–581) here led to this change in name. East peak resembles a dragon and another a tiger. The main peak is Sanmao Peak. Another important site is the Confucian temple here where Confucius is worshipped.

**Qingdao** with population 7.16 million borders the Yellow sea and is a seaside resort. The Pier, symbol of Qingdao, was constructed in A.D. 1891. It is a 440 m long and 10 m wide park which gives a good view of the sea. There is an islet called 'lesser qingdao' south of the pier with exquisite rocks and lushly growing trees. It has a white pagoda and a navigation park in the bay. Badaguan area has 200 villas and a cherry flower path.

**Sanya** is the second biggest city in Hainan Province with 18 bays and 209 km long coast line. 4.8 lakhs people-Han, Li and Miao-live here. The area has tropical fruits and landscape and is in fact a winter resort with mountains on 3 sides and sea on the other.

**Shenzhen** is a long and narrow city of 1.4 million people. It runs 81.4 km east to west with a width of only about 10.8 km. It is a tourist destination located 160 and 35 km respectively from Guangzhou and Hong Kong facing the sea with a mountain at its back. It has Pearl River mouth in the west and Daping Bay in the east.

**Shenyang** is in Liaoning province in North east China and has a population of 6.87 million composing of more than 30 ethnic groups. The main attractions here are Shenyang imperial palace (built in A.D. 1625), Imperial Mausoleums (Fuling and Zhaoling), Huishan Scenic Area, Magic slope and the former residence of Zhang Xueliang.

Sheyang Imperial palace (*pl.see page 230)* located in the center of the city of Mukden in Manchuria was built in A.D. 1625–36. It is of the Jin dynasty and the first three Qing emperors lived here from A.D. 1625 to 1644. It has 90 buildings and 300 rooms and is next in importance only to the Forbidden City. It is intact and has great historical and artistic value. Summer Palace Water world here is the largest amusement park in Asia large enough for 2000 people. In Meteorite Forest Park, ancient meteorites are scattered in Lixiang town and Yaoquian town over 168 sq. km. The largest is 100 m long, 50 m wide and 60 m high. These were formed 4.5 billion years ago, and dropped here 1.9 billion years ago.

The magic slope is in Qingshuita town at the western foot of the Maoshan Mountain. It is 80 m long and 15 m wide and slopes from west to east. If a car is stopped at the foot, it will go up and a bike will run with out pedaling. But for going down the slope, strong pedaling is needed.

**Splendid China** (*pl. see page 229*) is a miniature scenic area reflecting Chinese history and culture, art and architectural styles and minority customs, with miniatures of 100 places of interest. Chinese folk culture village demonstrates folk arts, customs, and architecture of residential house of various ethnic groups. Village life of 24 minority groups and customs of 56 minorities are displayed. 'Window of the world' in Shenzhen Bay covers 480000 sq. m with culture as the theme and famous scenic spots, natural attractions, folk customs, songs and dances of the world are on display. 'Sea world' covering an area of 185000 sq. m displays wonders on the bottom of the sea, performance of dolphins, sea lions and seals. Shark room and marine fish hall, diving performances, view of rare marine products and performances of sea world artists are interesting. Minsk aircraft carrier of USSR, at one time 5$^{th}$ largest carrier, which had become unoperational for war was purchased by ShenzhenMinskco in A.D. 1998 and is shown as a tourist attraction.

**Tianjin,** 120 km south of Beijing, bordering Bohai Sea in the east, has a population of 9.27 million. It is considered a bright pearl on the Beijing-Tianjin itinerary. Tianta Lake scenic area has a TV tower on water. The Drum tower in the heart of the old city is pedestrianised, but is good for shopping, leisure and sight seeing. Eight Immortals mountain, 35 km from Jixian county seat, has 10493 sq. m of secondary forest. A legend says that 8 immortals passing by were attracted by the forests, long valley, clean streams and beautiful scenery and sat on a rock giving it the name. Memorial hall of Chou En Lai and Deng Ying Chao opened on the 100 birth anniversary of Chou 1998 has a mammoth hall where shows, pictures, documents, cultural relics, etc. are on display.

**Urumqi** (population: 1.75 million), capital of Xinjiang Uygur Autonomous Region, was a transport hub on the Silk Road. The interesting sites around are Urumqi Tianshan International Skiing Field (65 km away), Shuimo Gully Scenic Area with ancient trees, spurting springs, ancient temples and terraces and the Heavenly Lake in Tianshan Mountains. The hot springs in the Gully scenic area are famous for presence of different elements like potassium, magnesium, radon, zinc and nitric acid which help to cure many skin diseases.

**Wuhan,** capital of Hubei Province, is at the confluence of Yangtze and Hanjiang rivers at the eastern edge of the Jiangshan plain. It is a 3500 years old cultural triple city of Wuchang, Hankou and Hanyang with a population of 7.68 million. It is also a transport hub of central Asia. The Yellow crane tower, symbol of Wuhan, is 51.4 m high and is 5 Storied. East Lake is the largest lake in cities in China with 33 sq. km in size and 99 turns and bends.

**Xining,** capital of Qinghai Province, is a 2000 years old city on the Silk Road with 1.78 million people, mostly Hans and ethnic minorities of Mongshan, Hui, Tibetan and Tu.

**Xiamen** on south east coast of China with 1.57 million people is a home land for overseas Chinese and also a native place for Taiwanese. Gulangyu Island separated from the mainland only by 500 m wide Lujiang river is famous as 'the garden on the sea'. 20000 people who love music and piano stay here and hence is also called 'Piano island'. It attracts millions of overseas Chinese and tourists. Sunlight rock is the highest part of the island and from here one can have a bird's eye view of the place and see rocks, pavilions, etc. under big towering trees around. Dragon Pond on the Beichen or North Mountain has 1000 m long water fall and 12 ponds resulting from it are called 'Dragon Ponds'.

**Yinchuan,** capital of Ningxia Hui Autonomous Region, has 1.44 million people and borders Helan Mountain in the north and Yellow River in the east. The interesting sites are Jade emperor pavilion, Jinshui garden, Shahu lake and Najiahu Mosque.

It is rich in tourist resources.Colourful customs of Hui people, rich cultural sites of the Western Xia dynasty, etc. make Ningxia an attractive place. Cliff engravings at Helan Mountain, 50 km off Yinchuan, show the scenes in the daily life of ethnic groups like xiongnu, xianbei, tujue, haiku, tubo and danxiang of north China. covering 50 sq. km.

**Western Xia tombs** (*pl. see page 230*), 35 km west of Yinchuan, are on the eastern side of the Helan Mountain. The kings of the ancient kingdoms were buried in nine tombs here. These equal in importance to the Song tombs in Gongxian County in Henan. These are some of the most intact imperial mausoleums in China.

South China Sea by Hainan.[22]

Splendid China Temple of Heaven.[23]

Dazheng Hall, Mukden Palace, Shenyang.[24]

Xia tombs.[25]

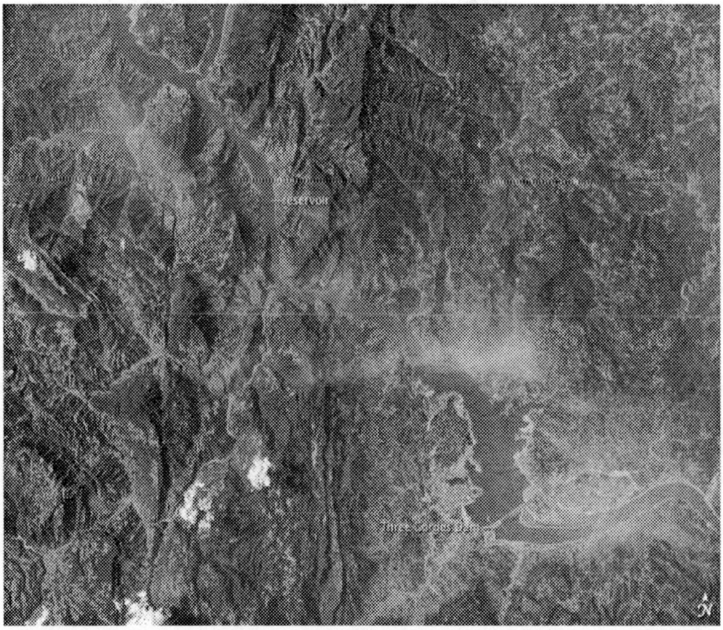

A Photo of the Three Gorges Area.[26]

Wuxia gorge.[27]

Long Sheng Rice Terrace.[28]

## Endnotes

1 From CIA Fact Book Photos—In public domain. Also all *
2 Ibid.
3 Ibid.
4 In public domain.
5 Ibid.
6 From CIA Fact Book Photos—In public domain.
7 In public domain.
8 Ibid.
9 Ibid.
10 Ibid.
11 From CIA Fact Book Photos—In public domain.
12 Ibid.
13 Ibid.
14 Ibid.
15 courtesy http://unesco.org/ext/field/beijing/whc/pkm-abc site.htm of Unesco.
16 From CIA Fact Book Photos—In public domain.
17 Ibid.
18 Ibid.
19 Ibid.
20 Ibid.

[21] Ibid.
[22] Ibid.
[23] Ibid.
[24] In public domain.
[25] Ibid.
[26] From CIA Fact Book Photos—In public domain.
[27] Given permission to use by Copy right holder Doug Janson.
[28] From CIA Fact Book Photos-In public domain.
* photo from CIA Fact Book Photos

## References

### Seen Marvels

*Beijing and adjoining areas*


a. http://en.wikipedia.org/wiki/Summer_Palace. (Dec. 28, 2009)
b. http://China SummerPalace.com.
c. http://kinabaloo.com/summer_palace.html.
d. www.travelchinatour.com.
e. www.hotelsbeijing.travel.
f. http://en.wikipedia.org/wiki/Forbidden_City. (Dec. 28, 2009)
g. www.warwick.ac.uk/./forbidden_14.jpg.
h. http://en.wikipedia.org/wiki/Tiananmen_Square. (Dec. 28, 2009)
i. http://worldisround.com.en.wikipedia.org/wiki/Great_Wall_of_China.
j. http://en.wikipedia.org/wiki/Great_Wall_of_China. (Dec. 28, 2009)
k. http://en.wikipedia.org/wiki/Ming_Dynasty_Tombs. (Dec. 28, 2009)
l. www.chinaculture.org.
m. http://travelchinaguide.com/attraction/shaanxi/xian/dinnershow/
n. http://travelblog.org/Bloggers/Chinaspring
o. http://irlbrl.com.cgi.ebay.com.my/Chinese-pearl-and-Green-jade
p. http://ebeijing.gov.cn/Life/Transportation/Ci
q. http://traveladdicts.connectfree.co.uk.


*Xian and adjoining areas*


a. http://en.wikipedia.org/wiki/Qin_Shi_Huang. (Dec. 27, 2009)

b. http://en.wikipedia.org/wiki/Terracotta_Army. (Dec. 27, 2009)
c. http://travelchinaguide.com/attraction/shaanxi/xian/citywall.htm

*Guilin and adjoining areas*

a. http://travelchinaguide.com/attraction/guangxi/guilin/flute.htm and a number of other references on Guilin area andits sceneries.

*Shanghai and adjoining areas*

a. http://destination-shanghai.com.
b. http://en.wikipedia.org/wiki/Shanghai_Museum. (Dec. 27, 2009)
c. http://chinahighlights.com/./shanghai-museum1.jpg.
d. http://skyscrapercity.com.
f. http://en.wikipedia.org/wiki/Oriental_Pearl_Tower. (Dec. 27, 2009)
g. http://studylanguages.org.
h. http://en.wikipedia.org/wiki/Nanjing_Road. (Dec. 27, 2009)
i. http://studylanguages.org/./shanghai-shopping.jpg.
j. http://spafinder.com/uploaded_images/1634814-Pe.

<u>**Unseen Marvels**</u>

*Beijing and adjoining areas*

a. www.travelchinaguide.com/attraction/beijing/beihai.htm.
b. en.wikipedia.org/wiki/Temple_of_Heaven. (Dec. 27, 2009)
c. en.wikipedia.org/wiki/Hutong. (Dec. 27, 2009)
d. www.chinavista.com/experience/hutong/hutong.html.
e. www.chinadaily.com.cn/english/doc/2004-1/14/content_298860.htm.
f. www.thebeijingguide.com.
g. en.paralympic.beijing2008.cn
h. en.wikipedia.org/wiki/Beijing_Temple_of_Confucius. (Dec. 27, 2009)
i. travelchinaguide.com/attraction/beijing/confucius.htm.
j. beijingguide2008.com.
k. http://www.travelchinaguide.com/attraction/beijing/yonghe.htm.
l. http://worldisround.com
m. http://en.wikipedia.org/wiki/Eastern_Qing_Tombs. (Dec. 27, 2009)

n. travelchinaguide.com/attraction/beijing/qing_mausoleums.
o. en.wikipedia.org/wiki/Beijing_Ancient_Observatory. (Dec. 27, 2009)
p. chinapage.com.
q. travelchinaguide.com/attraction/beijing/bell_temple.htm
r. travelchinaguide.com/attraction/beijing/fragrant.htm.
s. en.wikipedia.org/wiki/Fragrant_Hills. (Dec. 29, 2009)
t. dawnsay.multiply.com

*Xian and adjoinin areas*

a. http://en.wikipedia.org/wiki/Banpo(Dec. 29, 2009)
b. http://flickr.com.
c. http://en.wikipedia.org/wiki/Stele_Forest.(Dec. 29, 2009)

*Shanghai and adjoining areas*

a. http://travel.webshots.com .
b. http://travelchinaguide.com/attraction/shanghai/ residence-sun-yat-sen.htm.
c. http://chinaculture.org/gb/en_travel/2003-09/24/ content_33924.htm.

**Cities, Rivers and Hills linked Attractions**

a. China-2004, New Star Publishers, Beijing-100037. 152

*Rivers*

a. China-2004, New Star Publishers, Beijing-100037.
b. Waterside cities and towns inYangtze River delta, China National Tourism Administration.
c. China travel Guide, China National Tourism Administration.
d. http://en.wikipedia.org/wiki/Yangtze. (Dec. 30, 2009)
e. http://destination360.com.
f. http://chinaodysseytours.com.
g. www.chinahighlights.com/yell
h. en.wikipedia.org/wiki/Geography_of_China (Dec. 30, 2009)
i. http://muztagh.com/map-of-china/index.html
j. http://chinatour.com
k. http://en.wikipedia.org/wiki/File:Map_of_the_Yangtze_River.
l. China Mountains tour, China National Tourism Administration.
m. Shangrila, China National Tourism Administration.
n. http://en.wikipedia.org/wiki/Sacred_Mountains_of_China (Dec. 30, 2009)

CHAPTER 6

# Security Systems

Security related topics are dealt with under three heads viz., Public Security, State Security and Defense or Military matters. Public Security covers police functions (including People's Armed Police), Criminal Justice System (including Procuratorates and penal systems), Security of Government offices, vital installations, VIPs, and Embassies, border security, etc. The 1.5 million strong People's Armed Police deals with most of the pure security roles including border defense and assists the civil police when needed. State Security deals with activities of enemy agents, spies, subversion, revealing of state secrets, political dissenters, social advocacy, domestic and foreign Intelligence, etc. Matters relating to Defense Forces/PLA are covered under the head Defense/Military.

**Public Security.** The Ministry of Public Security (MPS) is a functional organization under the State Council (National Cabinet) in charge of nationwide public security work. It was created by removing the security service function from the Central Department of Social Affairs (CDSA) after the 1949 revolution. It is the domestic security agency, equivalent of National Police Agency in Japan or national police in other countries. It also administers the People's Armed Police, which undertakes paramilitary functions. It does not collect domestic intelligence since 1983, which is a primary responsibility of the Ministry of

State Security. Hong Kong and Macao have their own security bureaus/agencies and police forces.

The functions of the MPS include: prevention, suppression and investigation of criminal activities; fight against terrorist activities; maintenance of social security and order; fight against behaviors jeopardizing social order; control over traffic, fire, dangerous objects and special trades; administration of household registration, identification cards, nationality, entry-&-exit and stay, travel of foreigners in China; maintenance of border security; protection of state assigned persons, venues and facilities; management of rallies, parades and demons-trations; security inspection of public information networks; supervision and instruction of security work in state organs, societal associations, enterprises and important construction sites; and instruction on crime prevention work of community security commissions.

Public Security departments exist in Provinces and Autonomous Regions and metropolitan public security bureaus in Municipalities. Public security bureaus or their divisions look after the function in cities and prefectures and sub-bureaus in sub-regions of cities under the direct leadership of their superior public security agencies. Similarly, public security bureaus exist in counties and banners, under the leadership of their respective local governments and superior public security agencies. Dispatched police stations are directly subordinate to their superior public security bureaus and sub-bureaus in counties, cities and banners.

At higher levels, separate departments like Public Order Administration, Border Control, Criminal Investigation, Economic Crime Investigation Exit & Entry Administration, Fire Control, Security Protection, Public Information Network Security Supervision, Penitentiary Administration, Traffic Control, Legal Affairs, International Cooperation, Logistics and Finance, Drug Control, Science-&-Technology, Counter-Terrorism and Info-communications, etc. exist to look after respective functions. Railway, navigation, civil aviation, forestry and anti-smuggling public security departments are under the dual leadership of their superior administration and the Ministry of Public Security. Local municipal police used to be usually unarmed. Since 2006, all frontline personnel are given 9mm double-action revolver.

At lower levels of government, police have greater influence. Public Security Stations, which serve as the direct points of contact between police and ordinary citizens, are supervised by the public security sub-bureau as well as by local governments and procuratorates. The procuratorate can assume direct responsibility for any case that it chooses. It also supervises investigations of cases investigated by the public security station. A great deal of coordination occurs among the public security organs, the procuratorates, and the courts to see that a trial does not produce a surprise outcome. The Public Security station has broader responsibilities than a police station in the West, involving itself in every aspect of people's lives. In a rural area, a station typically has a chief, a deputy chief, a small administrative staff, and a small police force. In an urban area, it usually has a greater number of administrative staff and seven to eighteen patrolmen. The station's household section maintains a registry of all persons living in the area, births, deaths, marriages, and divorces confirmed through random household checks. The station regulates all hotels and requires visitors who remain beyond a certain number of days to register. All theaters, cinemas, radio equipments, and printing presses also are registered with the local public security station to enable it to regulate gatherings and censor information effectively. It also regulates the possession, transportation, and use of all explosives, guns, ammunitions, and poisons.

All residents over sixteen years of age, except those on active duty with the People's Liberation Army and the People's Armed Police and inmates serving prison sentences, are issued resident identity cards indicating name, sex, nationality, ethnicity, date of birth, and address of the bearer by the police. Cards for persons sixteen to twenty-five years of age are valid for ten years and those for persons between twenty-five and forty-five are valid for twenty years. Persons over forty-five are issued permanent cards. As of early 1987, only 70 million people had been issued identity cards, well below the national goal. Even those with resident identity cards prefer to use other forms of identification. As per regulations on re-education through labor, reissued in 1979, and the 1957 Order, "vagabonds, people who have no proper occupation, and people who repeatedly breach public order." could be apprehended and sentenced to 'reeducation through labor' with the approval of local labor-training administration committees. From early 1960s, sentences of three or four years were the norm and since 79, three years with the possibility of extensions in extraordinary cases. The Regulations Governing Offenses against Public Order empower the police to admonish, fine, or detain people up to fifteen days. A court or procuratorate is required to approve the arrest and in 24 hours, family of the arrested has to be notified of the detention "except in circumstances where notification would hinder the investigation or there is no way to notify them." The time that an accused could be held pending investigation is limited to three to seven days. Two officials are needed to conduct a criminal investigation. Except in cases of emergency search, police require a warrant for search of person, property, and residence of an accused and an injured person. They could intercept mail belonging to the accused. Police personnel can use their batons only in self-defense or when necessary to subdue or prevent the escape of violent criminals or rioters. Police officials are on long-term assignments and have counseling and role model functions too. "Cherish-the-people" months are observed, during which the police make special efforts to help local people, especially the aged and infirm. However, Criticisms about inability to deal with rising crimes and abuses of power exist. Insufficient salaries, poor training, low morale among the officers, etc.are also facts.

Selection to police is based on political loyalty, intelligence, and health, as it is for the PLA. Most recruits have Communist Youth League backgrounds or are former PLA personnel. Some say Hans get preference. Recruitment is from senior-middle-school graduates under twenty-two years of age, with a waiver to twenty-five years of age for those having a minimum of two years' experience in public security work. The leadership positions go to those who attend the police schools. There is at least one police school in every province. There are others operated by municipalities. Legal training is emphasized. Patrolmen are trained at the unit and on the job. Senior officers are often the products of Chinese People's Public Security University, University of Police Officers, Institute of Criminal Police, etc. which offer more than twenty special courses. University of Police Officers established in 1980 as the Institute of International Politics provides training for public security cadres, along with training for counter-intelligence and political security cadres.

People's Armed Police is PRC's main force in charge of the domestic security and social stability. It is simultaneously under the command of the CCP's CMC and the State Council. It was originally set up to function on military service lines with PLA forces on domestic defense duty and as the armed, frontier defense and fire-fighting police. It undertakes internal security duties and also functions as guards in co-ordination with the public security units, national-level construction works, etc. It has military and security missions like defense for borders and also has fire teams, traffic, public utility, woods and mobile divisions. Numbering over 1.4 million plus, though under the direct jurisdiction of the Ministry of Public Security, it gets equal treatment with PLA troops. At wartime, it comes directly under military command for battlefield security, anti-infiltration, and as coast guards. Since "the Democratic Movement June 4, 1989 in Tiananmen Square," the status and importance of the People's Armed Police have increased. Since June 1996, the status of the People's Armed Police GHO has been upgraded to a great military-region level. PLA field divisions were also included in the People's Armed Police. It is equipped with the light weapons-wheel armored vehicles, command vehicles, patrol cars, etc., and plays a mixed role between the military police and the police of the democratic countries. It has air patrol and helicopter units. Some units are trained with the PLA.

**State Security.** Ministry of State Security is responsible for foreign Intelligence work. It is also involved in domestic security matters. It has authority to arrest or detain people as regular police for crimes involving state security. The procuratorates and the courts also supervise its functions. Its current functions were earlier under the Central Department of Social Affairs (CDSA), the primary intelligence organ of the Communist Party of China (CPC) till 1949. Between 1949 and 1955, it was under the Communist Party Central Committee with the name Central Investigation Department (CID). Its present form was given in 1983 after the merger of the CID and the counter-intelligence elements of the Ministry of Public Security.

Its mission is to ensure "the security of the state through effective measures against enemy agents, spies, and counter-revolutionary activities designed to sabotage or overthrow China's socialist system." It gathers foreign intelligence from overseas. In the measures against counter revolutionary activities and non-official Christian churches and the outlawed Falun Gong religious group, it is allegedly involved in actions to maintain the rule of the Communit Party. Censoring of the Internet to prevent people from knowing what is going on outside the country also comes under this. It was very active earlier in the Greater China region (Hong Kong, Macao, and Taiwan) and among overseas Chinese communities. The most important target is said to be USA followed by Taiwan and Japan if we are to read between the lines from Susan L Shirks 'China: the fragile super Power'.

Its divisions are First Bureau for Domestic Affairs, Second Bureau for Foreign Affairs, Third Bureau for Hong Kong, Macao and Taiwan, Fourth Bureau for Technology, Fifth Bureau for Local Intelligence, Sixth Bureau for Counter Intelligence, Seventh Bureau for Circulation, Eighth Bureau for Research (Institute of Contemporary International Relations), Ninth Bureau for Anti-Defection and surveillance, Tenth Bureau for Scientific and Technological Information, Personnel and Education Bureau and Supervision and Auditing Bureau. Other offices/divisions are General Office, Political Department and Party Committee.

As per Chinese law, it handles activities carried out by organizations, groups and individuals outside the territory, or instigated and financed by them but carried out by others as well as those carried out by organizations and individuals inside the territory in collusion with organizations, groups and individuals outside the territory. These relate to: (1) plotting to subvert the government, dismember the state and overthrow the socialist system; (2) taking part in an espionage organization or accepting a mission assigned by an espionage organization or its agents; (3) stealing, secretly gathering, buying and illegally providing state secrets for an enemy; (4) Instigating, luring and bribing state personnel to rise in rebellion; and (5) engaging in other sabotage activities against state security. On the intelligence collection front, its tasks cover acquiring foreign military and civilian high technology, collecting information on adversary military planning, foreign policy, and foreign trade positions concerning China and monitoring Chinese dissident groups overseas.

The Military Intelligence Department (MID), like its counter part elsewhere, is responsible for basic order-of-battle intelligence, studies of foreign weapons systems, and analyses of the capabilities of foreign military organizations. It obtains information through military attaches, review of open source literature, clandestine HUMINT (human intelligence) operations, and joint business ventures.

The Technical Department, or Third Department of the General Staff Department of the Central Military Commission, is the national agency responsible for managing China's strategic SIGINT (Signal Intelligence) programme. The New China News Agency, the primary domestic and international news agency for the PRC, with a staff of over 5,000 operating out of over 90 bureaus and 300 offices in China and abroad, allegedly serves as a cover for clandestine Chinese intelligence operations. It also monitors newspapers, magazines, and broadcasts from around the world, and conducts open source analysis for the Chinese leadership.

Chinese intelligence services gather information about the United States, Taiwan, and Japan, countries bordering it like Russia, India, Vietnam and South Korea. In respect of US, High Tech areas are a focus. US's status as Super Power, its closeness to Taiwan, its position as the source of new Technologies and as the main market for Chinese exports are primary motivations. Intelligence collection to improve economic position in the global economy is a priority. Chinese diplomats are suspected to be extremely active to collect Intelligence about US. 3rd Department monitors telecommunication of foreigners. The focus of signal intelligence units in 1980s was Russia, Japan, Taiwan, South Korea, SE Asia and India. The 4th Department was for Electronics Intelligence. The Liaison Department was meant to support CPC elements in PLA. Political education, indoctrination, discipline and ideology related work for armies were also its priorities.

Some well-known successes include penetration of the US intelligence community and FBI. In the 1980s, Larry Wu-Tai Chin (Jin Wudai), a translator for the CIA's Foreign Broadcast Information Service, was arrested and charged with espionage in the service of the PRC. He had been recruited in 1944 while stationed in China as a US Army officer and went undetected for four decades. In 2003, Chinese-American Federal Bureau of Investigation source and Republican Party fund raiser Katrina Leung was arrested and accused of being a double agent for both the

FBI and the Chinese government, engaged in counter- intelligence, the collection of secrets and technology from other countries, and repressing internal dissent within China.

**Defense/Military.** According to United States' Department of Defense reports for 2006, China's military expenditure was estimated to be 80 billion US dollars though official Chinese figure was only 30 billion. It is kept shrouded in deep secrecy, perhaps to create the strategic advantage of uncertainty.

The active military personnel in 2006 were estimated at 2,255,000. Its Air Force is said to have 9,218 aircrafts of which about 2300 are combat aircrafts, operating from its over 490 air bases. Russian *Su-30 MK* and indigenously built *J-10* are the main fighter aircrafts. China's Navy is said to possess a fleet of 284 vessels, but its actual war experience is rather limited. It had no aircraft carriers, but was slated to build and induct one by 2010.

As per CIA estimates, China has produced and deployed a wide range of ballistic missiles, ranging from short-range missiles to intercontinental ballistic missiles (ICBMs). China's missiles are operated by the Second Artillery Corps. A transition is currently underway from relatively inaccurate, liquid-fueled, silo/cave-based missiles to more accurate, solid-fueled, mobile missiles and a new ICBM is believed to be under development. China is said to be replacing its older missiles with new varieties which could be equipped with multiple warheads.

China has not joined the Missile Technology Control Regime (MTCR), but has pledged to abide by its main parameters. In November 2000, China promised not to assist any country in the development of nuclear-capable ballistic missiles. In August 2002, China issued regulations and a control list restricting the export of missiles and missile technology. China ratified the Chemical Weapons Convention (CWC) in December 1996.Although China claims that it no longer possesses any CW stockpiles, the U.S. government believes that China has not revealed the full scope of its program.

According to the CIA estimates, China possesses nuclear weapons, a range of ballistic missile capabilities, and the ability to develop chemical and biological weapons. A key uncertainty is how ongoing military modernization efforts will ultimately reshape China's strategic nuclear capabilities, but US deployments of missile defenses are likely to be a key factor. China's proliferation of ballistic missile technology and its ability to control chemical items that could be used in the production of chemical weapons are some concerns expressed by western nations. But, some have been addressed by China, but many about nuclear and chemical weapons-related proliferation remain.

**PLA.** PLA was founded on August 1, 1927 during the Nanchang uprising when troops of the Kuomintang (KMT) rebelled under the leadership of Zhu De, He Long, Ye Jianying and Zhou Enlai shortly after the end of the first Kuomintang-Communist alliance. They were then known as the 'Chinese Red Army'. Between 1934 and 1935, the Red Army survived several campaigns by Generalissimo Chiang Kai-Sheik and engaged in the Long March. After the overthrow of Chiang KaiShek by Mao in 1949 and on assumption of power by Mao in the People's Republic of China, PLA became its Defence Force.

It is the Largest military force with 3 million members and a standing army of 2.26 million (and .8 million Reserves) 40% of which is armoured or mechanized. It has five main service branches consisting of the Ground Force, Navy (PLAN), Air Force (PLAAF), Second Artillery Corps (strategic nuclear or missile force), and the Reserve Force. The People's Armed Police (PAP), a Chinese paramilitary force under the dual leadership of the Central Military Commission and the Ministry of Public Security, though not its part ,is brought under its command in a war scenario. It is believed to have improved battlefield capabilities with satellite communications, digital radars, satellite network under severe electronic counter measures, network centric warfare capability with combat intelligence, surveillance and reconnaissance elements to form an integrated net work. Newer land based long range cruise missiles with the next generation capability were shown in the military parade on the occasion of the 60th anniversary of the communist revolution in Oct. 2009. Perhaps, newer high-powered lasers and microwave weapons, kinetic energy and particle beam weapons, etc. are under development utilizing the huge funds now available. Over the last 15 years, Defence expenditure has been continuously increasing by about 10% per year reaching 3% of GDP in 2009.

Its firearms were initially Soviet ones. Now the main infantry rifle is QBI -95, similar to AK-47. It also uses Ak-57 and Chinese type-56Assault rifle. Type 56 carbines with permanently attached bayonets are also used. Land based weapons consist of about 7500 MBT tanks, 5500 armored personnel carriers, 2200 Infantry fighting vehicles and 25000 artillery (11 armed brigades). 2/3 tanks are the Chinese version of RussianT-54 A. Overall, it is estimated to have a weapon holding of *34,281,000.*

PLA is said to have a Special Force for Counter Terrorism called 'Immediate Action Unit (IAU)'. It is believed to be a force for long airborne, amphibian and long-range reconnaissance operations. Described as "Sound of Southern China", it has army, air force and naval training. With 60% graduates, it is high technology driven, GPS based, cross-trained in various specialties and for different environments. It is tasked to respond to various contingencies in various regions "co-operating with other forces in attacks on islands". It is believed to be consisting of all weather versatile fighters, parachuters and those who can drive cars, boats, planes, etc.

It has Nuclear Weapons developed after the 1964 fission and '67 fusion tests with only a very short gap of 32 months. It also tested a neutron bomb. The series of nuclear tests in 1995–96 prior to China's signature of the Comprehensive Test Ban Treaty (CTBT), according to the CIA estimates, may have resulted in a smaller and lighter warhead design for the new generation of intercontinental ballistic missiles (ICBMs) now under development. China joined the International Atomic Energy Agency (IAEA) in 1984 and acceded to the Nuclear Non-Proliferation Treaty (NPT) in 1992 as a nuclear weapon state. It is believed to have ICBMs (100–160), IRBMs (100–150) and SRBMs (a few thousands of 300–600km range). It has solid fueled ICBMs in silos instead of liquid fueled ones. It has proclaimed the principles of minimum deterrence and no first strike.

In strategic nuclear defense and delivery systems, China is ahead. It is estimated to have about 400 strategic and tactical nuclear weapons, and stocks of fissile material sufficient to produce a much larger arsenal. China's highest yield is said to be of 4 megatons. Its nuclear delivery system is said to be quite advanced. The conflicts over Taiwan give China a strong incentive to beef up its military defence to counter the US military might.

Though PLA had, between 1990 and 2000, some commercial interests like farms, factories and guest houses, etc. managed by its private companies, these have been done away with the officers manning them retiring from the Force to continue their positions. Use of profits from them for Defence expenditure had started reducing the dependence on Government funds. Criticisms that the practice was affecting professionalism, increasing corruption, reducing loyalty to the Party, etc. prompted the Party leadership to gradually discontinue PLA's involvement with commercial activities.

Military service is compulsory, in theory, for all men who attain the age of 18; women may register for duty in the medical, veterinary, and other technical services at ages as young as 14. However, a draft in China has never been enforced due to large numbers of volunteers from China's huge population. Demobilized servicemen are carried in a ready reserve, which is reinforced by a standby reserve of veterans and by the militia.

The PLA is formally under with the Central Military Commission of the CCP. There is also an identical commission in the government, but it has no clear independent functions. The Ministry of National Defense, which operates under the State Council (cabinet) does not exercise any authority over it. The ministry assures continuing CCP control over the armed forces. Its primary role is that of a liaison office with foreign militaries. The political and military leaderships have made concerted efforts to create a professional military force restricted to national defense and provision of assistance in domestic economic construction and emergency relief. This conception of the role of the PLA requires the promotion of specialized officers who can understand modern weaponry and handle combined arms operations. Troops around the country are stationed in seven military regions and more than 20 districts. Chairman Hu Jintao has defined the missions of the PLA as: Consolidate the ruling status of the Communist Party, Help ensure China's sovereignty, territorial integrity, and domestic security in order to continue national development, Safeguard China's expanding national interests and Help maintain world peace.

The Central Committee of the Communist Party leads in all military affairs. The State President directs the state military forces and the development of the military forces is managed by the State Council. In order to ensure the absolute leadership of the Communist Party over the armed forces, every level of party committee in the military forces implements the principles of democratic centralism, the divisions and higher levels establish political commissars and political organizations, and ensure that the branch organizations are in line. These systems melded the party organization with the military organization in order to achieve the party's political and administrative leadership. This is the key guarantee to absolute leadership of the party over the military.

## References

1. Nationmaster.com
2. CIA world Fact book.

3. www.fas.org/irp/world/china/mss/index.html
4. www.fas.org/irp/world/china/program/humint.htm
5. www.fas.org/spp/guide/china/military/imint/index.html
6. www.fas.org/irp/nsa/ioss/threat96/part03.htm
7. www.fas.org/irp/world/china/mps/org.htm
8. En.wikipedia.org/wiki/People's_Liberation_Army
9. www.globalsecurity.org/intell/world/china/mps.htm, etc.

CHAPTER 7

# Emerging Scenario

The objective in this chapter is to project, taking into account the analyses in the earlier chapters and materials available from studies on the subject, the current and emerging scenarios in China. Though the prime focus is on economic aspects in view of the unprecedented economic growth since 1981, the likely changes in the political, cultural, educational, tourist, and other related fronts are also explored. The attempt is to give a balanced view highlighting the positive and negative aspects including the systemic problems confronting China.

**(a) Economics, Trade and Finance.** The unprecedented growth of GDP at about 10% per annum during the last three decades would marginally come down in the coming years, partly due to the law of diminishing returns in respect of huge FDI that had taken place in infrastructure. The economic slow down in Europe, Japan and US, would cause reduction in exports to these countries and FDI in China. Weak domestic demand when the stimulus measures begin to fade could reduce the growth in 2011. Difficulties could come from policies restricting excess production and energy consumption, plans for income redistribution, long term institutional reforms, needs for changes in household registration, boosting of private investments, medical care and education of rural agricultural workers, etc. But, in the global recovery process, the main beneficiaries would continue to be countries like China and India, which are emerging as the cheaper sources of supply for the richer nations becoming increasingly thrifty. Though the government's aggressive stimulus measures are boosting the domestic demand, the forecast for exports remains subdued.

China's trade surplus in the first quarter of 2010, compared to that of 2009, has been lesser, primarily due to increase in imports. In March 2010, there was a trade deficit though vis a-vis US and Europe, the surplus continued. 2010 was to end with a small favourable trade surplus compared to about 200 bn. US $ of 2008. The GDP, however, reportedly grew by 11.9%, 10.3%, 9.6% and 9.8% in the first, second, third and fourth quarters respectively of 2010 with an average of 10.3% for the whole year (Golden Sachs had estimated the growth around 10%) with increase in retails and private investments . Despite the waning of the impact of the stimulus package the, Chinese economy estimated to grow in 2011 by about 9.8% and in 2012 by about 8.4%. Though substantial growth would continue for the next few decades, neighboring countries like Vietnam, Cambodia, Korea, Thailand, Malaysia and India could attract part of the Huge FDI from MNCs now flowing to China due to factors like gradual increase in the exchange value of Reminbi, increase in labour costs due to the pressure of workers etc. Huge FDI flows from Chinese Diaspora would, however, sustain the momentum of growth at a higher level. Innovation flowing from a quantum jump in Higher education and return of capable R&D personnel from countries like US would also help.

China had for a few years ending in 2005 a constant trade surplus due to substantial favorable trade surplus with the US, despite the adverse trade balances with other countries. The surplus increased after 2005 and crossed 200 bn US $ in 2008 when recession began to reduce it. Management of its positive balance of trade with the US is a key issue. If exports to US decline, those to other countries will have to be improved. It could invite protective actions. Inflation will increase in US when the quantum of cheap Chinese goods gets reduced. The same could happen in Europe and Japan too. Undepreciated Yuan and cheap Chinese goods could create other problems for Japan, US and Europe. If US increases tariff on Chinese goods to force China to readjust the value of Yuan to a more realistic level, other problems could result.

The transformation of main Chinese Banks which had high very high Non-Perorming Assets becase of the huge quantities of bad loans given to State Owned Enterprises, which employ millions of workers, at the instance of Govermental authorities or on non-bsiness considerations, has been remarkable. Four of these (Agricultural Bank of China, Chinese Construction Bank, Bank of China and Industrial and Commercial Bank of China) now figure among the top ten in the world. They turned the corner after the Chinese government injected 420 bn US $ to rejuvenate them removing the bad loans and public offer of equities ranging between 8 and 22 bn US $. Their public offerings were well received in financial markets. Their loans went up from *102% of GDP in 2008 to 127% in 2009 as loans grow fast once top Chinese leaders order. The banks are making good money and can take shocks now, as savings in China are very high. The banks, better regulated now, have plenty of deposits with lending surging in 2009 as they pumped in stimuli very effectively. Agricultural Bank of China's earnings increased by 26%. The problems relating to other financial institutions in the state sector, co-operative banks and institutions etc. are yet to be addressed.* According to one analysis, China may become one of the dominant financial markets in the world by 2018, alongside the US and the EU, with a 13% share in global bond markets, 40% of equity markets and 18% of global banking.

In China, wealth is being made from the 'surplus value' being created basically by the industrial labour as most of the growth in GDP is from manufactured exports. As Chinese workers have no bargaining power, their wages are low. The wages, say, for a shop floor worker, is kept at about 5% of the wages of a US shop floor worker. A rise in wages in China will develop internal markets, but exports will decrease. Recently there have been increase in wages of 10 to 20% in different provinces and linking of wage increases to price index. This has followed a strike in a Honda plant and labour unrest in Foxconn employing about 400000 workers over wage related issues. As such increases in wages have a global impact, only gradual changes are perhaps possible.

**(b) Some problem areas.** Despite the rapid growth of GDP and rise in living standards, many millions were laid off from time to time as a result of the transitory unemployment. Though as per CIA estimates urban unemployment is only about 4.3% (with much higher unemployment in rural areas), increase in unemployment has potentials to create a crisis and bring down the economic and political systems. Foreign firms, which now produce more than the State Owned Enterprises, have already increased the pressure of competition on domestic firms by bringing out quality products using duty free advanced technology. WTO conditions would require opening up of the services sector including telecommunications and financial services and also their distribution. ISPs, services, etc. could also come as joint ventures. Financial services like banking, insurance, securities and asset management and distribution and after sales service have to follow. Chinese citizens will gain in many areas inefficiently managed now as also western companies who will deliver such services. Reduction in employment in the state sector inefficiently managing these will follow. It could result in labour unrests and demonstrations in northeast Provinces or other areas of low comparative advantage. Unhappiness among a large section of migrant labour (total 211 million) because of low wages and the absence of basic civic, health and educational benefits because of the rigidities of the 'Hukou' system is an indicator of simmering problems.

The growth has already created prosperity for some, social tensions and regional disparities. Inequalities between workers of SOEs and MNCs, rich and poor, urban and rural, coastal and interior areas, educated and the less educated, etc. have increased. According to a UN Human

Development Report, China (a socialist economy)'s 'Gini Index' (a commonly used statistical measure of inequality where 0 represents perfect equality and 1 the opposite) is higher than India (a mixed economy)'s (.47 against .365 of India). It is said to be approaching .5 It means the economic growth has actually widened the gap between the rich and the poor. To reduce the discontent resulting from evictions, decision to pay compensation at market rates has reportedly been taken. To reduce the inequalities, strengthening the rural financial systems, paying particular attention to development of viable credit markets in poor areas of rural China is suggested by some studies. Hence, sanction of more funds for rural health care and education, especially for rural schools, elimination of fees for rural students, co-operative medical care system for 80% of the rural areas, etc. are being done.

Initially, the widening disparity was perhaps useful as forced equality under Mao Zedong had demotivated people and reduced their initiative. But now, it increasingly contributes to social instability, as people, piqued by loss of their homes to make way for factories and developmental efforts, express displeasure sometimes in violent protests. As long as prosperity is spreading and the quality of life of the common man is improving, such challenges may be manageable. For this, the government would have to drastically improve its social services. The three major challenges that stand out are: the nation's changing work force, widening in the gap between rich and poor and severely constrained supplies of energy and environmental resources. Institutional reforms are also a priority. Factors that could boost the current success scenario are assessed to be strong and inclusive growth, economic integration and increased trade. China is thus said to be 'condemned' to continue a higher rate of growth to contain unemployment and avoid risks of increasing battles with its citizens and social instability.

Failure to implement tough reforms may also cause economic, social and ecological disruptions. China's working-age population will decrease after 2015 as a result of the delayed effect of its strict family-planning policies. The population is growing older and more urban and the Chinese industry is now less insulated from the adverse impact of the global economic downturns. China's urbanization rate is about 40% to 45% now, said to be lower than that of most west European and Latin American countries. But, it is said to be slowing down though increase in urbanization would continue for the next two or the decades more. Since urban workers earn more than three times as much as rural ones, the annual migration of more than 10 million farmers into cities had boosted the economy. A young and growing work force may have been responsible for a quarter of China's growth to date, says Wang Dewen, a demographer at the Chinese Academy of Social Sciences. Hence, it is said China will have to grow by making 'more productive use of fewer resources and working smarter'. Rapid growth has considerably depleted global supplies of cheap energy and raw materials and, also its own resources of clean air, fertile land and drinkable water. Without improvements in efficiency, China's growth could be constrained by the finite supply of essential resources. It is said that [1]if each Chinese (now using equivalent of 1.4 tons of oil) is to consume the same amount of energy as each person in the U.S. does (the equivalent of 7.82 tons of oil), China alone would consume nearly the energy the entire world uses now. Chinese government's effort to be more energy efficient has reportedly not made much progress though a lot of efforts and investments have been put in for new energy sources, development of solar power driven cars, etc. where China is clearly ahead of even US.

**(c) Growing Aging population.** China has an increasingly aging population with about 167 m, 12.5%of the total, above 60-years. 19 m are 80 or above which is again growing at about 1m p.a. Old age pensioners were 235 m in 2009, 7.3% more compared to 2008. The old age subsidy by Central Government increased by 69.7% last year. The retirement systems and economy and services are said to be too weak to handle the challenge.

**(d) New Thrust to R&D and Innovation.** The country has been making vigorous efforts to develop new technologies and innovative skills through research in order to improve manufacturing skills. It has also been spending more funds on R&D with focus on newer energy sources, solar energy, electric cars, high speed rails, nuclear power, space exploration, etc. A new thrust to improve quality 'made in China' products is also being made. Some of these have produced remarkable results. China is poised to emerge as the leading producer of high speed rails prompting Barrack Obama, President, USA, to tell university students in US that "If China is producing 40 high-speed rail lines and we're producing one, we're not going to have the infrastructure of the future," and that "The country that out-educates us today is going to out-compete us".

**High Speed Rails.** China, with a total length of 7055 km, is world leader in high-speed rail lines, which can carry traffic upto 350 kilometers per hour, faster than a Formula 1 racing car halving the traveling time between cities. One such line in the Yangtze River Delta region will have 92 pairs of high-speed trains operating daily. It will definitely become the big engine driving the modernization of the region, which contributed more than 22.1% of China's gross domestic product last year. It will force reduction of airfares. The government plans to build 16,000 kilometers of high-speed rail lines to link the major cities across the country by 2020, with travel speeds averaging over 200 kilometers per hour. A 1,318 kilometer line between Beijing and Shanghai, to open in 2012, will cut the travel time from 10 to 5 hours. Daily traffic has alredy peaked and reportedly reached 7.13 m on Feb. 19, 2010 during the Spring Festival season.

**Electric Cars.** Vigorous efforts are being made to become world leader in the manufacture of electricity driven cars, the next expected revolution in personal transportation. As China has been behind Germany, Japan, US, etc. in the field of internal combustion engines, the plan is to leapfrog the process in all related fields by huge investments when competitors are reeling under the adverse impact of recession. 16 Major State Owned Enterprises in the field have been asked to invest 100 bn Yuan to develop auto technology in 2 years seeing the high job and export prospects, less dependence on oil China imports in large quantities, and less pollution. It plans to put 5 lakhs electric cars on roads in China by 2012. 150 electricity driven buses are reportedly running in Beijing from Olympics days.

**Deep Sea exploration** is another front where China is set to emerge as the world leader. It would result in skills to explore deep and remote parts of sea rich in oil, minerals, trillions of dollar worth of mineral modules, objects of intelligence value, deep sea cables carrying diplomatic communications, lost nuclear arms, sunken submarines, 1000s of war heads of missile tests, etc. It is reported to have developed a small craft "jialong" which can do down to 7000 m under sea exceeding current Japanese record of 6500 m. It can search 99.8% of the seabed withstanding crushing pressures and darkness at such depths. It is thus set to edge out Japan S, Russia, and France active in the field. Field trials would continue till 2012. The device is useful for sea surveys and scientific research. 'Jialong' consists of a hollow sphere 7ft wide to house a pilot and 2 observers and a ship to which it is linked and a varieties of equipments of specialized nature.

**Innovation** is another area of focus as competitiveness comes from it. Modernization schemes for Higher education and Research, has development of innovative skills as an important aim. But, a scheme to attract outstanding among the Diaspora to return home capitalizing on the new opportunities at home, growing nationalist feelings, etc. has not produced much result. After more than a year and a half of its initiation, the numbers have stalled at about 600. Meanwhile, the number of wealthy Chinese essentially buying their way into the US and Canada via "immigrant investor" visas surged to record highs last year. It is said that deficiencies in fields like health care and education, and academic freedom are standing in the way showing that mere top-flight facilities are not enough to attract and retain top minds. A recent survey has shown that, given a chance, majority of youth are interested in going out.

**(e) Soft Power** China has been active increasing its soft power funding 270 Confucian institutions in 75 countries and propagating CCP's views of its history and culture to 100 m foreigners. Their number will increase to 1000 by 2020. Chinese diplomats selected from cream of the youth and given excellent cultural and language training are actively engaged in this effort. China also sends a large number of business, diplomatic and cultural delegations to all corners of the world to keep reputation of its economic and political systems high. The planned efforts to project achievements and hide failures are considered quite successful from their results. Westerners are generally unaware of the large number of unrests and fast growing inequalities in China. Compared to this, every body knows of India's poverty, disorder, etc.

On the whole, it could be said that China (and India) has managed the recessionary scenario very well because of its effective oversight and control systems by keeping the economy growing by over 9% when all developed nations are afflicted by crises on the employment, economic or financial fronts. China and India, by emerging stronger in the crisis, may reshape the economic future of the world. Goldman Sachs chief economist Jim O'Neill has predicted that the major emerging markets of Brazil, Russia, India and China could overtake the combined GDP of the G-7 nations by 2027, nearly a decade sooner than the forecast in a study a few years back.

**(f) Some Projections.** According to the studies of Sandra Polanski and Li Shantong,[1] Carnegie Endowment for International Peace, trade alone cannot solve challenges on the employment front, and hence domestic demand and government policies would have to be the main drivers of growth. Based on certain base line, optimistic and pessimistic assumptions about growth upto 2020, it was concluded that in all scenarios, the share of agriculture in employment and output would fall and that of secondary sector would grow through 2010 and then decline as growth in service industries would pull in larger numbers of workers. Pace of this transformation would depend on levels of domestic investment in human capital and growth in the technologically advanced service industries that serve manufacturing industries. The study concluded that agricultural workers would stand to gain the most in the optimistic scenario and may also face greatest losses if the risk scenario materializes. Labor-intensive service sectors like education and health care would be promising sources of new jobs. Technological advancement would be essential which would mean more and changing mix of skills. It would call for more educational services. In sum, the study concluded that growth upto 2020 would vary between a pessimistic level of 6% and an optimistic level of above 10%. It noted that by 2005, the urban/rural disparities in income had become pronounced with rural average income of $397 against urban average income of $ 1281. In fact, after 2005, the disparities have become more pronounced.

According to a Future Study on China and North Asia in the 'Future Study Series' of Free World Academy[2], China may grow at the current rate for another 5 to 10 years before slowing down. Another 20 years of speedy growth may also be possible. With 2004 as the base and growth rates of 8% upto 2020 and 9% from then to 2030 or another scenario of continuous 9% growth from 2004 to 2030, it was found that with a stable population and continued growth for the period 2004–2030, GDP can get multiplied nearly ten times, considerably raising living standards and making China prosperous. Chinese economy may equal US economy after 25 years.

Global Business Network[3], a San Francisco based Consultancy Firm involved in scenario planning, prepared the following four scenarios for the future of China. The basic objective was to project possible scenarios so that businesses could take suitable steps to avert mistakes. The scenarios were: (a) China grows peacefully and surpasses US by 2041 as predicted by Goldman Sachs study in 2003, (b) China's growth rate is short-lived and China becomes a bigger Brazil whose potential is not achieved. The country flounders in the face of environmental crisis, political unrest, poverty, and governmental corruption. (c) China grows as fast as its neighbors, enters an era of neo-regionalism and competes for resources with India, Japan, and Russia. Outsourcing leaves China and moves to safer Africa and South America. US companies align more with Latin America and Canada as the globe becomes more factional and regionalized. **More participants felt that this scenario was more likely.** (d) China grows very fast tipping all the scales in its favor and forces trade partners to play by its rules. Yuan replaces the dollar as the global currency and US loses world leadership.

Similarly, during a discussion[4] of business leaders, economists, financial experts, etc. participated by World Bank officials, the World Economic Forum developed three likely scenarios on the future of China mainly to prepare themselves for the unpredictables involved. These were: **(1) 'Regional Ties'** describing how China could continue on the path of reform despite an international environment that may become increasingly difficult. Chinese leadership strengthens regional ties overcoming historical enmities and restores prosperity. **(2) 'Unfulfilled Promise'** describing a China where the desire for economic development is not supported by the necessary structural reforms. Hence, in the resulting situation the promise made to people for inclusive economic development is largely unfulfilled. **(3) 'New Silk Road'** describing the flourishing economic and cultural rise of China achieved despite the presence of substantial internal obstacles. It thus recreates the original Silk Road by peaceful geopolitical integration and exchange of goods, services, investments and ideas. The **majority felt Regional Ties scenario was more likely.**

In an article by Andrew Batson and Jason Dean[5], China's current **economic gains giving way to a hazy future was forecast** because of "middle income trap". It quoted Homi Kharas, a scholar at the Brookings Institution and the World Bank's former chief economist for Asia, to say "the strategies that have helped China grow from poverty to its current levels will not yield the same dividends in the future". Lesser and older work force in the coming years, widening gap between rich and poor and severely constrained supplies of energy and environmental resources would be major constraints. Hence, more productive use of fewer resources and working harder and smarter would be needed. Also as people are becoming bolder in challenging the state, to avoid widening battles with them, the leadership has to find new ways to drastically improve the social services. Removal of inequalities, income-wise and regional, "a wedge issue among the ruling elites" will also have to be tackled. According to Shengman Zhang, former managing director of the World Bank[6], China has to change from the current economic growth mode characterized by low efficiency and excessive consumption of resources like water and energy and improve market operating and corporate efficiencies. Faster financial reforms, improved domestic consumption by reducing savings, elimination of inequalities between urban and rural areas and coastal and interior provincial areas, etc. are seen as essential to sustain its fast economic growth by many economic experts. According to an article 'China: Emerging Global Economic Player' by Panna Lal Chowdhury[7], through such steps and building a 'harmonious society', China could become comparable with US economy after about 25 years, but, superseding the American economy in its composition, size, per capita income and sophistication is not considered possible.[8] The same considerations may be relevant for comparison of China with Europe and other major economies.

Robert Fogel[9], Director of the Center for Population Economics at the University of Chicago Booth School of Business and winner of the 1993 Nobel Prize in Economics, in a recent article titled 'China will have a $123 trillion economy by 2040' opined that China's GDP would constitute 40 percent of the world GDP and may dwarf that of the United States (14 percent) and the European Union (5 percent) 30 years from now. Referring to a prediction in a recent study by the Carnegie Endowment for International Peace that by 2050 China's economy will be just 20 percent larger than that of the United States, he opined that such accounts fail to fully credit the forces at work behind China's recent success or understand how those trends will shape the future. Relative decline of a Europe plagued by falling fertility would, he feels, make the combined size of the economies of the 15 earlier European Union one-eighth the size of China's. The enormous investment China is making in education will improve its GDP as more educated workers are more productive workers. If China increases its high school enrollment rate to nearly 100 percent and the college rate to about 50 percent over the next generation as planned, it would itself add more than 6 percentage points to the country's annual economic growth rate. As output per worker in industry and services has increased, productivity is increasing even for those in rural areas, which constitute about a third of Chinese economic growth today. China's rapid urbanization, which shifts workers to industry and services, adds 3 percentage to the annual national growth rate. He opines that Chinese statisticians may be underestimating economic progress of the services sector as small firms often don't report their numbers to the government and officials often fail to adequately account for improvements in the quality of output. Rapid growth of China's services sector makes the underestimation more pronounced. In Europe's wealthy countries, people are not working longer hours to make higher salaries and accumulate more goods as they value long vacations, early retirements, and shorter workweeks over acquiring more stuff, at least in comparison to many other developed countries. This reduces the output of these countries. Though rising income inequalities, potential social unrest, territorial disputes, fuel scarcity, water shortages, environmental pollution, and an underdeveloped banking system are problems, these are no secret to China's leaders. Recent reforms, rationalization, injection of more state capital and public issue of shares of a number of Government banks have changed the face of banking in China. Today four of the world's biggest banks are Chinese. Hence, Robert Fogel rightfully feels that Chinese leaders are quite adept in tackling problems they have set out to address. The Government's increasing sensitivity to public opinion and rising living standards have improved popular confidence in Chinese leaders which would make major political instability unlikely. The notion of a rising China is, in Chinese eyes, merely a return to the status quo of 18 of the last 20 centuries when Chinese economy was the globe's top economy. But, such views have drawn severe criticisms from people like Gordon G Chang.

In his book 'Coming collapse of China', Chang speaks of the rot in the institutions in China and various forces that would end the communist party's monopoly on power. In his view, if the bad loans of the state owned banks to SOEs are added to the national debt, China's financial situation will be 'precarious'. A level playing field to be allowed to efficient foreign companies waiting for competition with inefficient SOEs and state run organizations in respect of the services sector, as per the conditionalities of WTO entry, will cause havoc and severe, at least transitional, unemployment. The above and consequences of failure to implement structural reforms, absence of political reforms due to eagerness to somehow hold on to monopoly power, corruption of party officials, lack of charismatic leadership, unrest from rising inequalities, evictions, high level of environmental damage, etc. could cause an 'implosion' in Chinese society and politics in a few years. He says: "Economic dislocations become social ones, with dark political overtones. At some point, there will be no solution. And then the economy and the Government will collapse.

One day the central government won't be able to face all who challenge it". According to him, while the Soviet Union showed the "collapse of going too fast on reforms, too slow reforms due to over caution by China are equally dangerous as misery can hit from either direction". While some factors cited are valid, the consequences predicted look like a dooms day forecast.

Susan L Shirk, in her 'China: The Fragile Super Power', also explains the **internal fragility of China's power structure.** She feels that after the 1989 Tiananmen Square massacre, CPC suffers from a lack of legitimacy and fear of its own people. This weakness and insecurity at the highest levels force the system to act belligerently to "foreign provocations" relating to Japan, Taiwan, and the United States. She sees it as the result of the decision to emphasize nationalism in education and the media in the post-Tiananmen era in the effort to shore up their legitimacy. Officials who are perceived as "soft" on Japan, Taiwan reunification, and the United States are seen as traitors and attacked. Leaders are forced by public opinion caused by the extreme segments and looser control of the new media to adopt a harder line reducing their freedom of action on issues relating to Taiwan, Japan, and US. In her view, the silent masses simply want an amicable solution to the Taiwan problem. But, because of the harder line by the military and media attention, Chinese officials sometimes make public statements accentuating foreign crises and situations. Japan is hated and it constrains CPC's efforts to mediate problems and disagreements with it. This has pushed Japan closer to the US and prompts it to think of scrapping its post-war constitutional restrictions on its military. Japan is more likely now to support its closest ally in any confrontation over Taiwan. Thus, in such a situation, leaders are under pressure to deliver economic growth and appease the military with large budgets. According to her, as seen from questions put to her by audiences in China, they had no doubts about the fragility of their government, but only about the super power status of China. On the other hand, audiences in US had no doubts about China's super power status coming from its economic might now, but only about the nature of its fragility.

According to Raghav Bahl's 'Super Power? The amazing Race between China's Hare and India's Tortoise', what is happening in China now is what Napoleon foresaw when he said, 'Let China sleep, for when China wakes up, she will shake the world.' As he says, China has woken up shocking and awing the world with its economic growth whose main thrust has come from capital spending on an unprecedented scale. In his view, China has built schools, hospitals, roads, railways, airports, bridges, ports, ships, skyscrapers, factories, malls, technology parks and new cities with 'spectacular and brutally effective' ambition. Bahl says it has proved the saying in the Red Army that quantity has a quality of its own. While Japan was investing only 30 per cent plus of its GDP for growth, China today is investing nearly half its GDP. Roy Ramos of Goldman Sachs paints a graphic picture of China's credit expansion by estimating that in less than ten months in 2009–10, China added 'the equivalent of India's banking industry twice over'. But, the classical economics says that hyper-investment would create a bubble that ends in a dreadful collapse as over investment or installation of capacity which can not be put to productive use causes ruin and destruction of wealth. He argues that China has consistently defied all such prophesies of doom as there is no sign that it could happen. If it continues to do so, it could be scripting, in his view, a new logic which could trump conventional theories. In his view, by investing on a scale hitherto unknown and untested, China may have defined a new 'escape velocity' of capital spending which may mean that if you pump so much capital into your economy, like extra fuel into a rocket, you can overcome the 'escape velocity' needed to get out of the gravitational pull of classical economics. If the bulk of capital is spent on infrastructure (roads, railways, schools, hospitals, ports), as against factories which produce toys and televisions, it would defeat 200 years of economic wisdom. Though big factories may create over-capacity, the mammoth infrastructure could trigger higher productivity and the ability to create wealth as life-enhancing social assets like education empower people. By rapidly educating the workforce, brilliantly executing gigantic projects, by importing expertise and dollars in a shrinking world, a 'shower of wealth and productivity' could develop so that consumption 'trickles through' quickly into the bubble. To quote, "the sheer scale of activities could end up swelling the tide in which everybody and everything rises together, a new model of `tidal wave investing' could buoy the whole ocean to a much higher watermark. Political economy teaches that genuine enterprise and innovation take place only when people are free and when individual genius soars unfettered as in America, Europe, Japan, Israel, South Korea, Brazil, India, Australia, etc., centres of wealth today". He feels China is "challenging this axiom too using ambition and infallible execution to trump democracy". He sees Chinese leaders "trading wealth for freedom", the logic which held ground for three decades and gathered in strength. The "quintessences of the new Chinese economic wisdom" in a rigidly controlled quasi-democracy, in reality a plain authoritarian system by western standards, are "mandated prices of foreign currency, wages and land" against free market discovered prices in a western democracy.

**(g) Education.** The rapid gains made by China on the educational front will get further consolidated in the coming decades and the sense of insularity which had marked China will get further reduced. As more youth with knowledge of English (the language of the new soft ware and international business) are coming out of universities as a result of the thrust on teaching English, more soft ware centers and soft ware exports are seen. China's software industry has grown 20 times in 10 years and it would break 1.2 Trillion Yuan this year. Nanjing declared as the 4th major software production center in the company of Shenzhen, Shanghai and Beijing would break 100 bn Yuan. Modernization and reforms on the educational front are thus enabling Chinese youth to better meet the challenges of international business.

**(h) Chinese Language.** Increasing tourist traffic and China's emergence as the lowest cost producer and an economic giant have already motivated many students in US to study Chinese language, already spoken by the 2nd largest number. One consequence foreseen by business leaders, academicians, and other experts when China tips all scales in its favour in the coming years by sustained rapid growth was that more Europeans would learn Mandarin than English. China is attracting more youth from abroad as a centre for Higher Education and all of them study Chinese.

**(i) Culture** The ancient Chinese culture is gradually getting weakened in centers like Beijing, Shanghai and other cities where economic activities based on FDI dominate the scene. Chinese youth thronging to western fast food joints, great fascination seen in the minds of the youth for western, esp. American systems, rapid spread of all modern gadgets and internet culture, etc. are some indicators of the decline of the traditional Chinese systems. Majority of Hutongs in Beijing, typical of the Chinese way of living, have disappeared thanks to the builders lobbies and increasing corruption. This is bound to increase as urbanization and development spread to interior areas. Thus insularity and exclusivity, which marked the Chinese culture for a long time, would get diluted more and more. But, certain intellectual aspects of Chinese culture like appeal to traditional religions, ancient Chinese Philosophies etc., looked down upon earlier by the Govt., now appeal to the modern youth as binding forces of Chinese culture and traditions. The government too, as part of the strategy to increase the country's soft power, is encouraging this through more cultural exchanges, establishment of more Confucian study centres and Institutes among the Diaspora, etc.

**(j) Sports and Games.** The 2008 Olympics in Beijing was a phenomenal success as it enabled China to emerge as a major sporting nation winning medals (total 100 including 51 Gold) in varieties of fields by systematic training and development of talents. The fillip given by this success would stimulate the country to take steps to retain its top position in sports and games too. The high level of literacy, fast growing middle class and urbanization, increasing economic prosperity, improvement in the quality of education and educational institutions will facilitate it. Hence, China will be in the forefront of sporting nations in the coming decades. The results of the 2010 Asian games held at Guangzhou recently have amply demonstrated China's dominance in sports in Asia. While it topped the list with 199 golds (total 416 medals), S. Korea and Japan which competed for the second position got only less than half its medals.

**(k) Tourism.** The interest in China is fast growing attracting more and more people to find out what is going on in the country. By 2007, China had become the world's fourth most popular **tourist destination** (behind France, Spain and the United States). In 2008, aided by the Olympics, it was to surpass the United States. The opening and closing ceremonies focusing on Chinese history and culture, watched by 200 millions all over the world, have increased the interest in China. China's remarkable resilience even when the developed world is in recession has also contributed to it. China is also opening up more places to showcase its attractions, great culture, historical places, unprecedented growth in infrastructure, etc. and hence tourist traffic to China is bound to go substantially up in the coming years. In 2009, 46.89 m international tourists visited China (ref.nationmaster.com/China) compared to a few millions in India. According to one estimate, the number of overseas tourists would reach136 million in 2010 and outbound Chinese tourists would touch 5.4 billion. The recently concluded 'Shanghai Exhibiton' was estimated to be seen by 70 million people. The 2010 Asian Games just completed at Guangzhou wherein China showed its dominance of the sports field in Asia also helped.

**(l) Military Might.** Along with the economic might, image and status among the community of nations, China has also been increasing its military might. It has also been emerging as a supplier of military hardware even to some controversial regimes, perhaps in its efforts to end the monopoly of US and other western nations. Its trade and financial relations and investments in the African continent and also in its neighborhood have shown a quantum jump perhaps keeping an eye on need for raw materials, new markets, etc. for its booming economy. It has also been joining in many peacekeeping and relief operations. Despite growing military might, it may not do anything which would hamper its economic gains as continuous rise in living standards and rapid economic growth are needed to maintain political and social stability. Needs to increase exports, international trade and other economic relations with the US, etc. are other compulsions. It is, however, unlikely to give up its claims in respect of territories like those relating to borders with India because of growing nationalism and as it believes some of the agreements, forced on China by countries like United Kingdom when it was weak during the Qing days, were harmful to its interests.

**(m) Image.** China's image in the world has been going up according to various recent studies conducted on the subject. A Pew Research Center survey, conducted in 22 nations from April 7 to May 8, 2010 found that in most Western countries, more people view China positively than those who view it negatively. It has favourable image in Latin America, Africa, and Muslim countries in general with the exception of Turkey and Russia. Only in France, Germany, Japan and Turkey negative feelings dominate. China's responsible stand on environmental issues, peace keeping operations, actions against pirates, increased willingness to "be a part of the solution to global issues" including on issues like the world economic crisis, Korean Peninsula denuclearization and the Iran nuclear issue have given it better respectability. Its efforts to promote better understanding of the country even in Europe and huge investments in Africa, though part of its strategy to improve its soft power and ensure availability of raw materials and other resources needed to sustain its economic progress can be reasonably expected to further improve its image in the coming years. Increasing stress to produce high-quality products as part of the effort to enhance the image of "made in China "is being laid. It is proposed to draw up a blacklist displaying the names of those firms breaching quality-related regulations, reward those companies that have good records for producing quality products with increased policy and funding support, and punish those with poor quality-control records. A campaign to allow enterprises to make promises on producing quality products, and work together with quality supervision authorities to incorporate the quality-based credit system of enterprises into the whole social credit system is on now. 156 Chinese firms have already signed a written proposal "promising to make quality products for the world," and called upon their peers in China to raise the quality of industrial products.

**(n) Religion.** The number of followers of Buddhism, Taoism, Confucianism and traditional religious practices has also been increasing as people have more freedom in a climate of increasing liberalization. Christianity, in the illegal house form, both of the Catholic and protestant varieties has perhaps the maximum growth with the estimate of total Christians varying between 30 m to 60 m. But, monitoring of tendencies to challenge the CPC continues. Growth of religiosity is also expected to grow as people become freer, richer and mix with people of other countries when Chinese travel more and tourism opens up China further. Religion may become more a private and personal issue and one with which the political power should be less concerned. The Government also has been gradually relaxing its rigid controls though any attempt even by religious people to challenge CPC's supremacy is severely dealt with. Vatican recently criticized the Chinese government for continued coercion over bishops who obey the Pope to compel them to follow Government approved Church's programmes. This shows the continuance of the dispute between Beijing and Pope over who should have the decisive say over the Catholic church in China.

**(o) Historical Perspective.** With about 5000 years of history and emergence as an empire as early as 221 B.C., the historical perspective is that the country would continue to march towards increasing strength and prestige. China has seen many revolutions, civil wars and chaos at the end of which again it preserved unity. The fact that the vast majority are Hans with one language and culture uniting them always helps. Today, the eyes of the Chinese youth, who are quite vibrant, are focused on fully developed countries like US with which only comparisons are generally made. Unlike in the past when empires could break up due to decline of the central authority, integrating forces are getting increasingly stronger through air, rail, road and water ways, power, communication and other infrastructural links. The highly successful conduct of the 2008 Olympics has boosted the nationalist feelings and the urge to emerge as a powerful country. Some writers like Susan L. Shirk have, however, highlighted the dangers of 'febrile' nationalism in China.

**(p) Youth.** One fact with considerable cultural significance is the changing attitude of the Chinese youth. The current vibrant youth of China has a dream like the 'American Dream', which pushes them to forge ahead. Young people below 25 numbering about 560 million, born in 1980s/1990s and who have not known the earlier communist period, form a very large section today. 400 million are aged between 20 and 39 and constitute a significant part of today's labor force. Majority of these are well educated, enthusiastic about business entrepreneurship and eager to do hard work. They are "clean, polite, civilized, and optimistic and focus on ethics and values with a real open mind". Most of them speak global English and are eager to travel. They are better prepared for the coming world and perhaps constitute the best asset and future of China. As a result of the 'one child' policy's delayed effect, the proportion of the youth who now constitute a major chunk of China's Labour Force, would, however, be getting reduced in the coming decades.

**(q) Corruption.** With increasing liberalization, growth of private enterprise and wealth, corruption has been emerging as a major problem. According to China's anti-corruption watchdog, 106,000 officials were found guilty of corruption in 2009, an increase of 2.5% over that of 2008. Many of them were involved in sex rackets too. Officials caught embezzling more than one million Yuan ($146,000; £91,000) in 2009 increased by 19% over the previous year. Chinese citizens consistently raise corruption as their prime concern. A survey published in the state-run China Daily indicated nearly 60% of respondents thought corruption was doing the most damage to China's reputation abroad. BBC reports speak of widespread anger at the ostentatious lifestyle enjoyed by some Communist Party officials, police chiefs and bosses of state-owned companies. Absence of independent oversight over the ruling communists, system of the government appointing executives to state-owned corporations and a lack of subsequent supervision allow corruption to flourish. A number of senior executives are already being investigated or have been convicted for taking bribes or for other charges, such as falsifying accounts. The former head of oil giant Sinopec was sentenced to death last year for taking nearly $30m in bribes. The head of the China National Nuclear Corporation—overseeing the country's nuclear industry—was dismissed and is under investigation over allegations of bid rigging in nuclear power plant construction worth $260m. Though CPC's Central Commission for Discipline Inspection says it would target corrupt executives of state-owned enterprises, corruption has only increased in an environment where to get rich is considered 'glorious'.

**(r) Political Reforms/Democracy.** Democratic tendencies like gradual loosening of controls, decisions based on consensus, devolution of powers to lower levels, elections with limited candidates at the lowest level, etc will go up in the coming decades. The right to private property provided recently, though only for long-term leases (30 years in rural areas and upto 50–70 years in towns) is another new change. It was again a compromise accommodating the views of those opposed to private property and compulsions of private business accounting for 65% of the GDP and more than 80% of the economic growth. More internal debates and compromises with the opposition are taking place-preferring pragmatism over ideology. Admission to CPC allowed even to capitalists, is a sign of progress towards democracy. Economic reforms have freed millions from party control. Women, lesser in numbers, are freer with more education and jobs. The current leaders like Hu Jintao and Win Biao have come up from an ordinary background by sheer merit of their performance. These have caught the imagination of people. But, before democratization gathers momentum, CPC would like to ensure great economic advancement and wealth to the common people so that they develop a vested interest in the system, which made them wealthy and happy with China itself becoming a fully developed nation. The fear of the lessons of the collapse of USSR and Tiananmen Square youth rebellion of June 1989 would prevent faster democratization.

According to Xinhua News Agency, Prime Minister Wen Jiabao, during a recent visit to Shenzhen has said that China has to pursue political reform to safeguard its economic health. He apprehended that without political restructuring, China might lose what it has already achieved through economic restructuring and the targets of its modernization drive might not be reached. He also spoke of guaranteeing People's democratic and legitimate rights and mobilizing People to deal with, in accordance with the law, state, economic, social and cultural affairs. Wen also wanted to "create conditions" to allow the people to criticise and supervise the government as a way to address "the problem of over-concentration of power with ineffective supervision". His comments reflect broader worries that unless the Communist Party embraces at least limited reforms to make officials more answerable, corruption and abuses may erode the country's economic prospects. Such urges for democratization would go up further as people become more educated, richer and exposed to practices in developed countries. In a few decades, communism in China, really the only big country where it is surviving, could ultimately become social democracy eschewing some of the democratic features in capitalist countries.

"Like the crew of a ship that must keep sailing forward or sink, Beijing needs to keep the economy humming to stave off ever greater social unrest. But economic growth itself feeds that unrest. Can China's technocrat leaders deal with that apparent contradiction? Indeed, can the country's unprecedented boom continue or must it inevitably collapse of its own weight, bringing unimaginable consequences? And abroad, what of Beijing's attempt to manage its transition from pariah state to global player, a performance that has so far met with mixed reviews, particularly when it comes to securing a supply of raw materials or handling unsavory dictators with nuclear ambitions? Can China's leaders manage their nation's growing nationalistic pride and global clout without clashing with existing world powers, notably of course the United States? The answers will sway the lives of generations." Simon Elegant/Beijing. How many of these question marks will be erased by the political sagacity and increased maturity of the emerging leadership and how the febrile nationalism will be managed may have a telling effect on the emerging scenario in China.

## CONCLUSION

In this scenario, let us consider what lessons can India, a maturing democracy with lesser literacy and population but on a similar developmental track with a smaller growth rate, learn from China's socialism based on market forces. While China was a united empire from from 221 B.C. to A.D. 1911 and has in general unity of history, culture, language, race etc., India is plagued by diversities of religions, races, languages, history and culture and other complexities like lack of emotional integration.

Perhaps, the first lesson to be learnt is the conspicuous unity and commitment to the objective of fast economic growth seen at all levels and regions in China. In India, even the best of schemes generate controversies. The next lesson is perhaps effective governance, execution styles, huge infrastructure built up for roads, rails, airports, ports, manufacturing and management systems in all major cities/ growth areas to facilitate massive FDI inflows. Unlike in India, where acquisitions of land even for major projects run into rough weather, collective ownership of land by the community/Government and absence of interfering laws and legal delays, have made allotment of land for projects very simple in China. China's highly successful 'one child' population policy, high literacy rate (91.6%), higher productivity of agriculture through better seeds and fertilizer use, better irrigation systems, etc. despite lower percentage of arable land also contributed to faster growth. Indian agriculture continues to be dependent on the vagaries of monsoon. The atmosphere of order and discipline, though perhaps artificial, is in contra-distinction to India's much published anarchies and bureaucratic delays. The recent upsurge in nationalism and increasing pride in its imperial past, Confucianism, Taoism and Buddhism, earlier looked down upon by Mao, is in contra-distinction to absence of true nationalism in the conflict zones of India. While corruption is a major problem in both countries, the hard working, literate, low cost and more productive Chinese labour attract investors. India has so far failed to modify outdated labour laws to facilitate smooth flow of FDI into manufacturing which has the potential to atleast partially solve India's unemployment problem. The fast systemic changes effected to speed up much needed FDI have made China the manufacturing capital of the world, and thereby created millions and millions of jobs for the rural unemployed. China too may have lessons to learn from democratic India's increasing growth rates, transparency, inclusive and genuine participative styles, legal and institutional infrastructure, better corporate governance and outstanding achievements of some private sector units emerging as multinationals vis-a-vis lacklustre performance of many purely Chinese companies and State Owned Enterprises. While the United States may play a balancing role to keep its dominance by 'friendly containment', in the emerging environment where China and India could lead the developing world, a strategy of 'co-operation and competition' between two emerging giants of the 21st century may be desirable for both. While China has perhaps crossed the highest point of its growth rate, India is yet to reach it and in the coming years is estimated to overtake China's growth rate.

## Endnotes

1 Sandra Polanski and Li Shantong, Sandra Polanski and Li Shantong reports, The Carnegie endowment. Paper No.83, April 2007. www.carnegieendowment.org

2 http://freeworldacademy.com/globalleader/china.htm

3 http://money.cnn.com/magazines/business2/business2_archive/2006/08/01/8382233/index.htm

4 http://weforum.org/en/initiatives/Scenarios/China Scenarios/index.htm

5 http://online.wsj.com/article/SB121958712606066933.html#mod=2_1339_leftbox.

6 www.globalpolitician.com/2530-chinaChina: Emerging Global Economic Player—Article by Panna Lal Chowdhury-4/5/2005

7 Ibid.

## References

a. http://weforum.org/en/initiatives/Scenarios/China Scenarios/index.htm-yes

b. http://globalpolitician.com/2530-china

c. http://freeworldacademy.com/globalleader/china.htm

d. http://business-standard.com/india/storypage.php?autono=331834

e. http://online.wsj.com/article/SB121958712606066933.html#mod=2_1339_leftbox

f. http://carnegieendowment.org/events/?fa=eventDetail&id=980

g. https://www.cia.gov/library/publications/the-world-factbook/geos/ch.html

h. http://www.adb.org/Documents/CERs/PRC/CER_PRC_2002.pdf

i. http://www.adb.org/Documents/CERs/IND/2001/ind_2001.pdf

j. http://www.forbes.com/commerce/2004/11/03/cx_1103mckinseychina1.html

k. http://www.chinadaily.com.cn/english/doc/2006-01/12/content_511523.htm

l. http://www.economist.com//countries/China/profile.cfm?\folder=profile%2Economic%20data

m. http://ddp-ext.worldbank.org/ext/ddpreports/ViewSharedReport?&CF=1&REPORT_ID=9147&REQUEST_TYPE=VIEWADVANCED&HF=N&WSP=N

n. http://web.worldbank.org/WBSITE/EXTERNAL/n.DATASTATISTICS/0contentMDK:20535285~menuPK:1192694~pagePK:64133150~piPK:64133175~theSitePK:239419,00.html

o. http://money.cnn.com/magazines/business2/business2_archive/2006/08/01/8382233/index.htm

p. http://www.wider.unu.edu/publications/newsletter/articles/en_GB/18-12- Feature-article/(july26, 200)

q. https://www.cia.gov/library/publications/the-world-factbook/geos/IN.html

r. http://www.globalpolitician.com/2530-china

s. http://www.weforum.org/pdf/scenarios/china_executive_summary.pdf

t. http://www.weforum.org/pdf/scenarios/China_report.pd

u. http://scenariothinking.org/wiki/index.php/Future_of_China_in_203

v. 'The coming collapse of China' by Gordon G Chang.

w. 'China: The Fragile Super Power' by Susan L Shirk

x. Reports of 'People's Daily',Xinhua news etc on different dates, etc.

# APPENDIX 1

| S No. | Name of the Province/ Muncipality/Auto.Reg/ Spl.Admn.Region | Area (Sq. Miles) | Capital | Population (Density/sq.m.) | GDP/2008 in US $ (m.) | GDP (nominal- Per capita) US $ | Remarks |
|---|---|---|---|---|---|---|---|
| 1 | Heilongjiang (NE) | 454000 | Harbin | 38170,000(83) | 119800 | 3131 | P |
| 2 | Jilin (NE) | 187400 | Chanhchun | 27090000(1450) | 92600 | 3388 | |
| 3 | Liaoning (NE) | 145900 | Shenyang | 42170000(289) | 194000 | 4506 | " |
| 4 | Qinghai (NW) | 721200 | Xining | 5390000(7) | 13900 | 2506 | " |
| 5 | Gansu (NW) | 454300 | LAN Zhou | 26190000(58) | 44700 | 1745 | " |
| 6 | Shaanxi (NW) | 20560 | Xian | 37050000(180) | 98700 | 2629 | " |
| 7 | Shanxi (N) | 156300 | Taiyuan | 33350000(213) | 100000 | 2925 | " |
| 8 | Hebei (N) | 187700 | Shijiazhuang | 68090000(363) | 233084 | 3348 | " |
| 9 | Sichuan (SW) | 485000 | Chengdu | 87250000(180) | 180200 | 2216 | " |
| 10 | Hubei (SC) | 185900 | Wuhan | 60160000(324) | 163300 | 2865 | " |
| 11 | Henan (SC) | 167000 | Zhen Zhou | 98690000(591) | 265035 | 1823 | " |
| 12 | Shandong (E) | 153800 | Jinan | 91800000(586) | 447375 | 4767 | " |
| 13 | Anhui (E) | 139700 | Hefei | 64610000(463) | 139400 | 2123 | " |
| 14 | Jiangsu (E) | 102600 | Nanjing | 75495000(736) | 436441 | 5695 | " |
| 15 | Yunan (SW) | 394000 | Kunming | 144150000(112) | 82200 | 1840 | " |
| 16 | Guizhou (SW) | 176000 | Guying | 39040000(222) | 176100 | 1293 | " |

*Appendix 1 contd..*

*.contd.. Appendix 1*

| *S No.* | *Name of the Province/ Muncipality/Auto.Reg/ Spl.Admn.Region* | *Area (Sq. Miles)* | *Capital* | *Population (Density/sq.m.)* | *GDP/2008 in US $ (m.)* | *GDP (nominal- Per capita) US $* | *Remarks* |
|---|---|---|---|---|---|---|---|
| 17 | Hunan (SC) | 210000 | Changsha | 66980000(316) | 160800 | 2823 | " |
| 18 | Jiangxi(E) | 167000 | Nanchang | 42840000(257) | 436441 | 5695 | " |
| 19 | Zhejiang (E) | 102000 | Hang Zhou | 47200000(414) | 309369 | 6082 | " |
| 20 | Hainan (SC) | 34000 | Haikou | 8180000(241) | 13100 | 2475 | " |
| 21 | Guangdong (SC) | 180000 | Guangzhou | 113040000(467) | 513957 | 5416 | " |
| 22 | Fujian (E) | 121300 | Fuzhou | 35110000(289) | 156000 | 4341 | " |
| 23 | Xingjian Yogurt (NW) | 1660400 | Urumqi | 196300009(12) | - | 2867 | A.R. |
| 24 | Inner Mongolia (N) | 1183000 | Hohhot | 23840000(20) | - | 4641 | " |
| 25 | Tibet (S) | 1228400 | Lhasa | 2740000(2) | - | 1997 | " |
| 26 | Ningxia Hui (N) | 66400 | Yinchuan | 5880000(89) | - | 2578 | " |
| 27 | Guanxi Zhuang | 236000 | Xian | 48890000(207) | - | 2156 | " |
| 28 | Beijing (N) | 16800 | - | 15810000(941) | - | 11,361 | M |
| 29 | Tianjin(N) | 11305 | - | 11519000(980) | - | 9136 | " |
| 30 | Shanghai (NE) | 6341 | - | 18450000(2622) | - | 10070 | " |
| 31 | Chongqing (E) | 82300 | - | 31442300(382) | - | 2597 | ." |
| 32 | Macao (E) | 29 | - | 520400(17310) | 14204 | About 33000 | S.R |
| 33 | Hong Kong(E) | 1104 | - | 6985200(6352) | 207171 | About 30000 | " |

P-Province. M-Centrally Administered Municipality.A.R.-Autonomous Region. S.R.- Specially Administered (by theCentre).* China hopes to make it too a Specially Administered Region. N-North, NE-North East, NW-North West, SC-South Central, E-East, SW-South Western, etc.

## APPENDIX 2

# CHINA—MAJOR URBAN CENTRES

| | | | *Urban* | *Total* |
|---|---|---|---|---|
| 1 | Shanghai | Shanghai Municipality | 9,495,701 | 18,542,200 |
| 2 | Beijing | Beijing Municipality | 7,296,962 | 17,430,000 |
| 3 | Hong Kong | Hong Kong SAR | 7,000,000 | 7,000,000 |
| 4 | Tianjin | Tianjin Municipality | 5,066,129 | 11,500,000 |
| 5 | Wuhan | Hubei Province | 6,660,000 | 9,100,000 |
| 6 | Guangzhou | Guangdong Province | 4,154,808 | 15,000,000 |
| 7 | Shenzhen | Guangdong Province | 4,000,000 | 8,615,500 |
| 8 | Shenyang | Liaoning Province | 3,981,023 | 7,500,000 |
| 9 | Chongqing | Chongqing Municipality | 3,934,239 | 31,442,300 |
| 10 | Nanchang | Jiangxi Province | 3,790,000 | 4,990,184 |
| 11 | Nanjing | Jiangsu Province | 2,822,117 | 7,100,000 |
| 12 | Harbin | Heilongjiang Province | 2,672,069 | 8,499,000 |
| 13 | Shijiazhuang | Hebei Province | 2,620,357 | 9,630,000 |
| 14 | Xi'an | Shaanxi Province | 2,588,987 | 10,500,000 |
| 15 | Chengdu | Sichuan Province | 2,341,203 | 11,300,000 |
| 16 | Changchun | Jilin Province | 2,223,170 | 7,400,000 |
| 17 | Dalian | Liaoning Province | 2,118,087 | 6,200,000 |
| 18 | Hangzhou | Zhejiang Province | 1,932,612 | 7,000,000 |
| 19 | Jinan | Shandong Province | 1,917,204 | 6,300,000 |
| 20 | Taiyuan | Shanxi Province | 1,905,403 | 3,413,800 |
| 21 | Qingdao | Shandong Province | 1,867,365 | 8,000,000 |

N.B. The first column shows urban population and the second total population.

# APPENDIX 3

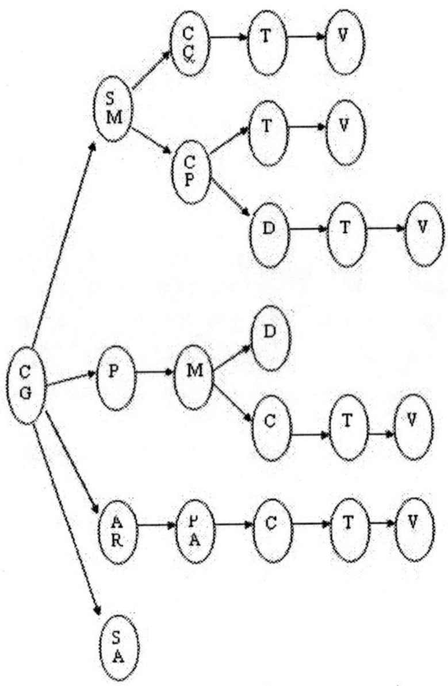


Structure of Local Administration.

## ABBREVIATIONS

CG : Central Government
SM : Special Municipalities
P : Provinces
AR : Autonomous Regions
SA : Special Administrative Regions
CC : Cities at County level
CP : Cities at Prefecture level
M : Municipalities
PA : Prefectures and Autonomous prefectures
T : Towns
D : Districts
C : Counties
V : Villages

APPENDIX 4

# GDP p.c. Nominal and PPP Basis for Major Cities

| *Rank* | *Provincial level* | *in RMB¥* | *in US$ (Nominal)* | *in US$ (PPP)* |
|---|---|---|---|---|
| 1 | Shanghai | 77,564 | 11,361 | 20,997 |
| 2 | Beijing | 68,750 | 10,070 | 17,974 |
| 3 | Tianjin | 62,403 | 9,136 | 16,315 |
| 4 | Zhejiang | 44,335 | 6,490 | 11,591 |
| 5 | Jiangsu | 44,232 | 6,475 | 11,564 |
| 6 | Guangdong | 40,748 | 5,965 | 10,653 |
| 7 | Inner Mongolia | 37,287 | 5,460 | 9,748 |
| 8 | Shandong | 35,893 | 5,255 | 9,384 |
| 9 | Liaoning | 34,193 | 5,006 | 8,939 |
| 10 | Fujian | 33,051 | 4,838 | 8,641 |
| 11 | Jilin | 26,289 | 3,848 | 6,873 |
| - | China | 25,125 | 3,678 | 6,568 |
| 12 | Hebei | 24,428 | 3,576 | 6,387 |
| 13 | Chongqing | 22,909 | 3,355 | 5,989 |
| 14 | Shaanxi | 21,729 | 3,181 | 5,681 |
| 15 | Heilongjiang | 21,640 | 3,168 | 5,658 |
| 16 | Hubei | 21,566 | 3,157 | 5,638 |
| 17 | Shanxi | 21,544 | 3,154 | 5,633 |
| 18 | Ningxia | 21,470 | 3,143 | 5,613 |
| 19 | Henan | 20,477 | 2,998 | 5,353 |
| 20 | Hunan | 20,226 | 2,961 | 5,282 |
| 21 | Xinjiang | 19,798 | 2,898 | 5,176 |
| 22 | Qinghai | 19,407 | 2,841 | 5,074 |
| 23 | Hainan | 19,166 | 2,806 | 5,011 |
| 24 | Sichuan | 17,339 | 2,538 | 4,533 |

*Appendix 4 contd..*

*contd.. Appendix 4*

| *Rank* | *Provincial level* | *in RMB¥* | *in US$ (Nominal)* | *in US$ (PPP)* |
|---|---|---|---|---|
| 25 | Jiangxi | 17,248 | 2,525 | 4,509 |
| 26 | Anhui | 16,391 | 2,400 | 4,285 |
| 27 | Guangxi | 15,821 | 2,316 | 4,136 |
| 28 | Tibet | 15,141 | 2,216 | 3,958 |
| 29 | Yunnan | 13,494 | 1,975 | 3,528 |
| 30 | Gansu | 12,836 | 1,879 | 3,356 |
| 31 | Guizhou | 10,258 | 1,502 | 2,682 |

APPENDIX 5

# People* of China—Some Characteristics

| | | | |
|---|---|---|---|
| Age wise distribution | 0–14, 19.8% | 15–64, 72.1% | 65 and above-8.1% |
| Median age | Total population-35.2 | Male-34.5 | Female-35.8 |
| Growth/birth/death rates (2010 est.) | Growth rate-.494% | Birth rate-12.17/1,000 | Death rate-6.89/1,000 |
| The sex ratio | At birth-1.14 males/female | Total population-1.06 males/female | The Infant mortality-16.51 death/1000 live births |
| Life expectancy (2010 est.) | Total population-74.51 years | Male-72.54 years | Female-76.77 years |
| Aids (2007 est.) | Percentage affected.-.1 | People living with Aids about 700000 | 39000 deaths (2007) p.a. |
| Literacy (2007) | Total population-91.6 % | Male: 95.7% | Female: 87.6% |
| School life expectancy (primary to tertiary-(2008) | Total-11 years. | Male-11 years. | Female-12 years |

*Appendix 5 contd..*

*contd.. Appendix 5*

| | | | |
|---|---|---|---|
| Urban/rural | Urban-43% | Rural-57% | Remarks-urban rapidly increasing |
| Ethnic groups (2000 census) | Main-Hans-91.5% | Minority groups-8.5% | Remarks-minority groups are Zhuang, Manchu, Hui, Miao, Uighur, Tujia, Yi, Mongol, Tibetan, Buyi, Dong, Yao, Korean, etc. |
| Religion | Main-Daoism (Taoism) and Buddhism | Minority religions-Christianity (3–4%) and Islam (1–2%) | Remarks-officially atheist. |
| Language | Main-Mandarin (Putonghua, based on the Beijing dialect-official) | Minority languages-Cantonese Shanghainese, Minbei, Minnan, Xiang, Gan, Hakka dialects. | |

* based on CIA Fact Book, China, People.

# Name Index

# Subject Index